9/11

BLOOMSBURY TOPICS IN CONTEMPORARY
NORTH AMERICAN LITERATURE

Series Editor: Sarah Graham

Bloomsbury's Topics in Contemporary North American Literature series offers authoritative guides to major themes in recent American writing. With chapters written by leading scholars in their field, each book surveys a wide range of writing in a variety of genres.

These informative and accessible volumes are essential reading for advanced undergraduate and graduate students, facilitating discussion and supporting close analysis of the texts covered.

Titles in the series:

The Vietnam War, edited by Brenda M. Boyle

9/11

Topics in Contemporary North American Literature

Edited by
Catherine Morley

Bloomsbury Academic
An imprint of Bloomsbury Publishing Plc

B L O O M S B U R Y
LONDON • OXFORD • NEW YORK • NEW DELHI • SYDNEY

Bloomsbury Academic
An imprint of Bloomsbury Publishing Plc

50 Bedford Square
London
WC1B 3DP
UK

1385 Broadway
New York
NY 10018
USA

www.bloomsbury.com

BLOOMSBURY and the Diana logo are trademarks of Bloomsbury Publishing Plc

First published 2016

© Catherine Morley and contributors, 2016

Catherine Morley has asserted her right under the Copyright, Designs, and Patents Act, 1988, to be identified as Editor of this work.

All rights reserved. No part of this publication may be reproduced or transmitted in any form or by any means, electronic or mechanical, including photocopying, recording, or any information storage or retrieval system, without prior permission in writing from the publishers.

No responsibility for loss caused to any individual or organization acting on or refraining from action as a result of the material in this publication can be accepted by Bloomsbury or the editor.

British Library Cataloguing-in-Publication Data
A catalogue record for this book is available from the British Library.

ISBN: HB: 978-1-4725-6970-7
PB: 978-1-4725-6968-4
ePDF: 978-1-4725-6967-7
ePub: 978-1-4725-6969-1

Library of Congress Cataloging-in-Publication Data
A catalog record for this book is available from the Library of Congress.

Series: Bloomsbury Topics in Contemporary North American Literature

Cover design: Jason Anscomb
Cover image © Getty Images

Typeset by Deanta Global Publishing Services, Chennai, India

*For my parents, Seán and Helen Morley ~
with love*

CONTENTS

List of contributors ix
Acknowledgments xii

Introduction: Cities of the dead
   Catherine Morley 1

1 Prosthetic fictions: Reading Jonathan Safran Foer's *Extremely Loud and Incredibly Close* through Philip Roth's *The Plot Against America*
   Debra Shostak 21

2 The Law of Ruins and homogenous empty time in Don DeLillo's *Falling Man*
   Aaron DeRosa 41

3 Absent presences: Paradoxes of representation and self-representation in (post)-9/11 comics
   David Brauner 61

4 Rebuilding after 9/11: The figure of the tower and poetics of the future
   Aimee Pozorski 83

5 Beyond belief: John Updike's *Terrorist*
   Mark Eaton 105

6   Desperate domesticity? Translocating the political into the personal in Lynne Sharon Schwartz's *The Writing on the Wall* and Paul Auster's *Man in the Dark*
    Sien Uytterschout and Kristiaan Versluys   125

7   "Anticipating the Fall": Art, memory, and historical reclamation in Colum McCann's *Let the Great World Spin*
    Hamilton Carroll   147

8   Jonathan Franzen's *Freedom* and "the great national tragedy"
    Paul Jenner   167

9   The architecture of memory and memorialization in Amy Waldman's *The Submission*
    Catherine Morley   185

Index 201

LIST OF CONTRIBUTORS

David Brauner is professor of contemporary literature at the University of Reading and executive coeditor of *Philip Roth Studies*. He is the author of three books: *Postwar Jewish Fiction: Ambivalence, Self-Explanation and Transatlantic Connections* (2001), *Philip Roth* (2007), and *Contemporary American Fiction* (2010). He is the coeditor of *The Edinburgh Companion to Modern Jewish Fiction* (2015) and of a special Lorrie Moore issue of the *Journal of American Studies* (46.3). His essays have appeared in a wide range of journals, including *The Yearbook of English Studies*, *Studies in the Novel*, *Modern Language Review*, *Canadian Literature*, *Studies in American Jewish Literature*, *Philip Roth Studies*, and *Journal of American Studies*.

Hamilton Carroll is associate professor in the School of English at the University of Leeds. He is the author of *Affirmative Reaction: New Formations of White Masculinity* (2011). He has published widely on contemporary American topics in journals such as *Modern Fiction Studies*, *Studies in American Fiction*, *Journal of American Studies*, *Television and New Media*, and *Comparative American Studies*, and in a number of edited collections.

Aaron DeRosa is assistant professor of twentieth-/twenty-first-century American literature at California State Polytechnic University, Pomona. His work on 9/11 has appeared in *Arizona Quarterly*, *Modern Fiction Studies*, *LIT*, and the anthologies *Portraying 9/11* (2011) and *Narrating 9/11* (2011). His current work articulates a clash of temporalities in the United States arising in the aftermath of 9/11.

Mark Eaton is professor of English and director of graduate studies at Azusa Pacific University, where he teaches American literature and film studies. He is coeditor of *The Gift of Story: Narrating Hope in a Postmodern World* (2006) and a contributor to *A Companion to the Modern American Novel, 1900–1950* (2009); *A Companion to Film Comedy* (2012); *Screenwriting* (2014); and *The Routledge Companion to Literature & Religion* (2015).

Paul Jenner is lecturer in English at the University of Loughborough. His work has appeared in *Stanley Cavell, Literature, and the Idea of America* (2012), and he is the coauthor of *The Contemporary American Novel in Context* (2011). He is currently working on a book-length study of the American philosopher Stanley Cavell.

Catherine Morley is senior lecturer of American literature at the University of Leicester. She has published *The Quest For Epic in Contemporary American Fiction* (2009) and *Modern American Literature* (2012). She has coedited *American Thought and Culture in the 21st Century* (2008) and *American Modernism: Cultural Transactions* (2009). She has written numerous essays on post-9/11 literature and culture for journals such as *Journal of American Studies, Review of International American Studies, Gramma*, and *Philip Roth Studies*.

Aimee Pozorski is professor of English at Central Connecticut State University where she teaches contemporary American literature and trauma theory. She is author of *Falling After 9/11: Crisis in American Art and Literature* (2014) and *Roth and Trauma: The Problem of History in the Later Works* (2011). She is editor of *Roth and Celebrity* (2012) and the critical insights volume, *Philip Roth* (2013).

Debra Shostak is Mildred Foss Thompson professor of English language and literature at The College of Wooster in Wooster, Ohio. Author of *Philip Roth—Countertexts, Counterlives* and editor of *Philip Roth: American Pastoral, The Human Stain, The Plot Against America*, she has published articles on contemporary American fiction writers, including Paul Auster, Jeffrey Eugenides, John Irving, and Maxine Hong Kingston, as well as on film. She is executive coeditor of *Philip Roth Studies*.

Sien Uytterschout holds a PhD in American literature from Ghent University (2013), which she obtained with a dissertation on post-9/11 fiction, entitled *Desperate Domesticity? Diagnosing Five 9/11 Novels*. She has worked as a policy advisor for higher education at the Flemish Interuniversity Council (Vlaamse Interuniversitaire Raad/VLIR), an umbrella organization that operates as a forum for university leaders and specialized staff members to create consensus on a broad range of topics. Recently, she has returned to her alma mater, now working for the Ghent University Educational Quality Office.

Kristiaan Versluys holds a PhD in comparative literature from Harvard University (1979). He is professor of American literature and culture at Ghent University (Belgium) and the founding director of the Ghent Urban Studies Team (GUST). He has published a study on city poetry and some sixty scholarly articles in international journals and collections. His book, entitled *Out of the Blue: September 11 and the Novel*, was published in 2009. His specialties are urban literature (especially the literature of New York) and Jewish-American fiction. Since 2008, he has been the director of education at Ghent University.

ACKNOWLEDGMENTS

I am grateful to Sarah Graham for inviting me to take on this book. I have long admired the series Sarah edits for Bloomsbury and was delighted and honored to be offered this opportunity. I am lucky to count Sarah as a friend as well as a colleague at the University of Leicester, where the Centre for American Studies and the School of English provide supportive environments for my research. I have wonderful colleagues at Leicester but would like particularly to thank Martin Halliwell, Nick Everett, Anne Marie D'Arcy, Gail Marshall, and George Lewis for their humor, kindness, and the many conversations that have gone into the making of this book. I thank all the students who have taken my New York Stories course at Leicester. Our debates, observations, and conversations have influenced my thoughts as articulated in the introduction to the volume. I would like to thank the University of Leicester for a period of study leave, which allowed me to complete the work on this book. I would also like to thank my editors at Bloomsbury, David Avital and Mark Richardson, for their patience, kindness, and encouragement from the very beginning.

This book would not be possible without the time, goodwill, and scrupulous scholarship of my contributors, all of whom have been gracious and responsive collaborators. My sincere thanks to David Brauner, Hamilton Carroll, Aaron DeRosa, Mark Eaton, Paul Jenner, Aimee Pozorski, Debra Shostak, Sien Uytterschout, and Kristiaan Versluys. It has been a pleasure to work with each and every one of you.

For their ongoing moral support, patient ears, and encouragement, I would like to thank my dear friends Anna Norman, Catherine Evans, Elleke Boehmer, Steve Matthews, and Rhys Sandbrook. And to my hugely supportive sisters, Deirdre Aherne, Elaine Morley, and Rachel Morley, I am eternally grateful.

Finally, and above all, my thanks and heartfelt love to Dominic Sandbrook for his enthusiasm for the project, intellectual energy, and expertise on video games, zombies and early British sci-fi. And thank you lovely Arthur Sandbrook for reminding me every day what it is all really about.

Without both of you, nothing would be possible.

Introduction: Cities of the dead

Catherine Morley

> *You can read me a story, the boy said.*
> *Cant you, Papa? Yes, he said. I can.*
> ~ CORMAC McCARTHY, *The Road* (2006)

A man, sleeping in the woods beside his son, has a dream. The two of them are in a cave, like pilgrims wandering inside some vast stone beast. Far off, across a deep, dark lake, a mysterious, hideous creature stares sightlessly into the void. The man wakes. Dawn comes. He gazes out across the countryside: "barren, silent, godless." His son wakes, and they set out across the wasteland, past the crumbling bridges and the deserted gas stations. Everything is old, broken, abandoned. Searching the building by the gas station, they find only the relics of a broken civilization: a ratchet; a metal barrel full of rubbish; an empty, purposeless cash register; and some old car manuals, ruined by damp. The man picks up the phone and dials an old number, pointlessly. "Dust and ash everywhere," he thinks. They press on, across the river valley, through a landscape charred and blackened. Wire straggles from the electricity poles. Fading billboards advertise long-forgotten motels. At the top of the hill, the man takes out his binoculars and studies the plain below, where "the shape of a city stood in the grayness like a charcoal drawing sketched across the waste." "Nothing to see," he thinks. "No smoke." The boy asks to have a look. "What do you see?" his father asks. "Nothing," says the boy (McCarthy 2006: 3, 4, 5, 6, 7).

So begins Cormac McCarthy's haunting novel *The Road* (2006), the moving story of an unnamed father and son wandering across a bleak postapocalyptic American landscape in the aftermath of some terrible unexplained catastrophe. *The Road*, which won the Pulitzer Prize, was McCarthy's tenth novel, and many critics saw it as a new departure, a foray into the realms of dystopian science fiction. As in so many postapocalyptic science-fiction novels, we never see the dreadful disaster that has brought civilization to its knees, but find ourselves plunged into its terrifying aftermath, although in the subsequent film adaptation, released in 2009, the director, John Hillcoat, added brief flashback sequences to emphasize the vast scale of the cataclysm. Interviewed by the talk-show host Oprah Winfrey, whose seal of approval worked wonders for his book's sales, McCarthy himself was cautious about discussing his inspiration. "Usually you don't know where a book comes from," he said, although in this case, he remembered exactly where he was when he first had the idea for *The Road*. Shortly after moving house to Santa Fe, and probably not long after September 2001, he had checked into an old hotel in El Paso with his son. At two or three in the morning, unable to sleep, he stared out of the window of their hotel room, gazing at the silent, gray city beneath him, and listening to the trains rattling sadly past in the night. He wondered what the city "might look like in fifty or a hundred years." And that set him thinking. "I just had this image," he told Winfrey, "of these fires up on the hill and everything being laid waste and I thought a lot about my little boy. And so I wrote those pages and that was the end of it" (Luce 2009: 8–9).

Although McCarthy himself never explicitly mentioned it, many critics were quick to spot echoes of the disaster that had overtaken New York City—not merely the crucible of twentieth-century modernity, but perhaps the most famous urban skyline in the world—on September 11, 2001. The story of the father and son wandering through a bleak, joyless wasteland was, wrote one critic in *Christianity Today*, "A timeless, ancient story of humanity that recalls the first spark of fire in the primeval caves; but . . . also a story of our time, perhaps the truest and most important piece of post-9/11 literature we have" (McCracken 2009: n. pag.). Meanwhile, the screenwriter who adapted the book for the cinema, the playwright Joe Penhall, thought that the horror of the World Trade Center (WTC) attacks had given McCarthy's work a new appeal for a mainstream audience. "My theory," he wrote later, "is that post-9/11, post-Katrina, post-Iraq, ordinary Americans can at last conceive of a world bereft of humanity—a world McCarthy has depicted for decades" (Penhall 2010: n. pag.). And when an interviewer for *The Guardian* asked Penhall why works like *No Country for Old Men* (2005) were so popular with Hollywood, he again looked back to the events of September 2001. "Post-9/11 we are frighteningly aware of what man is capable of," he explained,

> We've seen the randomness, the overheatedness, the irrationality of people's vengefulness in Islamist terrorism, in American imperialism, in British foreign policy. People see these examples of extreme behaviour on the news every night and don't know what to make of it, and McCarthy kind of does know what to make of it. By the time McCarthy's stuff gets to the screen we're not thinking, "What a radical, harsh vision"; we're thinking, "Yep, that's a world I recognise." (Penhall 2011: n. pag.)

The world of broken landscapes, deserted cities, unsettling absences, and terrifying, unspoken trauma is not merely the world of Cormac McCarthy's fiction; it is also the world of American culture in the wake of 9/11. In many ways, and like the other works discussed in this volume, McCarthy's novel represents an attempt to cope with the aftermath of the atrocity: to find consolation amid the rubble, and love among the ruins. Indeed, almost from the very moment that the dust began to settle on the wreckage of the WTC, writers were struggling to come to terms with what they had watched unfold. Norman Mailer famously told his fellow novelist Jay McInerney that he should "wait ten years" before trying to write about the events of September 2001. McInerney himself felt so traumatized that, for a time, "The idea of 'invented characters' and alternate realities seemed trivial and frivolous and suddenly, horribly outdated" (McInerney 2005: n. pag.). Yet right from the start, for many ordinary New Yorkers, language itself became a source of consolation. As Ulrich Baer has pointed out:

> In the first days after the attack, the astounding efforts by the rescue workers found a symbolic echo in the poems postered on walls and fences: first in makeshift memorials, then delivered to inboxes all over the globe. This spontaneous burgeoning of

poetry responded to a need—a need for words that then took the form of written scrolls hung on fences and walls along with donated pens and markers, allowing anyone to offer the language of poetry where little could be said. (Baer 2002: 2)

Perhaps it was little wonder, then, that even at a very early stage, some critics insisted that only novelists, with their special gift for seeing and ordering the world, could begin to make sense of the attack on the United States. "Swamped as we've been with a tidal wave of quite unbearable reality, it's the writers of fiction, contemporary masters such as Ian McEwan in Britain and Paul Auster in the US, who have come up with the words of comfort and clarity we crave in the midst of shock and desolation," wrote *The Observer*'s literary editor Robert McCrum. "People sometimes dismiss fiction as mere entertainment, but at times like this there's no question that novelists at their best have a privileged access to truths about the human condition denied to others" (McCrum 2006: n. pag.).

Yet the bombings of September 11, 2001 cast a dark shadow not just over literary fiction, but over American culture more generally. In this case, as in so many others, the dividing line between supposedly high and low culture, which is sometimes imagined to be a kind of literary equivalent of the Berlin Wall, often proved wafer-thin. Many writers dealt with the shock of the atrocity by retreating inward to the domestic interior and the politics of the ordinary American household: think, for example, of Ken Kalfus's *A Disorder Peculiar to the Country* (2006), McInerney's *The Good Life* (2006), or Claire Messud's *The Emperor's Children* (2006), each of which deals with the impact of the attacks on individual families and couples. A smaller number chose to focus instead on the figure of the terrorist, perhaps above all in John Updike's *Terrorist* (2006), which takes the reader into the mind of a home-grown jihadist, Ahmad Ashmawy Mulloy. Yet in popular culture more broadly, it is the postapocalyptic themes of *The Road* that have resonated most strongly. Indeed, the image of a man wandering through a bleak, postapocalyptic landscape, through abandoned cities and shattered suburbs, has been one of the most successful cultural devices of the early twenty-first century. It is this image, for instance, that dominates the video game *Fallout 3* (2008), which sold almost five million units in its first three months, as well as its sequel *Fallout: New Vegas* (2010), which sold a further five million units in a matter of weeks. In both games, the player controls a lone wanderer on a journey through the wreckage of postapocalyptic American society, searching for food and supplies amid the ruined detritus of mass consumerism just as McCarthy's unnamed protagonist hunts for sustenance in the abandoned garage in the opening scenes of *The Road*.

In the *Fallout* universe, as in *The Road*, the hero is threatened by those who have turned to violence in the wake of the apocalypse—raiders, looters, and cannibals. In both cases, too, the thrill for the player, or, indeed, the reader, partly derives from the sheer exoticism—the extremism, even—of the setting: a world at once immediately familiar, teeming with reminders of the old order, and yet utterly changed, plunged into a darkness almost beyond comprehension. Indeed, this sense of rupture—ripping apart the shroud of supposed innocence and invulnerability in which American culture had once been cloaked—is central to one of the biggest selling games of the millennium, *Call of Duty: Modern Warfare 2* (2009). As in *Fallout 3*, part of the game is set inside a war-ravaged version of Washington, DC, which has been attacked in this case by Russian ultranationalists. Once again the player is confronted with a landscape at once recognizably American—the White House, the suburbs of Virginia—and yet also terrifyingly dangerous, a place of violence and suffering. The effect, of course, could hardly be more different from the haunting melancholy of Cormac McCarthy's novel. But coming as they did only a few years after the most emblematic American city of all had been mutilated forever by terrorist bombers, it is not hard to see why both were immediately seen as cultural products of 9/11.

Among a host of other cultural reflections of the events of September 2001, one phenomenon is especially revealing. This is the comic book and television series *The Walking Dead*, conceived in 2003 by writer Robert Kirkman. The television show's popularity, in particular, can hardly be exaggerated: not only has it won a host of awards and broken all cable television records, but its fourth and fifth seasons, which ran between 2013 and 2015, reportedly attracted the biggest audience for any cable or broadcast show among the 18–49 age group. Both the comics and the series follow the adventures of an Atlanta sheriff's deputy who wakes from a coma to find himself in a postapocalyptic United States where the vast majority of the population has turned into flesh-eating zombies. The parallels with *The Road* and the *Fallout* games are obvious, while Kirkman made no secret of his artistic debt to the terrible tragedy of September 2011. Born in Kentucky in 1978, he had only just broken into the world of comics at the time of the 9/11 attacks. Indeed, among his first published works was a contribution to the edited volume *9–11: Artists Respond* (2002), which was published to support the WTC Relief Fund, the Survivors Fund, the September 11th Fund, and the Twin Towers Fund, and included pieces by a vast number of well-known comic writers and illustrators. Kirkman was already thinking of a new project that would involve zombies, set in a postapocalyptic version of Atlanta, Georgia. Years later, when asked why so many readers in the 2000s and 2010s were drawn to postapocalyptic fiction, he gave a very revealing answer:

> I'd like to think it's the news. Everyone watches the news, and it's always depressing, and there's always dire consequences and horrible things happening and it kind of leads to everyone thinking, "What if? What if the end of the world were to come?" It's always something that people fantasize about, and I think it's fun to kind of see a fictional version of that. I don't know. We got Gulf oil spills and massive hurricanes and crazy earthquakes and there's all kinds of madness going on . . .
>
> *Was there anything in particular, news-wise, that was in your head when you started writing the book?*
>
> Well, 9/11 was definitely a big part of it, just because that was something that was on everyone's minds. It was the first time that we'd ever really been attacked on that level, and it was definitely scary. Everybody was scared, and the future was uncertain. It was definitely on my mind. (Pappedemas 2010: n. pag.)

It is, of course, hard to miss the unintentional echoes of Joe Penhall's explanation for the success of *The Road*.

Yet the case of *The Walking Dead* illustrates a deeper point, reinforced by almost every essay in the current volume. Although this book is about American and world literature after 9/11, it is not as though the clock started on September 12. To put it another way, the fiction of 9/11 did not emerge in a vacuum. Take, for example, the first episode of the televised version of *The Walking Dead*. In its most arresting image, the protagonist, a Stetson-wearing

Rick Grimes, rides into a deserted, smoldering Atlanta, smoke rising from its high-rise skyline in a stunning long shot that immediately evokes the news footage of the burning Twin Towers on the morning of September 11, 2001. Many, perhaps most viewers, must have been reminded, if only unconsciously, of the famous images of that terrible day, just as many readers must have thought of New York when they read Cormac McCarthy's memorable words about "the shape of a city . . . like a charcoal drawing sketched across the waste"(McCarthy 2006: 7). And yet it is also distinctly possible that when viewers watched the episode's opening scenes, set in the eerily deserted hospital where Rick awakes from his coma, they thought of the remarkably similar scenes that open the British zombie film *28 Days Later* (2002), which were explicitly modeled on the first chapter of the British writer John Wyndham's novel *The Day of the Triffids* (1951). The threat in Wyndham's book, however, comes not from zombies, but from nature itself, in the form of colossal artificially engineered plants, or "triffids," which have been farmed for years for their oil. In the central traumatic event, which happens before the start of the novel, a mysterious shower of meteors sends everyone on the planet blind, except those people—like the narrator—who were for some reason not watching the skies. The rest of the narrative is strikingly similar to that in *The Walking Dead*, which, at the time of writing, is still continuing. Wyndham's narrator wanders across a bleak, ravaged landscape, escapes looters and criminals, and makes contact with other survivors, eventually finding sanctuary on the Isle of Wight. In Britain, at least, the book was enormously influential. The science-fiction writer Brian Aldiss once called it a "cosy catastrophe" (Aldiss 1986: 253–4). The same thing might be said of *The Walking Dead*—and perhaps of many other post-9/11 narratives, too.

The parallels between *The Road*, *The Walking Dead*, and *The Day of the Triffids* offer a nice example of the way in which the literary, artistic, and cinematic reactions to 9/11 so often drew on much older images of apocalyptic disaster, not just in American literature but in Western culture more broadly. The image of the modern city devastated by catastrophe, for example, is very familiar. So in Wyndham's book, as in *The Walking Dead* and *The Road*, we follow the adventures of a single protagonist, who wanders in horrified disbelief across a bleak, broken postapocalyptic landscape, where he is threatened as much by his fellow human beings as he is by nature. And although many critics have interpreted Wyndham's book as a reflection of the paranoia of the early Cold War, it actually has an older pedigree, stretching back to H. G. Wells's *The War of the Worlds* (1898). In both Wyndham's and Wells's novels, however, the city left smoldering and deserted in the aftermath of catastrophe is not Atlanta or New York, but a much older urban embodiment of capitalist modernity: London. In *The War of the Worlds*, for example, the narrator wanders through the broken British capital, "a city condemned and derelict," noting not just the corpses, but the closed shops, "the houses locked up and the blinds drawn, the desertion, and the stillness." As he goes on, "the profounder grew the stillness. But it was not so much the stillness of death—it was the stillness of suspense, of expectation" (Wells 2013: 122–3, 124). This sense of an uncanny, unsettling stillness is very common in postapocalyptic fiction. "I could not shut out the sense of loneliness," reflects Wyndham's narrator in *The Day of the Triffids*. "Until then I had always thought of loneliness as something negative—an absence of company, and, of course, something temporary.... That day I had learned that it was much more. It was something which could press and oppress, could distort the ordinary, and play tricks with the mind" (Wyndham 2014: 177). Stillness, loneliness, absence, and tricks played on the mind: here, of course, are some of the abiding themes of the post-9/11 novel.[1]

To many people who watched the horror of 9/11 unfold on their television screens, what made it so shocking and so traumatic was that it seemed so unthinkable. "These were the kind of events that Hollywood has been imagining these past decades in the worst of its movies," wrote Ian McEwan, just hours after the 9/11 attacks. "But American reality always outstrips the imagination. And even the best minds, the best or darkest dreamers of disaster on a gigantic scale, from Tolstoy and Wells to Don DeLillo, could not have delivered us into the nightmare available on television news channels yesterday afternoon" (McEwan 2001: n. pag.). But although McEwan's horror was perfectly understandable, his analysis does not ring entirely true. In fact, writers and artists have been imagining the death of great cities for generations, and to readers and viewers alike, the image of the scarred, deserted urban landscape, its proud towers torn down by some dreadful catastrophe, could hardly be more familiar. An obvious example is the Victorian novel that partly inspired *The War of the Worlds*: Richard Jefferies's book *After London* (1885). The hauntingly memorable opening lines—"The old men say their fathers told them that soon after the fields were left to themselves a change began to be visible. It became green everywhere in the first spring, after London ended, so that all the country looked alike."—conjure up a world in which industrial modernity has been traumatically overthrown, plunging England, then the world's most advanced capitalist and imperialist power, back into the equivalent of the Middle Ages, not unlike the scenario in *Fallout 3*, or, indeed, *The Road* (Jefferies 2010: 1). And as in so many postapocalyptic visions, the most memorable moments come when the wanderer—a familiar protagonist in works of this kind, and an obvious nod to the legacy of the classical epic—finds himself in the flooded remains of a great city. "The deserted and utterly extinct city of London was under his feet," explains the narrator. Indeed, the sense of layer upon layer of history and memory is made explicit in the very ground beneath his feet. "The earth on which he walked, the black earth, leaving phosphoric footmarks behind him, was composed of the mouldered bodies of millions of men who had passed away in the centuries during which the city existed" (Jefferies 2010: 248).

The idea of the death of the city has always fascinated writers. It is surely no accident that Jane Jacobs's celebrated attack on twentieth-century modernist urban planning, published in 1961 and focusing particularly on mid-century New York, was entitled *The Death and Life of Great American Cities*. Indeed, even John Dos Passos's novel *Manhattan Transfer* (1925), one of the most celebrated literary evocations of twentieth-century New York, capturing the relentless, restless energy of the city in the middle of the Jazz Age, explicitly reminds its readers that all cities die eventually. Here is the opening of the second chapter, "Metropolis":

> There were Babylon and Nineveh; they were built of brick. Athens was gold marble columns. Rome was held up on broad arches of rubble. In Constantinople the minarets flame like great candles round the Golden Horn. . . . Steel, glass, tile, concrete will be the materials of the skyscrapers. Crammed on the narrow island the millionwindowed buildings will jut glittering, pyramid on pyramid like the white cloudhead above a thunderstorm. (Dos Passos 2003: 11)

It is telling that of the five imperial cities referred to here, all five were either famously destroyed or fell into deep decline. Babylon, originally one of the greatest of all ancient cities, was sacked by the Assyrians, conquered by the Persians, and eventually abandoned by the Arabs. Nineveh, capital of the Assyrian empire, was destroyed by their former vassals: among them, ironically, the Babylonians. Athens, which flourished in the fourth and fifth centuries BC, was conquered by the Romans; it fell into virtual disrepair and never recovered its former glory. Rome itself, once the capital of a mighty empire, was the victim of some of the most famous sieges in history, being sacked by the Goths, the Vandals, the Normans, the French, and the Spanish, among others, and spending much of its subsequent history as a virtual ruin. And Constantinople, the city established as a "New Rome," was famously besieged and sacked by the Ottoman Turks in 1453. Indeed, only two years before Dos Passos published *Manhattan Transfer*, the city subsequently known as Istanbul was still occupied by Allied troops in the aftermath of the First World War—a telling reminder that all cities, no matter how glittering their palaces, how bustling their arcades or how lofty their pretensions, can be brought low eventually.

With its explicit reference to the "millionwindowed buildings" that were coming to dominate the Manhattan skyline in the mid-1920s, Dos Passos's book now reads like an unsettling prophecy of the tragedy that was to strike New York on September 11, 2001. Yet, it also obviously nods to another prediction of urban nemesis, the British writer Rudyard Kipling's poem *Recessional*. Kipling wrote his poem in 1897 to mark Queen Victoria's diamond jubilee, at precisely the moment that the first serialization of H. G. Wells's *The War of the Worlds* was terrifying readers with its portrait of a future Martian-occupied London. And although Kipling is remembered as the quintessentially patriotic poet of Empire, *Recessional* has a remarkably downbeat, even bleak message, warning his countrymen that, "drunk with power" and their own achievements, they are in danger of losing their sense of humility before God:

> Far-called our navies melt away—
> On dune and headland sinks the fire—
> Lo, all our pomp of yesterday
> Is one with Nineveh and Tyre!
> Judge of the Nations, spare us yet,
> Lest we forget—lest we forget! (Kipling 1897: 13)

The reference to Nineveh here, as in Dos Passos's *Manhattan Transfer*, is no accident. To readers familiar with the Old Testament, no city was more synonymous with hubris and destruction. The biblical book of Nahum, for example, is virtually dominated by denunciations of Nineveh's arrogance and predictions of God's impending vengeance. "And the Lord hath given a commandment concerning thee, that no more of thy name be sown: out of the house of thy gods will I cut off the graven image and the molten image: I will make thy grave; for thou art vile," reads Nahum 1:14. As an earlier verse puts it, "with an overrunning flood he will make an utter end of the place thereof, and darkness shall pursue his enemies" (Nah. 1:8). Another Old Testament prophet, Zephaniah, struck a similar note:

> And he will stretch out his hand against the north, and destroy Assyria; and will make Nineveh a desolation, and dry like a wilderness.
> And flocks shall lie down in the midst of her, all the beasts of the nations: both the cormorant and the bittern shall lodge in the upper lintels of it; their voice shall sing in the windows; desolation shall be in the thresholds; for he shall uncover the cedar work.
> This is the rejoicing city that dwelt carelessly, that said in her heart, I am, and there is none beside me: how is she become a desolation, a place for beasts to lie down in! Every one that passeth by her shall hiss, and wag his hand. (Zeph. 2:13-15)

It probably hardly needs pointing out how uncannily the Israelite prophet's prediction of Nineveh's doom, turning the city from a monument to human hubris into an abandoned "desolation," foreshadows the imagery of later urban apocalypses, from the relatively benign Victorian pastoralism of *After London* to the wastelands of post-9/11 fantasies such as *The Road* and *The Walking Dead*.

It says a great deal about the importance of the apocalyptic theme in the Judeo-Christian tradition that the prophecies of Nineveh's destruction are not even the best-known images of catastrophe in the Old Testament. The book of Genesis alone, for example, describes not only the Tower of Babel—a kind of primitive skyscraper, abandoned after God confused its builders' languages and scattered them across the earth—but also the destruction of the cities Sodom and Gomorrah, consumed by fire and brimstone as divine punishment for their debauchery and wickedness. Indeed, when rereading these biblical stories, it is hard not to be reminded of Don DeLillo's poignant words in December 2001: "The writer begins in the towers, trying to imagine the moment, desperately. Before politics, before history and religion, there is the primal terror. People falling from the towers hand in hand" (DeLillo 2001: n. pag.). Most famously, of course, there is the story of the Great Flood, which recurs in religious traditions across the globe, from the Mesopotamian epic of Gilgamesh to the flood myths of the Chinese and the ancient Greeks. In the best-known biblical version, God sends the flood as a punishment for mankind's sinfulness, though not before warning Noah to build an ark to save himself, his family, and a pair of every animal on the planet. And as Erik J. Wielenberg has argued, there are obvious parallels between the Flood narrative and the scenario in *The Road*, with the unnamed man cast as a kind of unwilling Noah in a postapocalyptic world where God's existence cannot be taken for granted. Just God charged Noah with keeping human life alive on Earth, so the man feels the awful responsibility of his son's survival. "He knew only that the child was his warrant," McCarthy tells us. "He said: If he is not the word of God God never spoke" (McCarthy 2006: 4). These, significantly, are the first words the man speaks in the novel. Similarly, the idea of the fire that his son carries within him, not unlike the Holy Spirit, is a time-honored religious image. And at the very end of the novel, after the man's death, his son is taken up by an obviously religious family. The mother, we are told, "would talk to him sometimes about God. . . . She said that the breath of God was his breath yet though it pass from man to man through all of time" (McCarthy 2006: 241).

No doubt, literary scholars will be debating the issue of religion in McCarthy's *The Road* for years to come. The broader point, though, is that what makes post-9/11 literature so richly intriguing is precisely that it draws on deeper religious, cultural, and aesthetic traditions, refining and reframing them for the twenty-first-century audience. To give just a couple of brief examples, it is no coincidence that Lynne Sharon Schwartz's novel *The Writing on the Wall* (2006), which is discussed in Sien Uytterschout and Kristiaan Versluys's essay, takes its title from the biblical book of Daniel, in which the prophet interprets a mysterious message that appears during the Babylonian king Belshazzar's feast. God has weighed Belshazzar's kingdom and found it wanting: that very night, proud, mighty Babylon falls to the Medes and the Persians. History, too, looms large in the post-9/11 novel. As Debra Shostak shows in her forensic discussion of Philip Roth's *The Plot Against America* (2004) and Jonathan Safran Foer's *Extremely Loud and Incredibly Close* (2005), both books address "the question of what traumatic history means in America," with the latter looking back to the bombing of Dresden in 1945, an urban catastrophe on a genuinely apocalyptic scale. In fact, the memory of the Second World War has cast a remarkably heavy shadow over American writing in the first decade of the twenty-first century, from the threat of domestic Nazism and anti-Semitism in Roth's alternative history of the early 1940s to the images of Auschwitz and Hiroshima that, as David Brauner reminds us, feature in Sam Glanzman's polemical story "There were tears in her eyes" (2002). And even though many of the first reactions to 9/11 treated it as an event without precedent in human history, it is remarkable how often writers and poets have reached back to their predecessors for inspiration. For as Aimee Pozorski writes in her essay contemplating the image of the tower and its fall, to read "a canonical poem such as William Butler Yeats's 'The Tower' or Hart Crane's 'The Broken Tower' is to witness a twentieth-century poem's foretelling of a twenty-first century trauma."

Perhaps what this suggests, therefore, is that even though writers initially treated 9/11 as a moment of extraordinary rupture, after which nothing would ever be the same again, it was actually much less exceptional than we often think. "After a couple of hours at their desks, on September 12, 2001, all the writers on earth were reluctantly considering a change of occupation," wrote Martin Amis a few months later (Amis 2002: n. pag.) But as we now know, none of them followed through: instead, many of them turned to the terrorist attacks for inspiration. Indeed, as early as September 30, the critic John Dugdale pointed that far from falling silent, writers had been remarkably quick to turn their shock into words. "Among the literary authors who have written about the World Trade Center bombing so far," he noted, "are Martin Amis, Peter Carey, Amitav Ghosh, David Grossman, Ian McEwan, Jay McInerney, Susan Sontag, John Updike and Jeanette Winterson" (Dugdale 2001: n. pag.). Only a week later, meanwhile, James Wood published a blisteringly powerful rejoinder to Jay McInerney's suggestion that, after September 2001, New York fiction would never be the same again. In fact, as Wood pointed out, the great fictions of the city—the likes of Stephen Crane's *Maggie* (1893), Theodore Dreiser's *Sister Carrie* (1900), Henry Roth's *Call It Sleep* (1934) and Saul Bellow's *Seize the Day* (1956)—had already explored precisely those themes that would obsess writers in the early twenty-first century. "As soon as one recalls these novels," Wood explained, "it becomes difficult to imagine the precise ways in which they would have been different had they had to accommodate a mutilation of the kind visited upon the city on September 11. And that is partly because they are already dark books, in which the city looms jaggedly. It is only the McInerneys, for whom Manhattan is a tinkle of restaurants, who are suddenly surrounded by the broken glass of their foolish optimism. The pessimist is already ruined, and knows it" (Wood 2001: n. pag.).

Time, of course, has proved him right: as the essays in this book show, far from dragging American fiction onto an entirely new path, 9/11 often reinforced trends that were already underway. Indeed, it is worth remembering that the novel has always dealt with moments of violence, rupture, and trauma, from the chaos of the battle of Waterloo in Stendhal's *La Chartreuse de Parme* (1839) to the shock of the Franco-Prussian War in Emile Zola's *La Débâcle* (1892). Even the figure of the terrorist has a long pedigree in literary fiction, being most famously represented by the anarchists in Joseph Conrad's *The Secret Agent* (1907). And American fiction is little different: indeed, given the republic's bloody and contested history, it is hardly surprising that so many memorable American works, from William Faulkner's *The Sound and the Fury* (1929) to Tim O' Brien's *Going After Cacciato* (1978) to Cormac McCarthy's *Blood Meridian* (1985), engage with precisely the same themes of violence, faith, trauma, loss, and absence that have dominated so much post-9/11 literature. So perhaps it is only a slight exaggeration to suggest that these are the themes, not merely of post-9/11 fiction but of all fiction, from the classical epic to the postmodern pastiche. "You can read me a story," the boy asks his father in *The Road*. "Cant you, Papa?" "Yes," says his father. "I can" (McCarthy 2006: 7). It is a story as old as humankind.

What unites the essays in this volume is not just their careful attention to detail or their sensitivity to language, but their eagerness to place post-9/11 fiction in a broader intellectual, cultural, literary, and ideological context. In her opening chapter, "Prosthetic Fictions," Debra Shostak reads Jonathan Safran Foer's novel *Extremely Loud and Incredibly Close* (2005) through Philip Roth's *The Plot Against America* (2004), showing how both writers explore the nature of historical trauma by using the innocent perspectives of child narrators, their responses "uncensored by familiarity with suffering or the mature practices of self-suppression." As Shostak argues, this choice enables a kind of "prosthetic imagination," allowing the narrator to manipulate images and retreat into counter-narratives as a reaction to trauma, falling back on a sentimental fantasy of prelapsarian American innocence. What both novels share, she suggests, is "the impulse to live *outside* of history, simply, and safe at home." By contrast, Aaron DeRosa focuses closely on Don DeLillo's haunting novel *Falling Man* (2007), which is concerned less with historical antecedents than with the collapse of the WTC's towers themselves. As DeRosa sees it, *Falling Man* has a quality of "purity" precisely because of its "willed refusal to see beyond the WTC and the fixed temporality of 'September 11, 2001'." What DeLillo's book presents, he argues, is 9/11 as "neither an end nor a beginning, but a static moment held in perpetuity," in which time itself is suspended. Yet, DeRosa also shows how *Falling Man* touches on the themes of waste and consumption explored in DeLillo's earlier work *Underworld* (1997), as well as in Walter Benjamin's description of the past as an accumulation of rubble in his celebrated essay on the philosophy of history. Ultimately, however, he suggests that, by shrinking from the future and deliberately eschewing historical connections, DeLillo's book is "as insular and self-contained as Cormac McCarthy's *The Road*, whose post-apocalyptic setting affords no beginning or end, but rather places its characters in a perpetual state of precarity and indistinction."

David Brauner focuses on the comics published in the wake of 9/11, from anthologies such as *9/11 Emergency Relief* (2002) to Art Spiegelman's best seller *In the Shadow of No Towers* (2004). Among other things, he examines graphic novelists' treatment of the WTC's twin towers, which have dominated theoretical discussions by thinkers such as Jean Baudrillard. In fact, Brauner suggests that "omnipresent though they are in one sense, the towers are also curiously absent from many of these works," and he looks closely at their depiction in works such as *In the Shadow of No Towers* and Sam Glanzman's "There were tears in her eyes." The latter, as we have seen, draws an explicit parallel between the attack on the WTC and the Nazi death camp at Auschwitz, and this nods in turn to the chillingly memorable scenes in Spiegelman's earlier work *Maus* (1991). Above all, Brauner asks whether the comics written after 9/11 betray an authorial anxiety about the "issues of self-representation," noting that none of them try to show events inside the towers. Instead, many use the distancing device of television—a device that, as Brauner sees it, "domesticates the narrative of national trauma." Meanwhile, images of falling towers also dominate Aimee Pozorksi's essay, "Rebuilding after 9/11: The figure of the tower and the poetics of the future," which examines the lineage of the figure of the tower in poetry in English, both before and after the events of September 2001. Pozorski suggests that it works to "define and exemplify a poetics of the future," which she traces back to Sigmund Freud's ideas about trauma, as well as to images of the tower by writers as diverse as Chaucer, Eliot, and Yeats. As Pozorski sees it, poets reacted to 9/11 by trying to rebuild what the towers of the WTC represented: "American power, confidence, indestructability." The towers stand as "Freudian symbols of prowess and ego—two qualities that appeal to twenty-first century writers seeking to write their way to a new poetic." The result is what Pozorski calls a "poetics of futurity," remaking us—readers as well as writers—in a more democratic image.

Mark Eaton's essay opens by discussing John Updike's poem "Icarus," which imagines an encounter with a suspected terrorist on an airplane, but which was actually published before the attacks of September 11. As Eaton shows, Updike's controversial novel *Terrorist* built on his long-standing interest in terrorism and, in particular, Islam: as early as 1989, in fact, Updike had written of his fascination with Islam and his horror at the cult of the suicide bomber. But Eaton also sets Updike's novel in a broader social and political context, from racial profiling at airports to a growing anxiety about the radicalization of Muslim immigrants in Western societies. And he looks closely at the way in which *Terrorist* meticulously sets out the process and psychology of radicalization, giving us "a glimpse into how religious, psychological, and socio-political motivations combine to create a potent cocktail of terror." For Eaton, *Terrorist* is a deeply serious novel, attempting to come to terms with the problem of religious violence, and offering some important observations "about the pathways to religious extremism and violence that have continued to inspire young men like Ahmad, both in the U.S. and abroad." By contrast, Sien Uytterschout and Kristiaan Versluys devote their chapter to two novels with a more introspective, domestic approach: Lynne Sharon Schwartz's *The Writing on the Wall* (2005) and Paul Auster's *Man in the Dark* (2008), whose protagonists tell themselves stories as a way of warding off the pain of the past. These are novels, they argue, about the "interconnection of public language and personal grief," intertwining narratives grand and little, and showing that so-called domestication is probably necessary to help individuals come to terms with such a profound national trauma. Perhaps above all, they argue that neither book deserves criticism for retreating into the domestic arena: for this, they write, "is not to be mistaken for a trivialization of the events, nor is it a mark of withdrawal from historical and political reality." Instead, according to Uytterschout and Versluys, their achievement is to throw that reality into sharper relief.

As Hamilton Carroll observes in his essay on *Let the Great World Spin* (2009), Colum McCann's achievement is to have written a book that never mentions the attacks of September 11 at all, but yet is clearly "a novel *of* September 11," with his account of Philippe Petit's tightrope walk between the towers of the new WTC raising unsettling questions about "art and death, spectacle and war, humanity and memory." As Carroll sees it, the attack on New York is "held apart in the novel, caught between a past (1974) that appears to fully anticipate it and a future (2006) in which it has already been overshadowed by the U.S.-led ground wars in Afghanistan and Iraq." McCann's book, he suggests, reworks the past, giving Petit's wire walk an ending and a meaning that the Frenchman could never have imagined. But he also draws attention to the novel's qualities as a literary text, not least its engagement with writers from Alfred Lord Tennyson to Philip Larkin—a thread of continuity that parallels what Carroll sees as the novel's abiding theme, the idea of "grace and community" and the human capacity to affirm life in the presence of death. Paul Jenner, meanwhile, approaches Jonathan Franzen's best-selling book *Freedom* (2010) with a similarly sharp eye for nuance. As Jenner shows, Franzen's novel, like so many post-9/11 fictions, wrestles with the problem of resolving the personal and the political, a challenge embodied by the character Joey, the young Republican sympathizer who leaves his roommate watching the terrorist attacks on television in order to hurry to a half-empty economics lecture. Yet for Jenner, characterizations of the book as merely an exercise in unreflective realism miss the point. Franzen, he shows, refuses one of realism's central principles, the idea that the author has a privileged access to truth. And while Franzen's characters struggle to work out "how to live" in an age dominated by anxieties about terrorism, war, and national security, one of his book's most notable characteristics is that it openly admits the difficulty of providing a controlling narrative.

Finally, the book concludes with my own chapter on Amy Waldman's novel *The Submission* (2011), which invents a scenario in which a Muslim architect is selected to design a memorial garden to the victims of the WTC attacks, provoking a firestorm of protest and controversy. As I hope to show, Waldman's book is a work of greatly complex plotting, with its structure mirroring the architect's design in the novel. But it also feels like an appropriate note on which to end, since it concludes with a section set some twenty years in the future, in which a grown-up son mourns his lost father, a victim of the 9/11 atrocity. Fathers and sons, grief and memory, and life and death: themes not just of *The Submission*, *The Road*, and a host of other post-9/11 novels, but of fiction itself.

Note

1 On the links between Wyndham, Wells and Jefferies, and the parallels with *Fallout 3*, I am indebted to conversations with Dominic Sandbrook, who discusses them in greater depth in his forthcoming book on the British imagination.

Works cited

Amis, Martin. "The Voice of the Lonely Crowd." *The Guardian*, June 1, 2002. Available online: http://www.theguardian.com/books/2002/jun/01/philosophy.society.

DeLillo, Don. "In the Ruins of the Future." *The Guardian*, December 22, 2001. Available online: http://www.theguardian.com/books/2001/dec/22/fiction.dondelillo.

Dos Passos, John. *Manhattan Transfer*. New York: Mariner, [1925] 2003.

Dugdale, John. "World Trade Center Bombing." *The Sunday Times*, September 30, 2001.

Jefferies, Richard. *After London*. London: Classic Pages, [1884] 2010.

Kipling, Rudyard. "Recessional." *The Times*, June 17, 1897, 13.

Luce, Dianne C. "Beyond the Border: Cormac McCarthy in the New Millennium." *Cormac McCarthy Journal* 6, no. 1 (Fall 2009): 8–9.

McCracken, Brett. "The Road." *Christianity Today*, November 25, 2009. Available online: http://www.christianitytoday.com/ct/2009/novemberweb-*only*/*theroad.html*.

McCrum, Robert. "The Need for Novelists." *The Observer*, September 23, 2001. Available online: http://www.theguardian.com/books/2001/sep/23/september11.society.

McEwan, Ian. "Beyond Belief." *The Guardian*, September 12, 2001. Available online: http://www.theguardian.com/world/2001/sep/12/september11.politicsphilosophyandsociety.

McInerney, Jay. "The Uses of Invention." *The Guardian*, September 17, 2005. Available online: http://www.theguardian.com/books/2005/sep/17/fiction.vsnaipaul.

Pappademas, Alex. "Dead Reckoning: Robert Kirkman Brings Zombies to Don Draper's Backyard." August 2, 2010. Available online: http://www.gq.com/blogs/the-q/2010/08/dead-reckoning-robert-kirkman-brings-zombies-to-don-drapers-backyard.html.

Penhall, Joe. "Last Man Standing: What Cormac McCarthy Made of My Adaptation of *The Road*." *The Guardian*, January 4, 2010. Available online: http://www.theguardian.com/film/2010/jan/04/the-road-cormac-mccarthy-viggo-mortensen.

Wells, H. G. *The War of the Worlds*. New York: Tribeca, 2013 [1898].

Wielenberg, Erik J. "God, Morality and Meaning in Cormac McCarthy's *The Road*." *Cormac McCarthy Journal* 8, no. 1 (Fall 2010): 1–16.

Wood, James. "Tell Me, How Does it Feel?" *The Guardian*, October 6, 2001. Available online: http://www.theguardian.com/books/2001/oct/06/fiction.

Wyndham, John. *The Day of the Triffids*. London: Penguin, [1951] 2014.

1

Prosthetic fictions: Reading Jonathan Safran Foer's *Extremely Loud and Incredibly Close* through Philip Roth's *The Plot Against America*

Debra Shostak

The most searing and uncanny image that Philip Roth provides in *The Plot Against America* (2004) is Alvin Roth's amputated stump. Marking the trauma that historically motivated violence places upon the body, Alvin's stump offers a figurative starting point to examine the havoc that traumatic events wreak in human lives. Like Roth, Jonathan Safran Foer in *Extremely Loud and Incredibly Close* (2005) is, as David Brauner has suggested, interested less in the lineaments of a specific historical trauma than in how it imposes on "the consciousness and conscience" of an individual, especially his "subjecthood, and subjectivity" (Brauner 2007: 201). Yet, published within a year of each other, the two novels followed hard upon the catastrophic events of September 11, 2001, in the United States and represent, either overtly, in Foer's case, or by indirection, in Roth's, the consequences of national injury and shock on the nation's most vulnerable citizens. Both Roth and Foer focalize their exploration of historical trauma within the innocent narrative perspective of children, whose responses remain uncensored by familiarity with suffering or the mature practices of self-suppression. Roth's novel need not be *about* 9/11 for its meanings to be inflected by that recent historical fact. The confluences between the two novels' implicit and explicit representations of national trauma are enough to suggest how, together, they answer the question of what traumatic history means in America—an answer that, in the end, ironically deflects the question.

Each novel interweaves a terrifying version of the mid-twentieth-century European theater of war into its narrative premises about American history. One might then conclude, as Alfred Hornung does of Foer, that the novels bear witness to a "transnational turn" (Hornung 2009: 172) in American fiction, enabled by the unusual formal and generic choices the writers make to accommodate their subject matter. Certainly, the specter of an attack against the United States, diabolically using its own instruments of commerce, politics, leisure, or media, affords a rare opportunity to conceptualize traumatic action as happening queasily both within and beyond the borders of self and nation. Foer's chapters interlace the narrative perspectives of three characters—the child Oskar Schell, whose father dies in one of the Twin Towers, and his paternal grandparents, who were devastated by the firebombing of Dresden during the Second World War. *Extremely Loud* thus urges contextualization of the historical trauma of early-twenty-first-century Americans within that of the 1940s German noncombatants, making of "history" a multiple reckoning, temporally and geographically. The doubling is differently conceived in *The Plot*. Roth's dystopic counterhistory of a United States growing increasingly fascist and anti-Semitic under the presidency of an isolationist Charles Lindbergh plays always against a reader's memory of "actual" history. The history that really happened remains unnarrated, however, except insofar as the novel ends by reinserting its two years of invented events back into the known past and includes an extensive postscript of Roth's research. Still, in the resonance of *The Plot*'s plot with the persecution and annihilation of Europe's Jews, Roth introduces a transnational perspective that boils down to the question, "What if the United States had been like Europe?"

Roth has insisted that his novel is not an allegory for the events and political aftermath of 9/11.[1] The shock of direct assault within the borders of the United States, however, unfelt since Pearl Harbor, deepens its power and enables its reading as an uncannily displaced response to an all too recent past. In this regard, Charles Lewis offers succinct distinctions between "the claim that a novel is 'about' 9/11, the proposition that a novel has been influenced by 9/11, and the observation that readers might be interested in a novel because of 9/11" (Lewis 2009: 249). Since Roth's novel falls between the second and third possibilities, it seems fair—and useful—to read through the palimpsest of its representation of the years 1940–1942, a figuration of the trauma of 2001. Indeed, *The Plot* provides a compelling scheme within which to understand the devices of *Extremely Loud*.

While for both novels the traumatic disruption of pastoral American complacencies seems to resituate the United States and its citizens' awareness within a transnational context, their thrust is not to pull American history into a global network of meanings. As Rachel Greenwald Smith argues about *Extremely Loud*, the novel's representation of trauma "leads to a reading of the event that is compatible only with a highly limited historical outlook, one that sees the events of 9/11 as isolated from any larger geopolitical frame" (Smith 2011: 157). Specifically, while both novels develop a counter-narrative that realizes and displaces trauma toward the past—whether a wholly invented or recognizably "real" past—both prompt historical reflection to give way to the insular needs of the wounded subject within this present moment of suffering. Roth's and Foer's novels depict this consequence in surprisingly similar terms. Despite fundamental differences in the narration, they share important structures and motifs, including a focus on a precocious, narcissistic boy's consciousness, exploration of his relationship to a father for whom the phallic power of the patriarch has been subverted by events, cultivation of surrogate father figures, chartings of the boy's solo quests through his city, a redemptive but sentimental narrative arc, and even a stamp collection. Together, these emphases move the novels inward rather than toward the historical world. Each finally reduces historical rupture to a personal rupture, the transnational to the domestic and, most notably, to the familial.

This is why I open with Alvin's stump and the contradictory fascination and revulsion, fear and adulation that young Philip exhibits toward Alvin, his wound, and his artificial leg. The central metaphor of the amputation in *The Plot*—Roth titles Chapter 4 "The Stump"—offers an interpretive framework for the engagement with traumatic history there, and in *Extremely Loud*, exposes the useful paradoxes of Roth's complementary trope of the *prosthesis*. Both novels turn the material notion of a *prosthetic device* into a *literary* concept. From the root sense of an *addition*—in ancient Greek, of a syllable to the beginning of a word—the therapeutic application of the term to physical absences has, since its introduction in the eighteenth century, implied an *artificial* substitute ("prosthesis," n. *OED online*). David Mitchell and Sharon Snyder summarize the anatomical application: "A prosthesis seeks to accomplish an illusion. A body deemed lacking . . . needs compensation" (Mitchell and Snyder 2000: 6). David Wills teases out a cluster of meanings as he applies the term literally to anatomy and figuratively to the act of writing: "Prosthesis [is] about . . . placement, displacement, replacement, standing, dislodging, substituting, setting, amputating, supplementing" (Wills 1995: 9). If, as is thought, trauma stops time for a victim, the prosthesis restarts it. Yet, the addition, the substitute, the artifice, the metaphor, or the illusion of wholeness is always an index to what is missing, the mark of a *thing* in place of *nothing*, even as it carries a wounded person past traumatic injury. As the supplement to fill a lack, the prosthesis is the mechanism by which one gets back on one's feet, as it were, returning to the world in time; yet as the device that at once covers and uncovers traumatic absence, it also relentlessly signifies what is forever lost. *Memory* is in this regard a fundamentally related function, and likewise fundamentally double-edged. As Michael Rothberg writes concerning Holocaust memoir, memory serves as "a kind of prosthesis, an instrument that keeps subjects both in touch with and separate from their past" (Rothberg 2000: 172). The prosthesis marks the point—the present—at which one is contrarily directed toward both the future and the past. If Roth and Foer have written fictions that are, by some measure, "prosthetic," they at once expose the rip in the fabric of American consciousness that was caused by trauma on a national scale, offer compensations, and yet still reveal themselves as artifice.[2]

It takes little familiarity with Roth's recurrent psychoanalytic framing for his novels to see Alvin's amputation as a symbolic castration. Alvin joins the Canadian army bursting with idealistic fury at American isolationism at the beginning of the Second World War and returns defeated, depleted, and disaffected; his physical impotence becomes both psychological and moral. Roth narrates *The Plot* in the first person, from the point of view of the child "Philip Roth," who admires Alvin as a young man larger than life—

a surrogate father figure—before he leaves. Philip's bewilderment about how to view the damaged man on his return foreshadows his shock when his own father, Herman, seems crushed by America's subsequent swing toward institutionalized anti-Semitism, which constitutes the primary focus of the novel.

Roth's detailed representation of Philip's obsession with Alvin's stump and prosthesis demonstrates the web of related psychoanalytic mechanisms underlying his response to the trauma of history that is brought home to him. Anticipating that Alvin's arrival at the Roth house will destroy its security, Philip cries, "No! Alvin can't stay here—he has only one leg!" (Roth 2004: 109). The truncated body is uncanny to him—in Freud's terms, the *unheimlich*, or unhomely, which signifies castration anxiety (Freud, "Uncanny": 219, n. 1). His sensory perceptions of Alvin, who smells "rotten" and whose empty trouser leg "startle[s]" him (Roth 2004: 127), suggest that Alvin's stump serves as a synecdoche for the body as a corpse. Philip expresses his fear and revulsion at the liminal state of Alvin's wounded body when he asks his mother, "Will I ever have to touch it?" (Roth 2004: 131).

Julia Kristeva describes such a feeling of revulsion in terms of *abjection*. Abjection breaks down the borders between death and life and is caused by that which "disturbs identity, system, order. What does not respect borders, positions, rules. The in-between, the ambiguous, the composite" (Kristeva 1982: 4). Abjection, which entails consciousness of the crude physicality of loss, breaks down the border between the "I" and an object; revulsion expresses viscerally the loss of subjectivity, as the "I" comprehends becoming a *thing*. Roth exemplifies such revulsion when Philip, obedient to the role he has taken on as Alvin's nursemaid, practices wrapping Alvin's bandages around his own leg, only to vomit when he finds a scab from the stump deposited on *his* leg, as if the very loss itself has been translated to him. *The Plot* dramatizes the act of psychological repression that follows upon the boy's recognition: whether the abject body is seen or invisible becomes crucial to Philip's vicarious experience of Alvin's traumatic wound. Philip's innocence allows him to hope that something will not *be* if it is not *seen*. Recounting "the fear of gaping merged with the terror of seeing" (Roth 2004: 128), and "afraid to see what came next, I sat on my bed and watched" (Roth 2004: 136), Philip attests to the contrary responses of the traumatized child to the abject which, Kristeva explains, "simultaneously beseeches and pulverizes the subject" (Kristeva 1982: 5). As Alvin's stump becomes a homegrown metaphor for the terrible world that enters his front door, Philip sees "what the word 'stump' describes: the blunt remnant of something whole that belonged there and once had been there" (Roth 2004: 136). The lost wholeness encompasses himself, his family, and his community of New Jersey Jews.

In this image of lack, Roth connects Philip's view of the uncanny stump with historical events and with the inability of his father to maintain the law that signifies social order and his phallic authority. Philip mourns the "new life" that Alvin's return begins, when "my father [fell] apart . . . crying like both a baby abandoned and a man being tortured" (Roth 2004: 113). The drastic changes under Lindbergh's administration—the brainwashing of Philip's older brother in the "Just Folks" program of Jewish assimilation, the relocation of Newark's Jews to rural Christian enclaves by the "Office of American Absorption" (Roth 2004: 84), and Kristallnacht-like violence against Jewish schools and synagogues—all this leads Herman toward breakdown, climaxing in his violent fistfight with a cynical Alvin, who has turned from Herman's earnest rectitude toward the criminal underworld. The loss of the father's omnipotence is what the traumatized boy had most feared from the "vengeful fury of the missing leg" (Roth 2004: 133).

The dual signification of the prosthesis emerges when Philip sublimates his abhorrence by devoting himself to the care of Alvin's stump and artificial leg, which he sees as "horrible and a wonder both" (Roth 2004: 142). The material prosthesis eventually accomplishes a normalizing function for Alvin. As Roth's counterhistory and the "perpetual fear" with which the novel opens take over the narrative (Roth 2004: 1), however, the prosthesis fails Philip's deeper need for a symbolic supplement to the growing absence of his childhood security. He thus seeks refuge in other ways: in his stamp collection, for example, whose loss psychically, when he dreams of the stamps defaced with swastikas, and literally, when a horse kicks him in the head and he drops the album into a dark field, foreshadows his rising hysteria along with that of his family and community; and in his stalking of supposedly Christian men through Newark, when, in an expression of magical thinking, he performs being a "lost boy" (Roth 2004: 116) to ward off the condition's inevitability. The stamp collection is a prosthetic object; the "following Christians" escapades are prosthetic actions.

Roth presses the metaphoric opposition of stump and prosthesis most overtly in relation to Philip's double, the neighbor boy Seldon Wishnow.[3] Seldon's father, in his cancer and suicide, has doubled Herman by embodying the failure to maintain the phallic power of the patriarch, a failure that is exacerbated when, to his horror, the orphaned son discovers his father's corpse, echoing Philip's encounter with the abject body of Alvin. Because Philip, in his child's narcissism, sees Seldon not empathetically but as a terrifying enactment of his own feared abjection, he develops an increasing aversion to this *real* "lost boy." When Philip conspires to have Seldon and his mother, instead of the Roth family, relocated to Kentucky, he satisfies his desire to make the child's threat to his consciousness and self-concept disappear. Philip's prosthetic act, a hideous betrayal, is reversed, however, in the final chapter, whose climactic events undercut the chapter "Perpetual Fear," thus underscoring the wavering commitment in *The Plot* to a reckoning with transhistorical trauma. When Seldon is orphaned, his mother slaughtered in an American pogrom sparked by Lindbergh's policies, Herman regains his position of the symbolic Father, restoring order by his heroic rescue of the wholly traumatized child. This allows Roth to explicate his central metaphor in the final line of the novel, when Philip proclaims that Seldon "was the stump" and "I was the prosthesis" (Roth 2004: 362).

If Philip can fill the gap in another's traumatic loss, replacing the lost father, he must in some measure be whole himself. Herman's recuperation—"My father was a rescuer and orphans were his specialty" (Roth 2004: 358)—militates against Philip's feeling the full burden of traumatic history, an easing that Roth also accomplishes in the preceding chapter when, by conveniently making Lindbergh disappear, he brings order to Philip's world, channeling the counterfactual events right back into America's relative triumph in the Second World War. The plot of *The Plot* ends, as Tim Parrish notes, "with a sense of relief and even celebration"; Parrish concludes that the novel "fail[s] to create a nightmare America equal to what European Jews experienced," because Roth believes that "in America 'history' has had a happy ending" (Parrish 2011: 157, 160). The novel plays the part of a prosthesis, marking loss but devising a wholeness that mends it. *The Plot* thus serves for Charles Lewis as a "prosthetic screen" (Lewis 2008: 248) for the recent events of 9/11—and for the Holocaust, to which it refers more overtly—but does not thereby move American experience into a transnational historical consciousness. The normalizing capacities of prosthetic fiction offer a palliative for national trauma; the fear is *not*, finally, perpetual. The Roth family makes it intact.

Like Roth, Foer figures prosthetic devices alternately in terms of a fetish for a material object, ritual or compensatory actions or speech, or the invention of counterhistories. The prosthetic devices that Foer deploys, however, are much more numerous and densely presented than in Roth's novel, and the writers' choices of narrative voice make for some fundamental contrasts in their meanings. First, the structure of *Extremely Loud* interweaves discontinuous stories of historical trauma—the aftermath of 9/11 with the Dresden firebombing of 1945, which Oskar's grandparents survived physically, if not psychologically. Foer intensifies the representation of trauma by expressing it equally among the three rotating first-person narrations of Oskar and his grandparents. In this balanced knitting together of their stories, with 2001 juxtaposed with 1945, Foer formally inserts the United States into transnational history. Second, whereas Roth presents his first-person narrative voice largely in the simple past tense—a choice signaled by the first sentence's announcement that he is recounting "memories" (Roth 2004: 1)—Foer's tenses are less stable, shifting between the past and present or present progressive. Roth's narrator is always an adult Philip looking back on his child self, conveying some distance on the counterhistorical events Roth invents; Foer's Oskar, however, exists often in the immediate moment of suffering. Third, Roth's narration is largely future-directed, where the "perpetual fear" concerns what *might* happen (or, given the tenses, paradoxically what might *have* happened), making *The Plot* pre- or "present"-traumatic. Foer's narration is directed toward what irreversibly *has* happened, making *Extremely Loud* fully posttraumatic.

The historically prior trauma of Oskar's grandparents' survival of the Dresden firebombing serves as the narrative and symbolic frame for Oskar's post-9/11 storytelling. Foer presents the couple as a paradigm of the posttraumatic condition, which he figures largely by way of their relationship to language. Grandfather, known to Oskar until the close of the novel only as "the renter," has lost his first love, Anna, and the child whom she is bearing; he remains in a permanent, static moment of loss, immersed in a memory from which he cannot budge into an ongoing present. Having immigrated to the United States, he marries Anna's sister; together, they construct a complex prosthetic system of rules and codes to structure—and sidestep—their shared traumatic loss. They name their intimate physical spaces, converting their entire environment into prosthetic signifiers. In their "Something Places," they tentatively confront their concrete existence in the world of the present, and hence the abjection that attends absence. Their "Nothing Places," however, offer "complete privacy ... in which one could temporarily cease to exist" (Foer 2005: 110) and in which, as Philippe Codde suggests, they "act out the emptiness that pervades their lives" (Codde 2011: 682). By this means, they oppose, in Freud's terms for the psychic confrontation with traumatic loss, mourning to melancholy. Roughly speaking, Grandfather remains trapped in perpetual melancholy, the timeless condition in which trauma is acted out in endless repetition, while Grandmother engages slowly in the process of working through, back into the temporal world, that Freud associates with the remediating condition of mourning.[4]

Foer figures the grandparents' traumatic trajectories in relation to the erasure of language. Grandfather's first chapter at once establishes that his loss strips him of his voice—that he loses all his words, from "want," "shame," and "loss" itself, finally to "I" (Foer 2005: 16–17)—as a clear representation of his abjected subjectivity and his repression of all desire and now, literally, of his unspeakable memories. Paradoxically, he compulsively fills his empty spaces with *writing*, but it is writing that, according to the novel's premise, has— with only one exception—no diegetic reader. Most notable are the many letters he writes but does not send to the son he has abandoned, Oskar's father, Thomas Schell, Jr., comprising the chapters appearing from his viewpoint. The letters bespeak his failure of will, his consuming fear of living in the present, and his obsessive need to articulate his pain and guilt, which is thwarted by his equivalent need to blot out his memories. Foer brings the Grandfather's contradictorily self-erasing language to a climax when, in his last chapter, he narrates his relationship with Oskar. Again addressing his son, he writes, "He was trying to find you, just as you'd tried to find me, it broke my heart into more pieces than my heart was made of, why can't people say what they mean at the time?" (Foer 2005: 279). Foer then represents the impossibility of saying what one means, if the meaning is traumatic absence, as Grandfather's writing squeezes together to the point of unreadability—in a typographical blackness, a palimpsest so dense as to be utterly blank—when he at last hears his son's final phone message. Writing becomes for him a failed prosthetic act, a silent shriek.

Grandmother, however, moves in a reverse direction with respect to language. Urged by Grandfather to write her life story on the typewriter he has rescued from their Dresden past, she busies herself in typing some thousand pages of "My Life" (Foer 2005: 120), which, when she has finished, Grandfather finds to be completely blank, having been tapped out without a ribbon. In his terms, this task—of her writing and his reading—might have been a prosthetic act of memorializing, and so he concludes that he has failed her (Foer 2005: 124). Yet, Grandmother's resistance to writing, her subversive welcoming of the blank pages, seems to function positively as her prosthetic act. She commits the past to silence and moves on, just as in concrete terms she has committed herself to an ongoing present, both raising the child whom Thomas, Sr. could not face, and devoting herself to Oskar. The pair is last seen, in stasis, planning to reside in the international terminal of the airport, suspended between the something and nothing places of their own historical geographies and inhabiting neither, in a pure betweenness of irresolution. At the same time, they have found their way by the insistence of her love into reconciliation with a provisional present that allows them to narrate to one another their most repressed memory of trauma, Anna's death.

The narrativity of trauma is, of course, highlighted in Foer's many metatextual devices and, indeed, Oskar's own devotion to textuality is one of the most compelling and complex features of the novel. Because others have offered nuanced analyses of how Foer deploys Oskar's many prosthetic uses of language—his prodigious reading, his writing, his correspondence with surrogate father figures, and his narrating—the remainder of this chapter will concentrate instead on some of the boy's material fetishes: the objects, or fantasized objects, that he constructs or invests with the meanings that Philip seeks in Alvin's artificial leg.[5] Indeed, perhaps as a function of his age, like Philip and unlike his grandparents, Oskar invests magical meanings in *things*, as if the material world might offer a stopgap to its own dissolution, and might even in its very concreteness reverse the abstract woundings of time.

Oskar, of course, faces a much more immediate raw wound than do his grandparents. This posttraumatic narrative temporality is essential to the effects of Oskar's narration, beginning with the first sentence. "What about a teakettle?" (Foer 2005: 1) opens the novel *in medias res*, and in interrogatory form, introducing the first of Oskar's obsessively imagined inventions. In repeated "what if" statements, he fantasizes devices to fill or fix the gaping absence in his life left by his father's death in one of the Twin Towers. Foer begins with conditional verbs that enable a speculative approach to rewriting the past as something other than what it was. The novel's third sentence slips the heartbreak into the discourse sideways— "I could invent a teakettle that reads in Dad's voice"—identifying the central lack for this grieving narrator to fill: the lack of his literally rather than, for Philip, figuratively missing father, with emphasis on the lost *voice* of the father which has for Oskar special traumatic resonance. Compared to Philip's natural, childish self-centeredness, Oskar's compulsive, narcissistic attempts to displace history—most egregious when he blurts out to his mother that he would have chosen her rather than his father to die (Foer 2005: 171)—seem nearly pathological. Yet, no wonder, as the trauma lies so intimately in his sight—and hearing, and feeling. Oskar proves Herman Roth's insight that *history* is "what happens in his house to an ordinary man" (Roth 2004: 180) when he arrives home from school on the bright morning of September 11 to hear his father's final calls from the tower that is about to fall. The world's brutality violates his most intimate domestic space; Oskar's loss of safety is almost as traumatic as the loss of his father. Thomas, Jr.'s voice—which Oskar both hears and refuses to hear—becomes the horrifying stump, as it were, of the boy's traumatic history.

Oskar's chapters are largely devoted to his numerous prosthetic activities and fetish objects, meant, as Kristiaan Versluys suggests, "to make reality malleable so that it conforms to his desires" to make a world "in which the unthinkable has not yet happened" (Versluys 2009: 102). Oskar often notes the "weird" consequences of real facts or those he imagines; his term "weird" at once denotes and tames his child's experience of the uncanny. He devises improbable inventions, which Versluys aptly identifies as "symptoms of a repetition compulsion" (Versluys 2009: 103), such as a skyscraper that can move people safely to the ground after being hit by a plane, a birdseed shirt that allows someone falling through the sky to be rescued by hungry birds in flight, and "portable pockets" that might grow large enough to "hold the universe" safely (Foer 2005: 3, 2, 71, 74). He beats his tambourine to give rhythm and order to his immediate experience.[6] He takes comfort in stories, especially memories of his father's fanciful reasoning, as when Thomas Schell,

Jr. explains that Oskar might change the "course of human history" just by moving a grain of sand in the Sahara (Foer 2005: 86). Throughout, however, "history" remains for Oskar a vague, abstract thing, marked only by the fall of the towers, as if in a vacuum, where time exists only as the instant of traumatic loss, the pivot point between *before* and *after*. Oskar possesses only a primitive version of the temporal sense that his grandparents, burdened for decades by memory, comprehend as an eternal present-tense loss.

Oskar's most important displacing gestures relate directly to his memory of his father. Each gesture offers compensations and at the same time, in exposing its threads, allows for its unraveling as a useful stop to trauma; moreover, each maintains "history" solely as an artifact of Oskar's circumscribed experience. Foer devotes a chapter to the "Sixth Borough," Thomas's prosthetic fantasy of a New York that disappeared from historical memory like Atlantis from the sea's surface. Foer alludes to the story of the Sixth Borough in the opening chapter (Foer 2005: 13–14) but does not narrate it until three-quarters of the way through the narrative, when Oskar approaches readiness once again to hear his father's voice, which is to say, to face his most traumatic memory. While not a material "thing" as such, the story offers to Oskar the vividly concrete *image* of a thing. The Sixth Borough is a substitute to which his imagination can cling, as if it were real. Thomas's story is the final, tangible gift he has left for his son.

Thomas's tale, which he tells Oskar on the night before he dies, thus frames the narrative, allegorizing trauma by linking temporal loss with geographical loss even as it contrarily offers hope through recovery of the world in storytelling. In this sense, the story itself is a kind of a fetish object. Its power as a prosthesis is implied by the placement of Thomas's narration, as if it might fill the gap in the novel's structure between the two grandparents' confessions of traumatic memory—Grandfather's, looking back toward Dresden, recounted in the suppressed letter to his son, and Grandmother's, telling her version of Oskar's "worst day" in New York. Thomas's whimsical Sixth Borough is an illusory space that becomes a geographical figure for absence, a hole in the known world that opens naturally but inevitably, the fault of no one. The hole in New York is Thomas's premonition of Ground Zero, a hole standing for the whole of New York's loss and, most importantly in the novel's emphases, for Oskar's own. As the mythical Sixth Borough begins to drift out to sea,

Thomas explains, the inhabitants unsuccessfully devise fantastical inventions—like Oskar's—to retain a connection to Manhattan by resisting time. "Revert[ing] to old-fashioned technologies" like magnifying glasses, harnesses, magnets, and "string-and-tin-can phone[s]" (Foer 2005: 219), the Sixth Boroughers clutch futilely at what they know because they "didn't want to change" (Foer 2005: 221). Thomas's parable encourages Oskar to move beyond traumatic losses; yet, he also provides a fatherly comfort about the future that his own death reveals to be as illusory as his premise about the past. He assures Oskar of the borough's permanence as an island that "moves across the planet, [and] acts like a frame, displaying what lies beneath it" (Foer 2005: 222).

It is a metaphor for the power of the imagination to capture and, in storytelling, restore what has been lost. At the core of the Sixth Borough lies the serendipitously named Central Park, the figure of a *presence*, a lost "center" and signified that, contrary to Derrida's nihilistic formula, appears to be rescued for meaning: in the last moments of the Borough, Thomas asserts, Central Park was with "enormous hooks . . . pulled by the people of New York, like a rug across a floor" (Foer 2005: 221) to Manhattan from the vanishing island. The names of some of the missing remain (Foer 2005: 222), he affirms; and the island drifts to Antarctica, where its inhabitants remain frozen in suspended animation as if waiting to be resurrected. Insofar as Oskar's "memory" of the place depends on remembering his father's storytelling, he recovers his father. How he remembers him— and keeps his voice alive—offers hope and wisdom. Nevertheless, Thomas is also a source of unreliable fictions, of a story as prosthesis that cannot finally fill the hole it would cover up.

The final image of Thomas's story—"On a frozen shelf, in a closet frozen shut, is a can with a voice in it" (Foer 2005: 223)—connects directly with Oskar's most absorbing prosthetic action, with which Foer drives the novel's momentum. Oskar seeks to puzzle out the mystery of a key he has found on a shelf in his father's closet, identified only by the word "Black," hoping to construct a story that might help him understand his loss. He embarks on a quest across the five boroughs for the "Black" who might possess the lock that the key will open—that is, to unlock the story of his father's death that remains closed to Oskar. In their games of "Reconnaissance Expedition" (Foer 2005: 8), Thomas has prepared Oskar to seek for obscure objects. Their last game, in Central Park, establishes the unresolvable epistemological quest of the novel: how to know what a "clue" is ("Is no clues a clue?") (Foer 2005: 8) and what to do with material "evidence" that adds up to nothing. The Expedition, that is, offers another of Foer's figurations of the problem of traumatic loss: since no answers exist to the "why" of suffering, the quest theoretically has no closure, and no prosthesis can ever close the wound. It is thus with Oskar's central quest, which displaces his desire to hear the voice of his father that, retained in the phone messages alone, he has repressed out of fear, guilt, and grief. According to the Freudian narrative, Oskar hopes to gain the phallic power of the "key" that penetrates to knowledge. Because he has no reason to believe that this fetishized key has anything to do with Thomas's disappearance in the Twin Towers, however, Oskar's quest exhibits the kind of magical thinking that Philip engages in when he follows Christians through Newark's streets. Oskar implausibly solves the mystery of the key, but the solution is anticlimactic, except insofar as Oskar at last confesses, to the "right" Black, his worst secret: his guilt at hearing his father's messages and hiding them from his mother. The father's voice was always there for him, but it finally yields up no more than Oskar has already heard. He fills in his own story but not his father's history, and certainly no global sense of *why* this history happened. The end of the quest offers no therapeutic satisfaction. Not only is the quest itself an illusion but Oskar also discovers that, having concluded it, he no longer has a purpose: "I found it and now I can't look for it" (Foer 2005: 304).

The novel's climactic action perhaps most clearly conveys the ambiguous position of the symbolic prosthesis, which covers but does not heal a traumatic wound. Oskar has expressed his fear of his own disappearance, asking his mother to "promise not to bury me when I die" (Foer 2005: 168), and angrily expressing his preternaturally mature understanding that the coffin the family has buried to commemorate his father, fulfill ritual obligation, and seek emotional solace, does nothing: "It's just an empty box" (Foer 2005: 169). Thomas's coffin, the object that speaks doubly of the yawning absence of traumatic loss—not only of his death but also of the disappearance of any material remains that might, like grief, be laid to rest—thus becomes the object most central to Oskar's compulsive questing. Oskar embarks, with the "renter," to exhume the coffin as "a simple solution to an impossible problem" (Foer 2005: 321), a phrase he takes from his correspondence with one of his surrogate father figures, Stephen Hawking. The problem, as he tells the renter, is that he must confront the truth, because "'Dad loved the truth.' 'What truth?' 'That he's dead'" (Foer 2005: 321). The solution is that he must *see* the truth in all its material finality, to look into the coffin and accept that he "is looking into the dictionary definition of emptiness" (Foer 2005: 321).

Yet, Oskar's grandfather to a degree protects him from altogether looking into the irremediable and uncanny void of his father's coffin, by turning the exhumation into his own private prosthetic act. Consistent with his fetishizing imagination, Oskar anticipates seeing the coffin only insofar as he can hope to fill it with objects to replace the missing corporeality of his father—with mementos of his father's life, or with things, such as the telephone on which he heard his father's final messages, that remind him of his own shame (Foer 2005: 321–22). But he is stopped short by the "renter's" reminder of the mechanism by which trauma may be repressed only temporarily: "Just because you bury something, you don't really *bury* it" (Foer 2005: 322). Instead, Grandfather fills the coffin with the thousands of letters he was unable to send to Thomas, Jr. His act, steeped in the ironies that the letters have not been read nor will they be in the future, becomes an almost literal metonymy for the failure of language to represent or compensate for past trauma.[7] Yet for Oskar, the hole left by trauma *is* filled to some degree, if in a displaced fashion; not only do the two suitcases' worth of letters fill the coffin materially, but also the event allows him to recover a lost paternal figure—even if a grandfather rather than a father. Foer emphasizes that this moment bears the force of a repressed trauma released to memory: "I don't think I figured out that he was my grandpa, not even in the deep parts of my brain. . . . But I must have understood something, I *must* have" (Foer 2005: 322), Oskar narrates. Insofar as the exhumation takes place under cover of night, as an act of stealth and danger in the darkened cemetery, it suggests Oskar and his grandfather's journey into the repressed material of the unconscious.

That the exhumation and reburial can do nothing to bring Grandfather from melancholy into mourning, however, is offset by its incremental effect on Oskar, an effect mainly implied by the placement of the scene in the structure of Foer's narrative. The scene ends just a few pages before the narrating voices conclude, juxtaposing, and seeming by narrative logic to prompt, Oskar's reconciliation to his life and to his mother's potential for a renewed life with her friend Ron, who has also suffered traumatic loss. Yet, Foer undercuts even this sense of progress in the prosthetic figures that dominate the novel's final pages.

The best prosthesis, of course, would erase the wound altogether, making a person whole without artifice by returning him or her to the condition before injury—a state, that is, of innocence or prehistory. It would be no prosthesis at all, but an artificial limb having become natural, grown seamlessly like Pinocchio's final nose. Foer indulges his characters in such fantasies. Oskar's grandmother dreams of reversing time during the firebombing of Dresden: "The collapsed ceilings re-formed above us. The fire went back into the bombs" (Foer 2005: 306). Foer's controversial conclusion to *Extremely Loud* engages the traumatized son in two like fantasies. First, Oskar reverses photos of a body falling from one of the towers into a flipbook that makes the body rise into the sky, reproduced as the final fifteen pages of the novel.[8] Second, like his grandmother, he imagines the "worst day" (Foer 2005: 11) in reverse time, leading back to his father's consoling story of the Sixth Borough, and concluding in the novel's last line with a final illusion: "We would have been safe" (Foer 2005: 326). Oskar's reversal of time "comprises," as Versluys argues with regard to another of the novel's episodes, "a sort of forgetting"(Foer 2005: 117).

Only with a prosthetic imagination—to manipulate images falsely or to play with the facts to construct a counterhistory—can one invent a reality that heals by causing forgetting. Roth's novel "forgets" its traumatic history by winding its way out of the Lindbergh labyrinth back onto the smooth path of Roosevelt's leadership, eliding the quasi-Holocaust and post-9/11 transnational histories it glancingly invokes, and leaving the Roths in late 1942, pained, wiser, but much as they were in mid-1940. Foer cannot bring Thomas Schell Jr. back, but he restores Oskar to a reconfigured, loving nuclear family, with his mother and a surrogate father, as well as two grandparents. The scope of Foer's closing is wholly intimate—there's no reckoning with the new "perpetual fear" of terrorism, or with Muslim Others, or even with the wider facts of post-9/11 New York. Or with the full comprehension of traumatic history, since Oskar's grandparents, who have supported the novel's transnational meanings, are "forgotten" in the narrative's redemptions; as Ilka Saal notes, they are left "in perpetual melancholia" in the "nothing-place of [an] airport" (Saal 2011: 471), as a final gesture to stop the time of traumatic remembrance.

In this regard, Roth's and Foer's choice of child narrator/protagonists is telling, because the choice enables both novels to retreat to sentimentality, to the innocence of a fantasized American prehistory—potentially, to the kind of isolationism that Roth skewers in his counterhistory of American politics. John Duvall and Robert Marzec refute the accusation that post-9/11 American literature "has retreated from politics into domesticity" by arguing persuasively for the effectiveness of an "oblique treatment of the root cause of a historical trauma" that they trace, for example, to Hemingway's *The Sun Also Rises* (1926) and Woolf's 1925 book *Mrs. Dalloway* (Duvall and Marzec 2011: 384). Certainly, Roth cloaks *The Plot* within an insistent historical context announced immediately in the novel's title, and repressed memories of 9/11 and the Dresden firebombing throb beneath almost every page of *Extremely Loud*. Still, as Smith suggests about Foer's novel, the constraining perspective of the boy narrators is so powerful that the concluding first-person pronouns, singular in Roth's novel and plural in Foer's, make it difficult to see beyond the immediate victims (the Wishnow and Roth families, the dead in the collapse of the World Trade Center towers) toward "the much more complicated geopolitical context of the event" (Smith 2011: 157–58). Perhaps this is because the prosthetic imagination can extend only toward the particulars of a particularized loss, an artificial limb to attach to a stump, not a simple solution to an impossible (geopolitical) problem. And insofar as *The Plot* and *Extremely Loud* demonstrate an historical impulse, it remains the impulse to live *outside* of history, simply, and safe at home. In the appeal to sentiment and fantasy lies the perpetual ambiguity of the posttraumatic condition: "posttraumatic" is, by the logic of the term, *never* temporally a condition that can end.

Notes

1 "Some readers," Roth wrote when the book was published in 2004, "are going to want to take this book as a roman à clef to the present moment in America." That would be a mistake ("The Story Behind 'The Plot Against America' C11). Nevertheless, readers have not been shy in committing precisely that 'mistake'."

2. Several scholars have preceded me in exploring the metaphor of prosthesis in Roth's work, but to rather different effects. Charles Lewis argues that *The Plot Against America* "offers a trope for reading the novel *as* a prosthetic device" (247) for 9/11 because it displaces the trauma to the past. Rachael McLennan focuses on how the figure of Anne Frank serves Roth in a number of fictions as a "narrative prosthesis to 'fix' or compensate perceived cultural impairments" (258). My reading is more specifically psychoanalytic and character-bound. Aimee Pozorski has also emphasized the "stump or prosthesis" as "the most powerful sign of the trauma" of the boys' lives in *The Plot Against America* (119).

3. Roth emphasizes the boys as doubles when Philip steals Seldon's clothes and plans to masquerade as Seldon to hide his own identity.

4. Freud's account of the opposing conditions appears in "Remembering, Repeating, and Working Through" (1914) and "Mourning and Melancholia" (1917). For a fine explication of Freud's terms, see Dominick LaCapra.

5. For excellent treatments of the novel's deconstructive foregrounding of textuality, see S. Todd Atchison, Mitchum Huehls, and Earl G. Ingersoll.

6. Oskar's tambourine, like his name, has prompted readers to argue for Oskar Matzerath in Günter Grass's *Tin Drum* (1959) as an obvious influence on Foer. See Kristiaan Versluys 198, n. 1. and, for more extensive comparisons, Sien Uytterschout.

7. Philippe Codde points out the poignant failure of the "words to ease the pain" that are meant to fill the "aporia at the heart of the traumatic experience" Foer represents ("Philomela" 245–46).

8. For excellent reflections on Foer's controversial incorporation of the "falling man" photos into the flipbook at the end of the novel, see Philippe Codde, "Philomela" 249–50; Naomi Mandel on the problem of fidelity to fact, especially 238–40; and Aaron Mauro on photographic history, especially 596–601.

Works cited

Atchison, S. Todd. "'Why I am Writing from where you are not': Absence and Presence in Jonathan Safran Foer's *Extremely Loud and Incredibly Close*." *Journal of Postcolonial Writing* 46, no. 3–4 (July/September 2010): 359–68.

Brauner, David. *Philip Roth*. Manchester: Manchester University Press, 2007.

Codde, Philippe. "Keeping History at Bay: Absent Presences in Three Recent Jewish American Novels." *Modern Fiction Studies* 57, no. 4 (Winter 2011): 673–93.

Codde, Philippe. "Philomela Revisited: Traumatic Iconicity in Jonathan Safran Foer's *Extremely Loud & Incredibly Close*." *Studies in American Fiction* 35, no. 2 (2007): 241–54.

Duvall, John N., and Robert P. Marzec. "Narrating 9/11." *Modern Fiction Studies* 57, no. 3 (Fall 2011): 381–400.

Foer, Jonathan Safran. *Extremely Loud and Incredibly Close*. Boston: Houghton Mifflin, 2005.

Freud, Sigmund. "Mourning and Melancholia." In *The Standard Edition of the Complete Psychological Works of Sigmund Freud*, vol. 14, edited by and translated by James Strachey and Anna Freud, 237–60. London: Hogarth, 1957.

Freud, Sigmund. "Remembering, Repeating, and Working-through (Further Recommendations on the Technique of Psycho-Analysis II)." 1914. In *The Standard Edition of the Complete Psychological Works of Sigmund Freud*, vol. 12, edited by and translated by James Strachey and Anna Freud, 145–56. London: Vintage, 2001.

Freud, Sigmund. "The Uncanny." In *The Standard Edition of the Complete Psychological Works of Sigmund Freud*, vol. 17, edited by and translated by James Strachey and Anna Freud, 217–56. London: Hogarth, 1955.

Hornung, Alfred. "Terrorist Violence and Transnational Memory: Jonathan Safran Foer and Don DeLillo." In *Transnational American Memories*, edited by Udo J. Hebel, 171–83. Berlin: Walter de Gruyter, 2009.

Huehls, Mitchum. *Qualified Hope: A Postmodern Politics of Time*. Columbus: Ohio State University Press, 2009.

Ingersoll, Earl G. "One Boy's Passage, and His Nation's: Jonathan Safran Foer's *Extremely Loud and Incredibly Close*." *The CEA Critic* 71, no. 3 (Spring and Summer 2009): 54–69.

Kristeva, Julia. *Powers of Horror: An Essay on Abjection*. Translated by Leon S. Roudiez. New York: Columbia University Press, 1982.

LaCapra, Dominick. "Reflections on Trauma, Absence, and Loss." In *Whose Freud? The Place of Psychoanalysis in Contemporary Culture*, edited by Peter Brooks and Alex Woloch, 178–204. New Haven: Yale University Press, 2000.

Lewis, Charles. "Real Planes and Imaginary Towers: Philip Roth's *The Plot Against America* as 9/11 Prosthetic Screen." In *Literature after 9/11*, edited by Ann Keniston and Jeanne Follansbee Quinn, 246–60. New York: Routledge, 2008.

Mandel, Naomi. "Fact, Fiction, Fidelity in the Novels of Jonathan Safran Foer." *Novel: A Forum on Fiction* 45, no. 2 (2012): 238–56.

Mauro, Aaron. "The Languishing of the Falling Man: Don DeLillo and Jonathan Safran Foer's Photographic History of 9/11." *Modern Fiction Studies* 57, no. 3 (Fall 2011): 584–606.

McLennan, Rachael. "Enabling Fictions: Philip Roth's Prosthetic Anne Franks." *Comparative American Studies* 7, no. 3 (September 2009): 253–67.

Mitchell, David T., and Sharon L. Snyder. *Narrative Prosthesis: Disability and the Dependencies of Discourse*. Ann Arbor: University of Michigan Press, 2000.

Parrish, Timothy. "Autobiography and History in Roth's *The Plot Against America*, or What Happened When Hitler Came to New Jersey." In *Philip Roth—American Pastoral, The Human Stain, The Plot Against America*, edited by Debra Shostak, 147–60. New York: Continuum, 2011.

Pozorski, Aimee. *Roth and Trauma: The Problem of History in the Later Works (1995–2010)*. New York: Continuum, 2011.

"Prosthesis, n." *Oxford English Dictionary Online*. Oxford University Press, March 2014.

Roth, Philip. *The Plot Against America*. Boston: Houghton Mifflin, 2004.

Roth, Philip. "The Story Behind 'The Plot Against America'." *New York Times*, September 19, 2004, C10–12.

Rothberg, Michael. *Traumatic Realism: The Demands of Holocaust Representation*. Minneapolis: University of Minnesota Press, 2000.

Saal, Ilka. "Regarding the Pain of Self and Other: Trauma Transfer and Narrative Framing in Jonathan Safran Foer's *Extremely Loud & Incredibly Close*." *Modern Fiction Studies* 57, no. 3 (Fall 2011): 453–76.

Smith, Rachel Greenwald. "Organic Shrapnel: Affect and Aesthetics in September 11 Fiction." *American Literature* 83, no. 1 (March 2011): 153–74.

Uytterschout, Sien. "An Extremely Loud Tin Drum: A Comparative Study of Jonathan Safran Foer's *Extremely Loud and Incredibly Close* and Gunter Grass's *The Tin Drum*." *Comparative Literature Studies* 47, no. 2 (2010): 185–99.

Versluys, Kristiaan. *Out of the Blue: September 11 and the Novel*. New York: Columbia University Press, 2009.

Wills, David. *Prosthesis*. Stanford: Stanford University Press, 1995.

2

The Law of Ruins and homogenous empty time in Don DeLillo's *Falling Man*

Aaron DeRosa

Do you think you are sufficiently decayed?
~ W. S. GILBERT, "There is Beauty in the Bellow of the Blast,"
The Mikado (1885)[1]

Although the "9/11 novel" is a complicated and arbitrary brand, insofar as Don DeLillo's *Falling Man* (2007) foregrounds the World Trade Center (WTC) towers and is profoundly fixated on their collapse, it is perhaps one of the "purest" novels in the canon, distinguished from other novels that privilege pre-9/11 naiveté (Andre Dubus; Claire Messud), the Homeland Security State (HSS) (Laila Halaby; Lorrie Moore), encounters with multiculturalism (Mohsin Hamid; Gerald Vizenor), historical antecedents (Philip Roth; Kamila Shamsie), and speculative futures (Cormac McCarthy; Colson Whitehead).[2] Instead, it seems aligned with a traditional traumatic realism that audiences might expect from "Literature" in response to a national tragedy. Indeed, this is perhaps why the novel has prickled many for being too conservative. Richard Gray noted early on that novels like *Falling Man* domesticate the tragedy by making it too familiar. Elizabeth S. Anker writes that in 9/11 novels like DeLillo's, nostalgia "encodes sentiments at once idealized and regressive, which is to say that these narratives partake of a longing to return to a bygone era of American omnipotence wherein white, heteronormative, patrician masculinity was still sacrosanct" (Anker 2011: 468). And in a different context, John Duvall implies DeLillo may have lost his satirical edge when he notes that Jess Walter's *The Zero* "seems like the novel that DeLillo or Thomas Pynchon might have written twenty years ago" (Duvall 2012: 187). These observations hint at the diverse expectations for 9/11 literature and the panoply of conversations that can and should take place in the wake of tragedy.

Falling Man is a compelling text in a growing chorus of literary voices precisely because of its "purity"—an arbitrary categorical description, not a qualitative one—which derives from the novel's willed refusal to see beyond the WTC and the fixed temporality of "September 11, 2001," and the political critique DeLillo levels from that position. The towers have certainly become a metonym for the post-9/11 nation in what Anker refers to as America's "melodramatic political discourse" (Anker 2014: 2). For Anker, the historical moment is cast in terms of "moral polarities of good and evil, overwhelmed victims, heightened affects of pain and suffering, grand gestures, astonishing feats of heroism, and the redemption of virtue" (Anker 2014: 2), and it is perhaps for this reason that the towers draw our attention more fervently than the other two sites of trauma from September 11: United 93 and the Pentagon. *Falling Man* recognizes the primacy of the towers in the American imagination. In a moment of self-reflexive paranoia, the German art critic Ernst Hechinger observes a Giorgio Morandi still-life painted a half-century earlier and remarks, "I'm looking at these objects, kitchen objects but removed from the kitchen, free of the kitchen, the house, everything practical and functioning. And I must be back in another time zone. I must be even more disoriented than usual after a long flight. . . . Because I keep seeing the towers in this still-life" (DeLillo 2007: 49). More than a traumatic ambiguity or the failures of aesthetic representation, Ernst's confusion registers an inability to collapse the temporal distance between the painting's composition and reception, between history and interpretation. The novel responds to such incommensurability and disorientation through a temporal and spatial fixity on the towers in which 9/11 is appropriated into the homogenous empty time of consumer capital, a condition of mass-produced and endlessly repeatable and replaceable moments. Such moments accumulate as a waste product of the contemporary condition and consign the tragedy and its victims to the scrapheap of American history.

The standing now

DeLillo's fiction has always been concerned with temporality in American culture, from the predictive game theory in *End Zone* (1972) to the protraction of his 2010 book *Point Omega*'s "24-Hour *Psycho*." One of the major threads of DeLillo scholarship deals with the writer's deep engagement in the apocalyptic impulse of the Cold War. Peter Boxall notes, "From *Americana* to *Libra* . . . DeLillo's novels have angled themselves towards and against the millennial apocalypse. . . . But from the very first moments of *Underworld* there is a sense that the deferral of the apocalyptic moment is over" (Boxall 2004: 177). Maciej Maslowski similarly notes that "DeLillo's oeuvre has been continuously informed by a sense of a radical incompleteness of history and may therefore be read as a project aimed at mapping the historical movement towards the millennial moment of ultimate denouement" (Maslowski 2011: 245). Yet, I would like to consider that the September 11, 2001, attacks rupture these eschatological preoccupations. Boxall gestures toward this in his provocative epilogue, written before *Falling Man*'s publication, in which the past and future collapse in on the present in works like *Cosmopolis* and *The Body Artist*: "If the past is present to us here, in its bleached out absence, so too the future has already arrived" (Boxall 2004: 225). DeLillo makes a similar remark about American culture in his December, 2001 *Harper's* essay aptly titled "In the Ruins of the Future." He notes that the post–Cold War euphoria that settled into American culture in the 1990s "summoned us all to live permanently in the future, in the utopian glow of cyber-capital" (DeLillo 2001: 33). Obliquely referring to Francis Fukuyama's claim that the collapse of the Berlin Wall signaled a successful conclusion to the world's teleological march toward globalized capitalism, DeLillo recasts the triumphalist "end of history" in light of this new tragedy: "The Bush Administration was feeling a nostalgia for the Cold War. This is over now. Many things are over. The narrative ends in the rubble, and it is left to us to create the counter-narrative" (DeLillo 2001: 34). DeLillo takes his own advice when he interrupts the essayistic article with a separate section that creatively renders the attacks. The narrative is ambiguous in its fictionality, but it shows DeLillo's first tentative steps toward what will become *Falling Man*. Here, he first uses the image that will open the novel, describing a world of "ash and near night" (DeLillo 2001: 37, 2007: 3). Similarly, DeLillo will return to his statement about narratives ending in the rubble: "These are the days after. Everything now is measured by after" (DeLillo 2007: 138).

The promise of new measurements and counter-narratives has led critics to cite this as an axiom in the dawning of a new postlapsarian "Post-9/11" era. Yet this claim belies *Falling Man*'s measurement of a nonprogressive time—a time that *doesn't* begin. The quotation comes from a conversation between protagonist Keith Neudecker and his fellow North Tower-survivor turned mistress, Florence. The latter asks, "Do you have to leave?," to which Keith responds, "I'll always have to leave" (DeLillo 2007: 137). Keith's response syntactically implies a ritual of arrivals and departures that never occur in the text. Indeed, these encounters are left ambiguous and hazy, like Keith's memory of the affair: "His experience with Florence was brief, maybe four or five encounters over a period of fifteen days. Is that possible, only that? He tried counting the times, sitting in a taxi at a stoplight, staring at a billboard. It all ran together now, with only the faint grain of something felt and held" (DeLillo 2007: 228). The vagueness of these events can be attributed to the fact that Keith and Florence occupy a perpetual present, caught in "the timeless drift of the long spiral down" the North Tower stairwell (DeLillo 2007: 137). Indeed, DeLillo revises the original axiom late in the novel with precisely such a presentism in mind: "These are the days after and now the years, a thousand heaving dreams, the trapped man, the fixed limbs, the dream of paralysis, the gasping man, the dream of asphyxiation, the dream of helplessness" (DeLillo 2007: 230). More than a traumatic return of the repressed, time does not progress for Keith.

Falling Man's very structure implies such a lack of progression, as it begins and ends with the image of an empty shirt falling through the Manhattan sky on September 11, 2001. The structure is often considered circular, implying a departure and then a return, or for many readers a traumatic repetition. But as the conversation between Keith and Florence indicates, the novel aestheticizes a failure of time: 9/11 is neither an end nor a beginning, but a static moment held in perpetuity.³ Keith endlessly defers his confession to Lianne—his estranged wife to whom he returns on 9/11—about his affair with Florence (DeLillo 2007: 161, 162, 166). Instead, he joins the poker tournament circuit to escape from time, and the "recovered domesticity" between them is frozen: Keith is "not set on doing anything permanent" (DeLillo 2007: 215), unprepared to leave or commit, and Lianne "lived in the spirit of what is ever impending" (DeLillo 2007: 212). The inheritor of this fixity is their son Justin who believes the towers were hit but did not fall. The suspension of historical time in Justin's imagination is a childish foil to Keith's own state of mind.

This fixity is evident from the beginning, where Keith limps away from the WTC plaza and hears the Tower collapse but envisions himself still there: "That was him coming down, the north tower" (DeLillo 2007: 5).⁴ The participle implies a moment of halted temporality: the towers are neither in the wholeness of their past nor in their collapsed future. It grammatically mimics the fall*ing* man of the infamous Richard Drew photo and DeLillo's titular character, a performance artist who stages jumps via a harness that arrests him in mid-fall. Indeed, a host of different media have attempted to recover this moment of arrest from Kerry Skarbakka (photography), Sharon Paz (installation art at the Jamaica Center for the Arts & Learning), Matthew Weiner (opening credit sequence of *Mad Men*), and Eric Fischl (sculpture).⁵ Analyzing the latter, Karen Lang invokes Hannah Arendt's vision of the present as a "standing now," the position between "the infinite forward-pushing force of the 'no longer' clashing against the infinite backward-driving force of the 'not yet'" (qtd. in Lang 2002: 29). Boxall argues that DeLillo's other post-9/11 fiction—*Cosmopolis* and *The Body Artist*—take place in an "evacuated time which has lost its narrative quality, which can neither inherit the legacy of the past, nor move towards the possibility of a new and undiscovered future. It is a time which has lost its sense of identity" (Boxall 2004: 216). And Maslowski extends this to say, "Deprived of the potential to transcend its own context, the present expands infinitely, absorbing the space traditionally occupied by the past and the future" (Maslowski 2011: 249). It is the failure of time that Boxall seems to be referring to as the lost "narrative quality." But whereas for Maslowski "the future does arrive" (Maslowski 2011: 253) and for Boxall the present is a "place of pure potentiality" (Boxall 2004: 232), I read DeLillo's temporality as closer to Leif Sorensen's claim about "the unthinkable possibility of a crisis so severe that it might not have a future at all" (Sorenson 2014: 560). For Sorensen, too, this is an eschatological impulse. But I think DeLillo's late work is less interested in end-times than the eradication of progress. In this figuration, 9/11 is a crisis so banal as to be appropriated within the temporal register of the mundane, whose future and past are subsumed into a homogenous, empty time. *Falling Man* erodes the idea of progressive time.

To illuminate this erosion, it might be best to start with the counter-narrative. If the Neudecker story is one in which time passes but does not leave its mark, then it is juxtaposed against the alternative temporality of Hammad and the hijackers. While the dominant plot surrounding Keith and Lianne is told in three parts, these are spliced with the narrative of Hammad's terrorist education under the guidance of Mohammad Atta. This storyline, though, is chronological, progressive, and death-driven. "The time is coming" (DeLillo 2007: 82), Hammad states, recognizing the promise of a conclusion to his story. "The end of our life is predetermined," he considers. "We are carried toward that day from the minute we are born. . . . This is not suicide in any meaning or interpretation of the word. It is only something long written. We are finding the way already chosen for us" (DeLillo 2007: 175). Time is marked out spatially in the chapter titles—"In Marienstrasse," "In Nokomis," "In the Hudson Corridor"—that delineate a terrorist pilgrimage from Germany to New York City. But unlike the character names of the novel's three major sections, the preposition in these subheadings locate Hammad in space and in time, moving along a preordained path toward the towers on September 11, 2001, and ultimately in collision with Keith's timeline.

Narratives of progress and fulfillment are here ceded to the terrorists; Keith and Lianne are left with rubble. But for DeLillo, such ruins are vitally important. Responding to Walter Benjamin's analogy that allegories are to thought what ruins are to things, Anker writes that "9/11 novels have widely employed allegory to confront the literal as well as figural debris of 9/11" (Anker 2011: 463). Anker implies the symbolic strategies these texts employ render them insufficient to the task of thinking through the tragedy, and although I regard the allegorical qualities in *Falling Man* as consciously compromised (through equivocation and circularity as the novel's revision of the "measured by after" axiom suggests), it is perhaps through the symbol of ruin that the novel most adeptly thinks through the caesura of 9/11.

Sufficiently decayed

On the day of the attacks, Keith walks "north through rubble and mud" (DeLillo 2007: 3) and passes "a car half buried in debris, windows smashed and noises coming out, radio voices scratching at the wreckage" (DeLillo 2007: 4). And Florence describes the WTC plaza as "a bombed-out city, things on fire, we saw bodies, we saw clothes, pieces of metal like metal parts, things just scattered" (DeLillo 2007: 58). Such depictions of ash and debris are a staple of 9/11 fiction, but DeLillo draws on a different historical trajectory; the waste, we are reminded, preceded the attacks. When Keith returns to his apartment building, he notices the windows had been broken out by people taking "desperate shelter" on 9/11, but that "the entrance hall reeked of garbage uncollected in the basement" (DeLillo 2007: 26). He juxtaposes the "streets and cars ... surfaced in ash" against the "garbage bags stacked high at curbstones and against the sides of buildings ... and a stink in the air that infiltrated the skin" (DeLillo 2007: 24–25). The scenes echo the depictions of the 1968 NYC sanitation worker strike DeLillo depicted in his earlier novel, *Underworld* (1997): "A hundred bags on one corner and a smell so summer-lush it enveloped the whole body, pressing in like a weather system" (DeLillo 1997: 376). That is, *Falling Man* gestures toward another form of waste and a counter-narrative to the devastation of 9/11.

In *Underworld*, a sprawling novel that concatenates America's Cold War nuclear legacy with the nuclear waste management of the 1990s, garbage is no longer figured as a consequence and byproduct of American consumption, but rather precedes and outlives it. Nick confesses that he and his partner

> saw products as garbage even when they sat gleaming on store shelves, yet unbought. We didn't say, What kind of casserole will that make? We said, What kind of garbage will that make? Safe,

clean, neat, easily disposed of? Can the package be recycled and come back as a tawny envelope that is difficult to lick closed? First we saw the garbage, then we saw the product as food or lightbulbs or dandruff shampoo. How does it measure up as waste, we asked. (DeLillo 1997: 121)

The waste precedes the consumption; in fact, is built into the production itself. Vance Packard analyzed the production side of this model in his influential 1960 critique, *The Waste Makers*. He delineated three modes of "planned obsolescence" through which businesses stoked consumption by conceptualizing their products as waste.[6] Considering a product's "death date" in its construction reverses the logic of the durable good for the waste product. DeLillo approaches the same idea from the consumer side, recognizing that now consumers consider the type of waste they will create through their buying practices. And this is tied to a hidden identity politics within American consumer culture: "Waste is the secret history, the underhistory, the way archaeologists dig out the history of early cultures, every sort of bone heap and broken tool, literally from under the ground" (DeLillo 1997: 791). Such waste is no longer a byproduct, but an artifact of cultural identity and belonging.

So DeLillo leads readers to believe in *Underworld* when he triangulates the Watts Towers in Los Angeles—a series of sculptures made from refuse like discarded rebar, bottles, and tiles—with the Twin Towers and the Fresh Kills Landfill in Staten Island, New York. Surveying the latter tower of refuse, Nick finds "the sight inspiring. All this ingenuity and labor, this delicate effort to fit maximum waste into diminishing space. The towers of the World Trade Center were visible in the distance and he sensed a poetic balance between that idea and this one" (DeLillo 1997: 184).[7] The "high gloss of modernity" and its underworld of waste conjoin at the point of global consumption. And while the world's formerly tallest towers practically fit maximum productivity into the diminishing space of Manhattan Island, there is also a sense in which the WTC's global production is, as Packard would argue, also waste.

We might telescope this architectural critique further back in DeLillo's fiction, to his description of the "Law of Ruins" in *White Noise* (1985). DeLillo describes the Law of Ruins as an aesthetic model envisioned by Nazi architect Albert Speer who desired to "build structures that would decay gloriously, impressively, like

Roman ruins. No rusty hulks or gnarled steel slums" (DeLillo 1985: 246). First theorized by John Ruskin in the mid-nineteenth century, the Law of Ruins holds that the final record of a civilization is its architecture, and thus the chief purpose behind architectural design should be posterity:

> Therefore, when we build, let us think that we build for ever. Let it not be for present delight, nor for present use alone; let it be such work as our descendants will thank us for, and let us think, as we lay stone on stone, that a time is to come when those stones will be held sacred because our hands have touched them, and that men will say as they look upon the labor and wrought substance of them, "See! this our fathers did for us." For, indeed, the greatest glory of a building is not in its stones, nor in its gold. Its glory is in its Age. (Ruskin 1849: 243)

An age, Ruskin continues—and as the epigram from *The Mikado* notes—that begins to show: "For there is an actual beauty in the marks of it" (Ruskin 1849: 244). Speer, addressing the Reich's fascination with Roman ruins, applies this logic to his architecture:

> It was hard to imagine that rusting heaps of rubble could communicate these heroic inspirations which Hitler admired in the monuments of the past. My "theory" was intended to deal with this dilemma. By using special materials and by applying certain principles of statics, we should be able to build structures which even in a state of decay, after hundreds or (such were our reckonings) thousands of years would more or less resemble Roman models.[8] (Speer 1970: 56)

DeLillo's fiction thus ties architectural production to waste, and specifically a waste product that is deeply nationalistic in its decay. The narrator of *White Noise* remarks that building the ruin into the creation "shows a certain nostalgia behind the power principle, or a tendency to organize the longings of future generations" (DeLillo 1985: 246).[9]

It is hard not to see in these descriptions the echoes of Benjamin's Angel of History. Commenting on Paul Klee's "Angelus Novus" in *Theses on the Philosophy of History*, Benjamin depicts the past as an accumulation of ruins. The Angel "sees one single catastrophe, which unceasingly piles rubble on top of rubble" that "grows sky-high" (Benjamin 1969: 257), while the Angel is ineluctably drawn into the future by the storm of "progress." For Benjamin, the present is a moment in which the past is brought into the fullness of its meaning and potential through interpretation. This is what *Underworld*'s Nick succeeds in doing when he juxtaposes the towers of industry of America's "white hot future" (DeLillo 2001: 34) against the landfill's towers of waste of an ineradicable past. He maps a relationship between the past and the future that *Falling Man*'s Ernst expressly says he cannot do when viewing the Morandi paintings in the aftermath of 9/11. The collapse of the WTC is yet another accumulation in a single catastrophe, undifferentiated in time.

Considered as such, we might return to DeLillo's depiction of power's nostalgic impulse and consider its manifestation in *Underworld* and *Falling Man* not as complicit in, but deeply critical of, post–Cold War narratives of American exceptionalism. Rather than accepting that decay can be nationalistically productive in the vein of Ruskin and Speer, DeLillo points to the hollowness of these constructions. In fact, Speer worried that anticipating the failure of the Reichstag through decayed buildings would render the buildings, the government, and the nation hollow, and draw the ire of the Führer. Building the ruin into the creation foregrounds their emptiness and replaceability. In a telling passage in *The Waste Makers*, Packard writes, "The new mood of the disposable era was reflected in the pages of the *Engineering News Record*, which observed: 'Nowhere in the world except in the U.S. would a skyscraper office building in sound condition be torn down merely to be replaced by another one'" (Packard 1960: 42). The twinned construction of the WTC towers is thus significant. Phillip Wegner, referring to the Soviet Union's second atomic blast and its importance for DeLillo's *Underworld*, notes that "only when an event happens the *second* time can it be said to mark the beginning of something new, be it a genre, institution, or historical period. The second occurrence establishes the historical necessity of the original case, reinscribing it, *after the fact*, as the first in a series" (Wegner 2004: 60). This reproducibility, then, reifies the towers as symbolic of American consumption, as the "'second tower' that is the projected/rejected surplus of the West" (Hardack 2013: 153). DeLillo suggests as much when he considers the Twin Towers as "a behemoth of mass production, units that roll identically off the line" (DeLillo 1997: 377). While not intentionally replaced, and certainly not designed with their destruction in mind, the WTC possesses a symbolic logic deeply enmeshed in American national identity and capitalist decay. All of this prompts Ernst to pontificate:

> But that's why you built the towers, isn't it? Weren't the towers built as fantasies of wealth and power that would one day become fantasies of destruction? You build a thing like that so you can see it come down. The provocation is obvious. What other reason would there be to go so high and then to double it, do it twice? It's a fantasy, so why not do it twice? You are saying, Here it is, bring it down. (DeLillo 2007: 116)

For Ernst, the promise of the WTC towers' ruin—more than its realization on 9/11—is what generates their aura and justifies their metonymic position in the national imaginary of progress.

And as we have seen, the WTC remains marketable. As the first (and second) landmark(s) of the American empire to crumble under a reconceptualized Law of Ruins, the towers became a glorious commodity in their destruction. The WTC's pillared tridents now stand in the 9/11 Memorial Museum alongside a host of other detritus from the attacks, all viewable for the low price of $24 per ticket ($1 cheaper than admission to the MoMA or The Met). Tourism to NYC has increased, and the memorial receives more visitors than the Statue of Liberty does. This spectacle was promoted from the beginning. Within weeks of the attacks, a private viewing platform had been constructed for 9/11 families to survey the site. The intrigue was overwhelming, though, and needed expansion: "'It was chaotic, and it was extraordinary', [architect Kevin Kennon] said of the site. 'There were an extraordinary number of people. People were climbing fences, it was unsafe'" (Greenspan 2013: n. pag.). By December, a new public platform would be designed and opened. Even Rudy Giuliani recognized the potential that the ruins would become a tourist attraction, but he conceded in his mayoral farewell speech: "To deny people access to the site would be like denying people access to other sites of historic significance, like Gettysburg or Normandy. I'm sure there are people that go to all those places for the wrong reasons, but most go for the right reasons" (Cardwell 2001: n. pag.).

The two popular battlegrounds Giuliani cites convey the difficulty of differentiating memorial and tourist spaces, in that insofar as the former registers a collective grief it must also recognize itself in terms of the latter.

Sutured time

The metaphor of accumulated rubble rests at the heart of Benjamin's critique of capitalism, time, and progress. Under capitalism, Benjamin argues, time is perceived in terms of discrete units of measurement, where each unit—minutes, hours, and weeks—is identical to every other. The result is the felt sense that the units of time are interchangeable, indefinitely repeatable, and empty of meaning: what he calls "homogenous, empty time" (Benjamin 1969: 261). Guy Debord similarly notes that "commodity-time, is an infinite accumulation of equivalent intervals. It is the abstraction of irreversible time, all of whose segments must prove on the chronometer their merely quantitative equality. . . . This is time devalued, the complete inversion of time as 'the field of human development'" (Debord 1983: 147). Debord links commodity time to the failure of progressive narratives, and the devaluation of time. Together, Benjamin and Debord return us to Klee's rubble piled at the feet of the Angel of History. History is an accumulation of ruins made comprehensible in moments of immediacy. *Falling Man* tracks this sentiment in the interchangeability of Keith and Lianne's lives after their separation, which "had been marked by a certain symmetry, the steadfast commitment each made to an equivalent group. He had his poker game, six players, downtown, one night a week. She had her storyline sessions, in East Harlem, also weekly, in the afternoon, a gathering of five or six or seven men and women in the early stages of Alzheimer's disease" (DeLillo 2007: 29). The routinized experiences are denoted through quantitative values and parallel structures.[10]

The September 11 attacks promise a rupture from such mundanity, a moment of immediacy in which alternative temporalities might break through. "The card games ended after the towers fell" and "the [Alzheimer's] sessions took on a measure of intensity" (DeLillo 2007: 29). The novel gestures toward the post-9/11 rhetoric that "9/11 changed everything." David Wyatt argues that "the day and all it called forth are marked by a return to feeling, an upwelling of unironized emotion that writing has attempted to honor, represent, and contain" (Wyatt 2009: 149). Thus in the opening pages of the novel, the attacks seem to reunite Keith and Lianne, and calendrical time is shot through with affect: "It wasn't just those days and nights in bed. Sex was everywhere at first, in words, phrases, half gestures, the simplest intimation of altered space" (DeLillo 2007: 7). Routinized temporal order is replaced by an affective impulse that gestures toward what Benjamin might consider the messianic. But as the novel makes plain, Keith and Lianne's revived relationship after September 11 is also interchangeable. Lianne's mother reminds her that the revived sexuality between them echoes their early (failed) marriage, a critique that Keith justifies when he commits adultery with Florence, and again when the novel hints that Keith seeks similar connections from the women in Las Vegas (DeLillo 2007: 226). The affect is interchangeable. In addition, Lianne's writing group is quickly restored to its entropic monotony (the "slow and certain decline"), and Keith returns to the timelessness of poker (DeLillo 2007: 125). Thus if the novel offers the promise of radical change that "this was the world now" (DeLillo 2007: 3), it also negates this by appropriating 9/11 within the normative timelessness of capitalist consumption.

Keith's return to poker is particularly suggestive of this critique. Michael Rosenthal argues that "gambling is a pastime devoted to the here and now, a perfect pastime that uses the endless calculations of profit and gain that define a life of *negotium* in the dawn of the new capitalist era" (Rosenthal 2012: 263). Keith's pre-9/11 poker games are entropic, a dwindling horizon of possibilities. Each time the group gathers they create increasingly rigid rules about the games they could play, the food they could eat, and the conversations they could have. Like Lianne's Alzheimer's group, whose routinized writing practices attempt to stave off the growing chaos of the world, the poker games create an artificial order that bind the players together. After 9/11, Keith begins frequenting the tables in Las Vegas, which he seeks out for its ability to cast him outside of time: "He checked his watch again. He knew time and day of week and wondered when such scraps of data would begin to feel disposable" (DeLillo 2007: 189). He does ultimately achieve this goal: "There were times . . . when he glanced at one of the screens and wasn't sure whether he was seeing a fragment of live action or of slow-motion replay. It was a lapse that should have unsettled him, an issue of basic brain function, one reality versus another, but it all seemed a matter of false distinctions, fast, slow, now, then" (DeLillo 2007: 211). Insofar as the gambler is the consummate capitalist, subsumed into homogenous empty time, Keith occupies this position. Like the accumulated rubble the Angel of History surveys, Keith's life becomes a mass of undifferentiated and empty experiences. As he sits at the poker table, he considers, "These were the times when there was nothing outside, no flash of history or memory that he might unknowingly summon in the routine run of cards" (DeLillo 2007: 225).

Furthermore, we might also understand gambling through Benjamin's contention that gambling hollows out experience because it is a game of exact repetitions, where "no game is dependent on the preceding one. Gambling cares about no assured position.... Winnings secured earlier are not taken into account" (Benjamin 1969: 177). Keith believes as much, thinking that losing money "hasn't happened and it won't" (DeLillo 2007: 216). His reflections on poker "would all go flat at the end of the night, win or lose, but that was part of the process.... Days fade, nights drag on, check-and-raise, wake-and-sleep" (DeLillo 2007: 226). Gambling manifests this temporality because, as much as the shock of winning or losing disrupts the game, the game is fundamentally about repetition: "This starting all over again is the regulative idea of the game, as it is of work for wages" (Benjamin 1969: 179). Rosenthal argues that the game mediates two different experiences of time: one that places us within a "continuum of events" and another that "loosens the experience from its context" (Rosenthal 2012: 272).[11] Keith's gambling anesthetizes the former temporality and promotes the alienating sensibility of the latter. The narrator writes that Keith thinks "not in clear units, hard and linked, but only absorbing what comes, drawing things out of time and memory and into some dim space that bears his collected experience" (DeLillo 2007: 66). Keith is released from time.

Keith is the gambler-laborer, as Rosenthal observes, "contained within the repetitive motions of the gambler is a different kind of stimulation, one that moves his body to act without rational direction" (Rosenthal 2012: 271). Analyzing an Alois Senefelder lithograph, Benjamin notes that gamblers "are capable only of a reflex action.... They live their lives as automatons and resemble

Bergson's fictitious characters who have completely liquidated their memories" (Benjamin 1969: 178). The financial metaphor is apt for Keith who views his time at the poker table precisely in terms of cashing in his memories in exchange for a release from time. Echoing the patients from Lianne's Alzheimer's group, whose presence is premised on their ability to retain accumulated memories, Keith figures himself as the automaton: "He wondered if he was becoming a self-operating mechanism, like a humanoid robot that understands two hundred voice commands, far-seeing, touch-sensitive but totally, rigidly controllable" (DeLillo 2007: 226). His memories liquidated and temporal identity evacuated, Keith is rigidly controllable and assimilated back into the national collective imaginary. His experiences of September 11 are appropriated into the homogenous empty time of American capitalism and its perpetual present.

Such forms of national appropriation are clearly evident at Ground Zero, where the WTC towers have been reinstalled at the site, incorporated back into the national imaginary of the "anonymous community" (Redfield 1999: 62), and the WTC towers are replaced with the "Freedom Tower" at 1 WTC. What potential existed for counter-narratives, as DeLillo sought in "In the Ruins of the Future," is lost. Instead, homogenous empty time sutures the wounds of the community and inoculates itself against individual narratives. Defining the nation as an imagined community of perceived simultaneity, Benedict Anderson relies on Benjamin's theses on history: "The idea of a sociological organism moving calendrically through homogenous, empty time is a precise analogue of the idea of the nation, which also is conceived as a solid community moving steadily down (or up) history" (Anderson 1998: 26). This collective temporality yields affective and associative bonds between disconnected members, the same types of bonds the novel attributes to Lianne in her search for religion, and even Hammad, who seeks the path already laid out for him. The difference for Keith is that, unlike the terrorist's narrative that envisions a future still to come, the American narrative in which Keith and Lianne operate privilege an eternal presentism that negates the authority of the past and future.

Falling Man underscores a pressure in the post-9/11 moment toward fixity and homogenous empty time. At best, DeLillo's work closes down myths of progress; at worst, it associates progress with fundamentalism—secular-capitalist or politico-religious. DeLillo's novel thus operates at the leading edge of a temporal concern within literary studies after 9/11. While Samuel Huntington suggested the post–Cold War world order would be articulated in a clash of civilizations defined by religion, region, and ethnicity, Harry Harootunian argues instead that the dominant concern should be a "collision of temporalities" arising in the wake of modernity (Harootunian 2007: 474). Not all progress is achieved uniformly, as Donald Pease and Samuel Cohen argue in a different context. They point to the failings of Huntington's argument that shows that "civilizational" differences do not mark the clashes of the globalized world, but rather the temporal differences between those who can progress, and those left in "endless delay" (Harootunian 2007: 474). Thus the fruitful interrogations of space—the nation and the homeland, Abu Ghraib and Guantanamo Bay, and the camps and the commons—represent just one axis in contemporary scholarship. Over the same period, the United States has consistently raised temporal questions about fostering an enduring freedom, waging preemptive strikes against *ancien regimes*, and conducting strategies of shock-and-awe immediacy to pave the way for long-term occupation. And while American concerns about time are not new, their post-9/11 register is unique in the profound tension that arises between futurity and nostalgia, and the uncertainty that attends to the present.

Elsewhere, I attribute this concern to the incongruence of two temporal narratives made evident after 9/11.[12] If the Cold War "National Security State" (NSS) sought to secure the future of liberal democracy abroad from Latin America to the Far East, then the War on Terror "Homeland Security State" promotes domestic security and is fundamentally nostalgic in orientation. Between these two poles—one anticipatory, the other retrospective—America has had to recalibrate its sense of national time. The resulting tension arises not only in the prelapsarian sentimentalism evident in Claire Messud's *The Emperor's Children* or the WTC Memorial, or the utopian impulse found in Joseph O'Neill's *Netherland* or Barack Obama's 2008 "Yes We Can" campaign; contemporary American literature also articulates a future that can no longer be attained, and a nation unraveling under this new arrangement. Writers like Colson Whitehead, Lydia Millet, and Gary Shteyngart demonstrate an American anticipation of retrospection: imagining a future in which the present ceases to progress.

DeLillo's *Falling Man* registers a similar crisis, but locates it in the WTC plaza on September 11, 2001. Such fixity comes at a cost. DeLillo's novel is largely critiqued for lacking broader vision. Compared to other fiction in the 9/11 genre, *Falling Man* is narrow in its historical connections and makes little gesture toward futurity. It is as insular and self-contained as Cormac McCarthy's *The Road*, whose postapocalyptic setting affords no beginning or end, but rather places its characters in a perpetual state of precarity and indistinction. John Carlos Rowe makes the excellent assertion that *Falling Man* is "hypernational" in its attempt to "incorporate and thereby domesticate global problems" (Rowe 2011: 134). Yet, DeLillo's text also seems to recognize within this hypernationalism the precarity of our experiences. Keith and Lianne's appropriation into homogenous empty time consigns their lives to an undifferentiated scrap heap of American history, their memories trucked off to the Fresh Kills Landfill to be sanitized and restored to Ground Zero. DeLillo thus seems to retreat from the claim he made in "Ruins of the Future" that the narrative ends in the rubble. Rather, the undifferentiated ruins mark a personal trauma held in perpetuity, and a national trauma subsumed back into the field of capitalist presentism.

Notes

1. Acknowledgments: Thank you to the Don DeLillo Society panel participants and audience members at ALA 2014, the Don DeLillo Society, and John Duvall.
2. It is perhaps for this reason that DeLillo's text has been so controversial, "failing" to speak to the aftermath of the attacks beyond its own Manhattanite bubble. The novel tells us little about the contemporary moment of increased militarization in the homeland security state, nothing about the wars in Afghanistan and Iraq, and little about anti-Arabic sentiment.
3. Charles Sumner noted DeLillo stylistically represents this fixity: "DeLillo uses conventional formal techniques to render Keith's psychic life because the politico-economic and cultural forces determining it are unaltered by 9/11" (Sumner 2014: 2).

4. An alternative reading posed by John Duvall argues that the pronoun "him" is misdirected and actually refers to Keith's friend, Rumsey, whom Keith left in the towers.
5. For more on the juxtaposition of art and terrorism across media, see Duvall's "Witnessing Trauma."
6. Having worked as an advertiser—one of the industries Packard takes to task in *The Waste Makers* as well as an earlier critique, *The Hidden Persuaders*—DeLillo certainly understood this leg of American consumption.
7. While *Underworld* is predominantly a novel about nuclear waste, fallout is similarly juxtaposed against scenes from the 1970s NYC sanitation workers' strike and the entropic gleam of futurity DeLillo will eulogize in "In the Ruins of the Future." Eerily, Nick pontificates about this relationship standing at the Fresh Kills Landfill where, four years after *Underworld*'s publication the detritus of the collapsed WTC towers will be hauled.
8. To some, Speer's philosophy was heretical because it imagined a future in which the Third Reich no longer existed.
9. DeLillo explored a similar idea in terms of the Parthenon in *The Names* (1982): "And this is what I mainly learned up there, that the Parthenon was not a thing to study but to feel. It wasn't aloof, rational, timeless, pure. I couldn't locate the serenity of the place, the logic and steady sense. It wasn't a relic species of dead Greece but part of the living city below it. This was a surprise. I'd thought it was a separate thing, the sacred height, intact in its Doric order. I hadn't expected a human feeling to emerge from the stones but this is what I found, deeper than the art and mathematics embodied in the structure, the optical exactitudes. I found a cry for pity. This is what remains to the mauled stones in their blue surround, this open cry, this voice we know as our own" (DeLillo 1982: 330).
10. Keith revels in the routinization of his poker games, as the players create an ever-stricter set of rules to bring even greater homogeneity to the evening's events. Conversely, Lianne tries to find narratives of progress in her Alzheimer's patients' stories, an effort critiqued by her supervisor who tells her that such narratives of progress are not open to these patients.
11. For Rosenthal, this is the "possible rupture in capitalist society, one that has revolutionary political potential" that he seeks to restore to Benjamin's critique of capitalism (Rosenthal 2012: 264).
12. See DeRosa, "The End of Futurity" and "Nostalgia for the Future."

Works cited

Anderson, Benedict. *Imagined Communities*. New York: Verso, 1998.
Anker, Elisabeth R. *Orgies of Feeling: Melodrama and the Politics of Freedom*. Durham: Duke University Press, 2014.
Anker, Elizabeth S. "Allegories of Falling and the 9/11 Novel." *American Literary History* 23, no. 3 (2011): 463–82.
Benjamin, Walter. *Illuminations*. Edited by Hannah Arendy. Translated by Harry Zohn. New York: Schocken, 1969.
Boxall, Peter. *Don DeLillo: The Possibility of Fiction*. London: Routledge, 2004.
Cardwell, Diane. "First Viewing Platform Opens to the Public." *New York Times*, December 30, 2001. Available online: http://www.nytimes.com/2001/12/30/nyregion/a-nation-challenged-ground-zero-first-viewing-platform-opens-to-the-public.html.
Cohen, Samuel. *After the End of History: American Fiction in the 1990s*. Des Moines: University of Iowa Press, 2009.
DeBord, Guy. *The Society of the Spectacle*. Detroit: Black & Red, 1983.
DeLillo, Don. *Falling Man*. New York: Scribner, 2007.
DeLillo, Don. "In the Ruins of the Future." *Harper's* (2001): 33–40.
DeLillo, Don. *Underworld*. New York: Scribner, 1997.
DeLillo, Don. *White Noise*. New York: Penguin, 1998.
DeRosa, Aaron. "The End of Futurity: Proleptic Nostalgia and the War on Terror." *LIT: Literature Interpretation Theory* 25, no. 2 (2014): 88–107. Rpt. in *REAL: Yearbook of Research in English and American Literature*. Vol. 30, edited by Winifred Fluck and Donald Pease. Tübingen, Germany: Narr Francke, 2014.
DeRosa, Aaron. "Nostalgia for the Future: Exceptionalism and Temporality in Twenty-First Century Fiction." In *Narrating 9/11: Fantasies of State, Security, and Terrorism*, 98–117. Baltimore: Johns Hopkins University Press, 2015.
Duvall, John. "Fiction and 9/11." In *The Cambridge Companion to American Fiction After 1945*, 181–93. Cambridge: Cambridge University Press, 2012.
Duvall, John. "Witnessing Trauma: *Falling Man* and Performance Art." In *Don DeLillo: Mao II, Underworld, Falling Man*, edited by Stacey Olster, 152–68. London: Continuum, 2011.
Gray, Richard. *After the Fall: American Literature Since 9/11*. London: Wiley-Blackwell, 2011.
Greenspan, Elizabeth. "The Story Behind the First Piece of Public Architecture at Ground Zero." *The Atlantic*. TheAtlantic.com. September 11, 2013. Available online: http://www.theatlantic.com/

national/archive/2013/09/the-story-behind-the-first-piece-of-public-architecture-at-ground-zero/279488/.

Hardack, Richard. "World Trade Centers and World-Wide-Webs: From *Underworld* to Over-Soul in Don DeLillo." *Arizona Quarterly* 69, no. 1 (2013): 151–83.

Harootunian, Harry. "Remembering the Historical Present." *Critical Inquiry* 33, no. 3 (2007): 471–94.

Lang, Karen. "Eric Fischl's Tumbling Woman, 9/11, and 'Timeless Time.'" *Future Anterior* 8, no. 2 (2002): 21–35.

Maslowski, Maciej. "'Like Nothing in This Life': The Concept of Historic Time in Don DeLillo's *Falling Man*." In *The American Uses of History: Essays on Public Memory*, edited by Tomasz Basiuk, Sylwia Kuźma-Markowska and Krystyna Mazur, 245–54. Frankfurt: Lang, 2011.

Packard, Vance. *The Waste Makers*. New York: McKay, 1960.

Pease, Donald. *The New American Exceptionalism*. Minneapolis: University of Minnesota Press, 2009.

Redfield, Marc. "Imagi-Nation: The Imagined Community and the Aesthetics of Mourning." *Diacritics* 29, no. 4 (1999): 58–83.

Rosenthal, Michael. "Benjamin's Wager on Modernity: Gambling and the Arcades Project." *The Germanic Review: Literature, Culture, Theory* 87 (2012): 261–78.

Rowe, John Carlos. "Global Horizons in *Falling Man*." In *Don DeLillo: Mao II, Underworld, Falling Man*, edited by Stacey Olster, 121–34. London: Continuum, 2011.

Ruskin, John. *Seven Lamps of Architecture*. London: Electric Book Company, 1849. ProQuest ebrary.

Sorensen, Leif. "Against the Post-Apocalyptic: Narrative Closure in Colson Whitehead's *Zone One*." *Contemporary Literature* 55, no. 3 (2014): 559–92.

Speer, Albert. *Inside the Third Reich*. London: Sphere, 1970.

Sumner, Charles. "Don DeLillo's *Falling Man* and the Protective Shield Against Stimuli." *American Imago* 71, no. 1 (2014): 1–27.

Wegner, Phillip E. "October 3, 1951 to September 11, 2001: Periodizing the Cold War in Don DeLillo's *Underworld*." *Amerikastudien/American Studies* 49, no. 1 (2004): 51–64.

Wyatt, David. "September 11 and Postmodern Memory." *Arizona Quarterly* 65, no. 4 (2009): 139–61.

3

Absent presences: Paradoxes of representation and self-representation in (post)-9/11 comics

David Brauner

When I look out of the window in the direction where the twins used to stand, I see this ENORMOUS hole in the sky. I'm slowly getting used to its presence.
~ HENRICK REHR, *Tribeca Sunset: A Story of 9–11* (2005)

Nothing like commemorating an event to help you forget it.
~ ART SPIEGELMAN, *In the Shadow of No Towers* (2004)

Unsurprisingly, given the startling, spectacular nature of the event itself and the gravity of its geopolitical ramifications, the destruction of the World Trade Center (WTC) on September 11, 2001, has generated an extraordinary amount of writing, both nonfictional (political polemics, cultural critiques, and eyewitness accounts) and fictional (novels, short stories, poems, and plays). This body of work has attained sufficient critical mass to become a category in its own right—what Marc Redfield calls "9/11 discourse" (Redfield 2007: passim)—and, in common with other discourses, to have developed its own set of conventions and parameters. Alongside these written responses, there have also been visual responses, including photographs, paintings, and sculptures, which have shaped, and been shaped by, what might be called an iconography of 9/11: the "jumpers" in freefall; the firemen and police wading through the rubble and smoke; the planes streaking across the blue skies; the ash, smoke, debris, and detritus that contaminated Manhattan in the hours, days, and weeks following the collapse of the towers; and, of course, the towers themselves, depicted again and again in various stages and states: pristine and apparently indestructible before the first plane struck; with smoke and flames issuing from them; like bleeding wounds; but still standing; collapsing; and in ruins.

Many of the most memorable cultural engagements with 9/11 have been produced in media that combine words and images, in films such as Michael Moore's independent documentary *Fahrenheit 911* (2004) and Paul Greengrass's Hollywood movie *United 93* (2006), and in the work of comics authors, many of whom were among the first artists in any field to publish work on 9/11, working in forms ranging from single-page images to graphic novels. Within a few months of the attacks, three anthologies had appeared: *9/11 Emergency Relief* (2002), a collection of strips from "alternative" comics artists and writers, commissioned to raise money for the relief efforts of the American Red Cross; and two volumes, entitled *9/11 Artists Respond Volume One* (2002) and *9-11 September 11th 2001: The World's Finest Comic Book Writers and Artists Tell 9-11* (2002), whose proceeds were donated to the victims of the attacks, comprising short strips by many of the most eminent names in contemporary comics. At the same time, Art Spiegelman, author of one of the foundational and unquestionably the most acclaimed of graphic novels, *Maus* (1980–1991), was working on "a series of ten large-scale pages about September 11" (Spiegelman 2004: n. pag.) that were eventually published, together with two accompanying essays and several comic strips from the "golden age" of comics, as *In the Shadow of No Towers* (2004). In the following year, Henrik Rehr's *Tribeca Sunset: A Story of 9-11* (2005) was published, followed by Sid Jacobson and Ernie Colón's *The 9/11 Report: A Graphic Adaptation* (2006) and *After 9/11:*

America's War on Terror (2008), as well as Alissa Torres's *American Widow* (2008).

Representing 9/11 has posed and continues to pose profound problems—aesthetic and ethical, formal and cultural, and generic and political—for writers and artists. Some critics have argued that graphic novels, by virtue of their very form, are uniquely well suited to dealing with these problems. Simon Cooper and Paul Atkinson point to "the uncanny resemblance between the starkly rendered political landscape of the 'war on terror' and the moral universe of the mainstream comic book," before asking how self-reflexive "comic books might react to a world that had seemed increasingly to resemble its fantasized constructions" (Cooper and Atkinson 2008: 60). Stefan Hall claims that "because 9/11 could barely seem to be part of anything but a fantastic realm, those working in cartoon strips, comic books and other sequential art took to the subject as a way to make sense of something that strained comprehension" (Hall 2011: 18). Tim Gauthier argues that "since the initial narratives were largely conveyed through images, it stands to reason that a medium that incorporates both text and image, such as the graphic novel, might have more success [in dealing with the 'unrepresentability' of 9/11]" (Gauthier 2010: 370). These critics emphasize different characteristics of the comics genre: for Cooper and Atkinson, it is the Manichean framework of the "classic comic book" that makes it a natural fit for representing the "fantasti[c]" events of 9/11 (Cooper and Atkinson 2008: 60); Gauthier sees an intrinsic affinity between the graphic novel and the "initial narratives" of 9/11 based on the centrality of "images"; and Hall implicitly invokes the "fantastic" tradition of "sequential art" as the key to its capacity to "make sense" of the events of 9/11. However, they all agree that 9/11 "strained comprehension" to such an extent that it is essentially "unrepresentable." In this way, their claim for the privileged position of comics rests on a paradox: the idea that it can represent an actual historical event authentically precisely because its "fantastic" nature precludes claims to realism or authenticity. In this essay, I want to interrogate this claim, focusing particularly on the ways in which comics writers have explored and exploited this paradox and others in their representations of, and responses to, 9/11.

What Gauthier calls the "unrepresentability" of 9/11 arguably derives from two distinct but related sources: the nature and circumstances of the reporting of the event in the media and the theoretical paradigms in which the reporting of this reporting have been situated. There is a critical consensus among academics who have written about 9/11 and its representations that there was something unreal about the images of the attacks on the twin towers that were broadcast live on 9/11 and in the ensuing days and weeks. Gauthier observes that "9/11 was a distanced and mediated experience ... [imbued with] a sense of unreality [and] a touch of cinematic déjà vu." (Gauthier 2010: 369) and furthermore that "it would [soon] be difficult to distinguish September 11, or '9/11', from what we had seen on our television screens" (Gauthier 2010: 369). Similarly, Marc Redfield claims that "there has never been a more utterly mediated event" (Redfield 2007: 65–66), while Slavoj Žižek reflects that "when we watched the oft-repeated shot of frightened people running toward the camera ahead of the giant cloud of dust from the collapsing tower ... the framing of the shot itself [was] reminiscent of spectacular shots in a catastrophe movie" (Žižek 2002: 11). What is notable here is the insistence on the "mediated" nature of the media footage of 9/11 and the recurring analogy between that footage and images made familiar by Hollywood films. I will return to the cinematic 9/11 trope later, but for now I want to interrogate these claims about the "mediated" nature of 9/11.

If it is true, as Redfield claims, that "wherever one looks in 9/11 discourse ... the event disappears into its own mediation" (Redfield 2007: 56), then this should be understood as at least in part a self-fulfilling and self-perpetuating phenomenon, the product of postmodernist tropes so familiar that they have become naturalized, ironically hardening into precisely the sort of grand narrative that postmodernist critics have always been determined to deconstruct. For a generation of academics on both sides of the Atlantic who were taught, and then themselves taught others, about postmodern theory and practice, two critical touchstones were Baudrillard's essay "Simulacra and Simulation" (1981)—in which simulation is defined as "the generation by models of a real without origin or reality" (Baudrillard 2011: 1)—and Don DeLillo's novel *White Noise* (1985)—in which Jack Gladney and his colleague Murray Siskind watch tourists "taking pictures of taking pictures" at the site of "the most photographed barn in America" (DeLillo 1986: 13). Given the foundational nature of these texts for the concept of "mediation" and the fact that the events of September 11, 2001, were almost immediately situated in this postmodernist paradigm in 9/11 discourse, it is perhaps unsurprising that Baudrillard and DeLillo were among the first authors to publish their reflections on 9/11 in essays that have themselves been repeatedly "mediated" in 9/11 discourse (a process in which I too am implicated as I write this chapter).

However, the relationships of these essays on 9/11 to their earlier texts are very different. Baudrillard embraced 9/11 as a vindication of his theories, declaring that "the two towers of the World Trade Center embodied perfectly, in their very double-ness (literally twin-ness) . . . [the] definitive order" (Baudrillard 2001: n. pag.), in terms that self-consciously recalled his formulation in "Simulacra and Simulation" that "things are doubled by their own scenario" (Baudrillard 2011: 24). Invoking the "phantasm" of numerous disaster movies and at one point referring to 9/11 itself as "Manhattan's disaster movie," Baudrillard asks "What happens then to the real event, if everywhere the image, the fiction, the virtual, infuses reality?" He concludes that although "one might perceive [in the events of 9/11] a resurgence of the real," in fact "reality has absorbed the energy of fiction, and become fiction itself," so that, paradoxically, the "collapse of the towers of the World Trade Center is unimaginable, but that is not enough to make it a real event" (Baudrillard 2001: n. pag.). In contrast, DeLillo argues that "the event asserts its singularity" and that it was unreal only in the sense that "when we say a thing is unreal, we mean it is too real, a phenomenon so unaccountable and yet so bound to the power of objective fact that we can't tilt it to the slant of our perceptions" (DeLillo 2001: n. pag.). These differences can be explained in terms of their opposing perspectives, literal and metaphorical: DeLillo is a New Yorker whose family was caught up in the events of 9/11, and whose essay includes a tribute to the cultural diversity and inclusiveness of the city, while Baudrillard has always viewed what he calls in his essay "the banality of American everyday life" (Baudrillard 2001: n. pag.) with a lofty contempt. However, their accounts converge on one point: the symbolic importance of the twin towers. For DeLillo, "the World Trade towers were not only an emblem of advanced technology but a justification, in a sense, for technology's irresistible will to realise in solid form whatever becomes theoretically allowable"

(DeLillo 2001: n. pag.), while Baudrillard describes the implosion of the tower as the "symbolic collapse of a whole system" in which the towers were metaphorically complicit: "By suiciding, the towers ... complete[d] the event" (Baudrillard 2001: n. pag.). In the light of these comments, I now want to explore the ways in which the towers themselves are represented, mediated, and appropriated in 9/11 discourse, focusing particularly on Art Spiegelman's *In the Shadow of No Towers* and a number of short strips in two 9/11 comics anthologies.

In his essay "Virtual Trauma: The Idiom of 9/11" (2007), Marc Redfield observes that

> a society keyed to spectacle is necessarily an intensely if narrowly verbal society, and it is above all as a name that September 11 has become part of everyday American cultural life. The array of images—photographs and video recordings—remain on call in the archive, forever ready to reappear in the media or to be accessed via the Internet; but far more available, endlessly and unavoidably available . . . are the keywords themselves: the name-date, "September 11" or "9/11" and, shadowing it, an atomic-era military idiom, "ground zero," turned toponym. (Redfield 2007: 55)

Conspicuously absent from Redfield's discussion of the "keywords" of 9/11 are the main targets of the attacks mounted on that date in 2001. The sheer proliferation of terms for these structures is striking: they are variously named the World Trade Center (sometimes abbreviated to WTC, sometimes elaborated as World Trade Center One and World Trade Center Two), the World Trade towers, the North Tower and South Tower, and finally the Twin Towers (which itself is often abbreviated either to simply "the towers" or "the twins"). These different terms carry their own particular connotations: the WTC emphasizes the functionality of the buildings, their unity (in this denomination the towers are treated as a single entity), and their symbolic claim simultaneously to represent a hub of economic activity with a specific geographical location (reinforced if referred to as World Trade Center One and Two) and a concept—global capital(ism)—which transcends national borders. The tension between these centrifugal and centripetal impulses is mirrored in the way that the formulation "twin towers" implicitly both monumentalizes and humanizes the structures, as can be seen most clearly in its abbreviations; whereas "the towers" invokes ancient historical monuments, "the twins" lends an anthropomorphic quality to the buildings.

This linguistic multivalency is correlative with the wide range of visual representations of the towers in comics. Redfield's comments on the nomenclature associated with 9/11 discourse are again relevant here: he argues that "no cultural study of the September 11 attacks ... can afford to ignore the rhetorical and political work performed by ... the name-date itself, for which no synonyms exist and which anchors all talk and all analysis of 'September 11' to a powerful, haunting catachresis" (Redfield 2007: 55–56). As we have seen, there are many synonyms for the towers but, just as the ubiquitous use of the "name-date" to signify the terrorist attacks in 2001 has colonized September 11, eclipsing its significance in any other historical or cultural context, so any reference, post-9/11, to "the towers" is implicitly understood to signify the WTC, as the use of the definite article implies. Moreover, the catachresis that Redfield refers to applies equally to the representation—visual and verbal—of the towers in 9/11 comics. Omnipresent though they are in one sense, the towers are also curiously absent from many of these works; in fact, one might say that, paradoxically, they become invisible precisely of their omnipresence, which is to say that their ubiquity means that it becomes difficult to register their presence— to see them—meaningfully, so that their presence becomes a sort of absence. Furthermore, they are often represented as already mediated images—that is to say, in photographs, in artworks or children's drawings, and, most frequently, on television screens (a point I shall return to later). As signifiers, they are both overdetermined and intractably indeterminate. The towers function both as metonyms for the terrorist attacks of 9/11 (absorbing and displacing the attack on the Pentagon and the fate of the United Airlines plane that never reached its intended target) and as meta-metaphors, symbols that have been evacuated of all meaning other than to signify the power of symbolism itself. Nowhere is this duality more evident than in Art Spiegelman's *In the Shadow of No Towers*.

In the prefatory essay to the book, "The sky is falling," Spiegelman draws attention to an image that he claims does not belong to what Redfield refers to as "the array of images—photographs and video recordings—... in the archive":

> The pivotal image from my 9/11 morning—one that didn't get photographed or videotaped into public memory but still remains burned onto the inside of my eyelids several years later—was the image of the looming north tower's glowing bones just before it vaporised. I repeatedly tried to paint this with humiliating results but eventually came close to capturing the vision of disintegration digitally on my computer. I managed to place some sequences of my most vivid memories around that central image but never got to draw others. (Spiegelman 2004: n. pag.)

This passage establishes the parameters of, and rationale for, *In the Shadow of No Towers*. It is a work predicated on paradoxes: the notion, implicit in the title, that the towers are more powerfully present in their absence than prior to their destruction, when their very familiarity as part of the city skyline made them invisible (in other words, the "hole in the sky" left by their collapse makes them more conspicuous than they were before 9/11); the claim to authenticity and victimhood, resting on the author's status as an eyewitness of the attacks on the towers (the memory of which remains "burned" in his consciousness, suggesting an unresolved trauma), qualified by the implicit acknowledgment of subjectivity (and therefore unreliability) in the use of the personal pronouns ("my 9/11 morning ... my eyelids ... I repeatedly tried ... I managed to place ... my most vivid memories"); and of course, the fundamental impossibility of "capturing" something at the moment of its "disintegration." The implicit gulf between the official version of 9/11 (the authorized version of events enshrined in "public memory") and Spiegelman's personal vision (reconstructed from his private "vivid memories") manifests itself in the way that he represents the towers in *In the Shadow of No Towers*. Rather than depicting the towers with smoke and flames issuing from them after being struck by the planes, or in the moments before the second plane struck, or post collapse, as a pile of smoldering rubble (the archetypal archival images), Spiegelman chooses to reproduce an architectural skeleton of the north tower without its twin, a surreal frame of "glowing bones." This image—of one tower emptied of all its contents (there are transparent spaces between the orange gridlines where there would have been furniture, interior walls, corridors and, of course, people)—is the leitmotif running through the book: it appears at the top of pages 1 and 5, at the bottom of page 2, as a vertical left-hand panel on pages 3, 4, 6 (the "bones" rendered in the last of these in chalky white), and 9 (where it has other panels superimposed on top of it in the lower half of the page), in the first two panels of page 7 (in the second of these the lines seem to be in the process of disintegrating), and in the antepenultimate panel of the final page of Spiegelman's narrative, on page 10, where it is followed, in the last panels of the comic, by two faded, gray images of the towers in outline.

The insistent replication of these variations on the central theme of the book seems to me both evidence of the sort of compulsive repetition associated with trauma and the artist's way of negotiating the problem of mediation that has determined so much of 9/11 discourse. By defining his image against those that have been mass reproduced, Spiegelman is trying to see, and by extension make his readers see, the events of 9/11 afresh; by choosing to focus only on *one* of the towers and making the image of that tower stylized rather than realistic, he is subverting the iconic image of the "twin towers," defamiliarizing it, trying to capture *the experience* of witnessing the burning tower. Yet by reproducing his own image— a self-consciously "unreal" image—of the towers over the course of the ten pages of his narrative, he also implicitly invokes some of the key critical tropes and debates that have pervaded 9/11 discourse: the contention that the events of 9/11 were "fantastic" and therefore "unrepresentable"; the notion that the towers can only be understood as simulations, replicas both of each other and of a concept with no recoverable origin; and the theory that "9/11" itself is an endlessly mediated phenomenon. As Richard Glejzer observes, "The glowing tower presents a radically particular image, an image that cannot be universally reproduced . . . it draws attention to the very mechanism of image reproduction, to how the image dissipates and fragments" (Glejzer 2008: 108). At the same time, however, within the pages of *In the Shadow of No Towers*, the image *is* repeatedly reproduced, its persistence paradoxically preserving the tower in a perpetual state of disintegration. In doing so, Spiegelman exploits the fluidity offered by the comic format. As Spiegelman points out in "The Comic Supplement," the essay that intercedes between his reflections on 9/11 and the reproduction of "golden-age" comic strips that functions as a sort of appendix to the *In the Shadow of No Towers* volume, "Comics pages are architectural structures—the narrative rows of panels are like stories of a building" (Spiegelman 2004: 11). This observation is somewhat complicated, however, by the fact that Spiegelman chose to publish *In the Shadow of No Towers* in broadsheet format, thereby considerably extending the vertical planes of the "architectural structure." As the title of the work suggests, the images of the tower in *In the Shadow of No Towers* foreground its destruction—since it is almost invariably depicted in the process of disintegration—but also metaphorically reconstructs it, because it is the dominant image of the book, colonizing so much of its architectural space. Similarly, the digitized image that Spiegelman decides is preferable to his initial "humiliating" attempts to paint the towers on the cusp of collapse is in one sense alienating in its artifice but in another sense highlights the opacity of the actual towers, or at least of their facades. As Tim Gauthier points out, during the events of 9/11:

> Thousands of people died; we merely witnessed two buildings imploding . . . the sheer immensity of the towers guaranteed that we could barely glimpse those trapped inside . . . the very scale of the buildings required a long camera shot to encompass the calamity . . . the very horror of the events . . . elicited a reflexive self-censorship. (Gauthier 2010: 369)

By depicting a tower that looks as though it is being "vaporised" in a pulp science-fiction comic, Spiegelman replicates the dehumanizing scale not just of the attacks but of the towers themselves. Paradoxically, however, the towers of *In the Shadow of No Towers* also arguably represent an attempt to restore a sense of the very human suffering that was obscured by the glass and steel of the actual towers and by the tacit consensus in the media not to show those who defenestrated themselves from the burning buildings. As Redfield points out, "Karen Engle, in *Visual Culture and 9/11*, plausibly suggests that the quasi-anthropomorphic towers came to substitute for the bodies of the victims, so many of which had been annihilated or utterly fragmented, and were in most cases forbidden objects of media representation." (Redfield 2007: 71). Certainly, Spiegelman's description of the shimmering orange gridlines as "glowing bones" suggests that his vision of the towers is self-consciously anthropomorphic, as does his paradoxical description of them as "arrogant boxes . . . rascals, icons of a more innocent age" (Spiegelman 2004: 2). Perhaps the very characteristics that had seemed to make the towers inviolable—their immensity, their steely opacity, the fact that they were replicas of each other—paradoxically encouraged this anthropomorphism. At any rate, this anthropomorphizing strategy—symbolized by Kieron Dwyer's untitled single-page contribution to *9–11 September 11th 2001*, which depicts the towers with hundreds of faces (presumably representing the victims of the terrorist attacks) superimposed onto their structures (Dwyer 2002: 14)—is one that recurs in a number of 9/11 comics and graphic novels, and I want to look at some examples of this before returning to *In the Shadow of No Towers*.

In his contribution to the *9/11 Artists Respond* anthology, "Close to Home," Chris Eliopoulos refers to the towers as "the twins" and "America's twins" and explicitly identifies them with his children, who are identical twins (Eliopoulos 2002: 127). In Henrik Rehr's graphic novel, *Tribeca Sunset*, one of the characters demonstrates a similar sentimentality, asking "Why did they have to hit the twin towers? I loved the twins. The sight of them always reminded me of home," which prompts the artist to ask the man's pregnant wife: "You're not by any chance having twins are you?" (Rehr 2005: 32). Jo Duffy, Todd Nauck, and Jamie Mendoza also personify the towers but with a different inflection. "Gemini Falling," their contribution to the *9-11 September 11th 2001* anthology, consists of three panels taking up one page, offering three views of the towers: first, pristine, in the foreground; second, still intact, in the background with the Statue of Liberty (wearing a concerned expression) in the foreground; and finally, from a distance, after collapse, with a huge pall of dark smoke filling the space where they used to stand. The accompanying text boxes refer to them as "twins . . . beautiful, vital," a "buddy story, told in concrete, glass and steel" and then simply "Gone now" (Duffy, Nauck, and Mendoza 2002: 39). This brief strip mobilizes a number of different allusions in order simultaneously to mythologize and domesticate the tragic fate of the towers. The title of the story invokes the myth of Castor and Pollux, who were unified—and glorified—in death in the form of the stellar constellation; the reference to the "buddy story" situates the towers in the context of contemporary popular culture, particularly Hollywood cinema, in which the buddy movie has become a staple, and the visual juxtaposition of the Statue of Liberty with the towers emphasizes the iconic status that they shared but also, because of the female features of the Statue (accentuated by the artists in the panel in which she appears), implies a gendered opposition between the singular Liberty and the (implicitly) male companionship attributed to the towers through the "buddy" metaphor.

The conjunction of the Statue and the towers also appears in Sam Glanzman's "There were tears in her eyes," a passionate, polemical story that utilizes aspects of both elements of Glanzman's identity as an American Jew to argue for a swift military response to 9/11. The Statue of Liberty appears twice—once in a verbal reference at the start of the story in which the artist represents himself watching the television coverage of 9/11, thinking "it's as if they raped the statue of liberty" (Glanzman 2002: 207) and once visually, in a panel showing the face of the Statue in profile with a single tear on her cheek. Glanzman's verbal analogy between the Statue and the towers couches the terrorist attacks in terms that make it seem as though their real victims are the towers themselves—as though his distress has been displaced from the human casualties onto the idea that the structures have been violated. However, this is complicated by the fact that (uniquely in the collection) in his opening panel, showing the towers in flames, he includes two human figures (in black silhouette) falling, on the right side of the right-hand tower. Even more audaciously, the image of the Statue of Liberty occupies the lower right-hand corner of a page that is dominated by a large panel in which a huge mound of emaciated bodies lie in a ditch in the foreground, while in the background smoke issues from the top of three tower-like chimneys to the right of a building that is clearly based on the SS administration building at Auschwitz. The analogy between the two historical events is reinforced by the fact that the panel containing the Statue actually overlaps with the bottom right-hand corner of the Auschwitz panel, obscuring some of the corpses, while a box containing the words "Will we wait? until it is too late?" straddles the two panels (Glanzman 2002: 210). These questions refer back to Glanzman's contention, at the top of the page, that the Nazi genocide "could have been prevented" had the allies "acted earlier" (Glanzman 2002: 210) and also to the image on the previous page, where Glanzman depicts the mushroom cloud created by the atomic bomb dropped on Hiroshima, accompanied by text that claims that it "spared . . . millions of American and Japanese lives" (Glanzman 2002: 209). But these images also return us, intertextually, to Spiegelman.

Glanzman's representation of the pile of corpses at Auschwitz recalls one of the most (in)famous moments in Spiegelman's *Maus*: the opening page of the "Time Flies" section of the second volume, in which Spiegelman's surrogate self, Artie, appears as a diminutive figure wearing a mouse-mask, slumped over his drawing board agonizing over the repercussions of the commercial success of the first volume, while flies buzz around him, circulating above a mound of corpses with mouse-heads at the bottom of the page. This image is of course itself a reworking of photographs of the mass graves of Jewish victims of the Holocaust, so whether Glanzman was alluding to this episode from *Maus* is a moot point, but it was certainly very much in Spiegelman's mind when he was writing *In the Shadow of No Towers*. The latter is packed with references, visual and verbal, explicit and implicit, to the author's earlier graphic novel. In fact, one might say that *In the Shadow of No Towers* is, itself, in the shadow of *Maus*.

It is there in the author's repeated representation of himself with the same mouse-head he had given himself and other Jews in *Maus*: on page 2, in the final panel of a vertical sequence of self-portraits of the artist looking at himself in the mirror, with the text "issues of self-representation have left me slack-jawed" (Spiegelman 2004: 2), which are themselves superimposed over an image of the artist with a mouse-head slumped over his desk with caricatures of Osama bin Laden and George Bush on either side of him, an image glossed by the bold, capitalized caption: "EQUALLY TERRORIZED BY AL-QAEDA AND BY HIS OWN GOVERNMENT"; in two series of panels on page 3, the first of which represents the artist recalling "my father trying to describe what the smoke in Auschwitz smelled like.... The closest he got was telling me it was 'indescribable'.... That's exactly what the air in Lower Manhattan smelled like after Sept. 11!" (Spiegelman 2004: 3); in the final panel of page 6, in which the artist represents himself as a young child with a mouse-head who has fallen out of bed as the result of a nightmare; in the final panel of page 8, in which the artist appears to be holding a large stick of dynamite that resembles one of the twin towers; in a panel on page 9, in which the artist throws his cat out of the frame in his rage at the antics of George Bush's governments (the main satirical target of the book), while a box in the bottom left-hand corner offers the mock "disclaimer" that "no creatures, other than the artist, were abused in the creation of the strip" (Spiegelman 2004: 9); and again on the final page, in which the artist and the other members of his family are represented with mouse-heads, at the front of a crowd otherwise made up of famous cartoon characters, cowering from a shower of cowboy boots (signifying George W. Bush's exploitation of 9/11 for his own political purposes) that rain down from the sky. It is there in the echoes of the "Time Flies" motif in the first sentence of the final paragraph of "The sky is falling!" ("Still, time keeps flying and even the New Normal gets old") and in the central panel on page 8, which reads: "Time passes. He can think about himself in the first person again, but deep inside the towers still burn. The killer apes learned **nothing** from the twin towers of Auschwitz and Hiroshima ... and nothing changed on 9/11" (n. pag., 8, bold font in original).

In one sense, Glanzman's and Spiegelman's analogies between the Holocaust and 9/11 (and their references to Hiroshima) are diametrically opposed. Whereas Glanzman urges the United States not to delay military action as it had in the Second World War, Spiegelman is dismayed by what he sees as the US government's knee-jerk military response, identifying the jingoism, xenophobia, and suppression of domestic political dissent that he sees in the aftermath of 9/11 with the fascism of the Nazis (the cowboy boot implicitly corresponding to the jackboot). Yet, in another sense, Spiegelman, like Glanzman, is positing a parallel between the persecution of Jews by the Nazis and the attacks by Al-Qaeda on the natives of New York. In fact, Spiegelman pushes this correlation further than Glanzman by virtue of his personal, biographical connection with the Holocaust. In this context, the subtext of the insistent echoes of *Maus* in *In the Shadow of No Towers* is that, for Spiegelman, the events of 9/11 increased his identification with the victims of the Holocaust. Like Glanzman, Spiegelman makes a connection between the chimney towers of the crematoria at Auschwitz and the WTC. In *In the Shadow of No Towers*, however, this becomes the basis of an expression of empathy with German Jews in the 1930s: "I finally understand why some Jews didn't leave Berlin right after Kristallnacht!" (Spiegelman 2004: 4). Yet, as the allusions to the "Time Flies" section of *Maus* suggest, at the same time as Spiegelman draws on the cultural capital of *Maus* and the connection it affords him to the Holocaust—representing himself as particularly sensitized to the trauma of 9/11 as a result of the transmission of the trauma of his parents' Holocaust experiences—

he is acutely, uncomfortably aware of the aesthetic and ethical problems with exploiting this connection. After all, "Time Flies" explicitly explores Spiegelman's feelings of guilt at having benefitted artistically, and profited commercially, from his family connection to the Holocaust and Spiegelman's self-representation in a mouse-mask implies that there is something inauthentic and perhaps disingenuous about his identification with the victims of the Nazis. This self-indictment is both reinforced and challenged in the opening paragraph of "The sky is falling," which invokes Spiegelman's identity as the son of Holocaust survivors and, by extension, his treatment of this precarious, fraught subject-position in *Maus*:

> Before 9/11 my traumas were all self-inflicted, but outrunning the toxic cloud that had moments before been the north tower of the World Trade Center left me reeling on that faultline where World History and Personal History collide—the intersection my parents, Auschwitz survivors, had warned me about when they taught me to always keep my bags packed. (Spiegelman 2004: n. pag.)

On the one hand, this passage seems to validate Spiegelman's credentials as an eyewitness and victim of the terrorist attacks. The image of the artist "outrunning the toxic cloud" generated by the collapse of the north tower (reinforced by a round panel that bisects the text of the top half of this opening page of the book, depicting a crowd running in terror while buildings seem to be toppling behind them)[1] places Spiegelman at the heart of the action and the metaphor of the "faultline between World History and Personal History" is offered as a vindication of the cautionary advice the author received from his survivor parents. On the other hand, Spiegelman's confession that his traumas prior to 9/11 "were all self-inflicted" complicates the notion that he has inherited what Marianne Hirsch (in an essay on *Maus*) calls "postmemory" of the Holocaust, and this in turn calls into question his status as a victim of 9/11, since this seems to rest at least partly on the claim to Holocaust victimhood (Hirsch 1993: n. pag.).

Like *Maus* then, and partly through its intertextual relationship with that earlier graphic novel, *In the Shadow of No Towers* is a text that interrogates its own tropes and deconstructs its own narrative. Just as Spiegelman draws attention to the vexed question of his own role in *Maus*, so throughout *In the Shadow of No Towers* he grapples with what he calls "issues of self-representation," representing himself not just with a mouse-head but also in a bewildering number of other guises.[2] Arguably, the most provocative of these occurs in the vertical panel on the left-hand side of page 6, when he depicts himself in free fall (in a sequence of five different positions) by the side of a skeletal tower, a clear visual allusion to those who jumped to their deaths from the towers. Once again, this seems to me a fundamentally paradoxical move: at once a bold confrontation of one of the taboo images of 9/11 and a potentially insensitive appropriation of these images in order to posit what is arguably a spurious correspondence between his own 9/11 trauma and that of the workers at the WTC. What complicates this further is that what might otherwise seem to be a naive or cynical overidentification with the victims can also be read as a knowing exposure of such overidentification, the visual equivalent of the self-indictment symbolized by the mouse-mask he has Artie wear in the "Time Flies" section of *Maus*, particularly in the light of the text that accompanies his self-portrait as a "jumper":

> He keeps falling through the holes in his head, though he no longer knows which holes were made by Arab terrorists way back in 2001, and which ones were always there . . .
> He is haunted now by the images he *didn't* witness . . . images of people tumbling to the streets below . . . especially one man (according to a neighbor) who executed a graceful Olympic dive as his last living act. (Spiegelman 2004: 6, italics and ellipses in original).

This text implies not only that the image of Spiegelman tumbling down is a metaphor for a precipitous psychological descent but that the catalyst for this figurative fall might not have been 9/11 at all. The acknowledgment that "he no longer knows which holes . . . were *always* there" echoes the opening lines in which Spiegelman confesses that he "tend[s] to be easily unhinged" and that the traumas he had suffered prior to 9/11 were "all more or less self-inflicted" but also raises the possibility that his 9/11 trauma, too, is as much, or more, the product of an innate mental fragility and/or a propensity for self-dramatization than a direct consequence of the terrorist attacks themselves. This suggestion is reinforced by the mediated nature of the account that he receives of the tragic trajectory of the jumper, by the contrast between this description of a "graceful Olympian dive" and the inelegant nature of his own fall, by the fact that this fall stops before the artist hits the ground, and by the paradoxical assertion that "he is haunted by the images he *didn't* witness" (Spiegelman 2004: 6).

All of this emphasizes the distance between Spiegelman's experiences of 9/11 and those who died in the attacks and, by extension, Spiegelman the author's ironic distance from the version of himself who appears in the pages of *In the Shadow of No Towers*, in my view complicating Glejzer's contention that "whereas *Maus* offered Spiegelman distance from the events he describes, *In the Shadow of No Towers* is about the failure to achieve such a distance" (Glejzer 2008: 100). The ellipses in the passage also seem to express this distance as well as being visual lacunae that correspond to the present absences of the images that he has not seen that haunt the artist. Conversely, the verbal repetition of "holes" invokes the "hole in the sky" left by the collapse of the towers, the dominant absent presences of the book, as well as anticipating the central image on page 8 of the artist drilling into his own fissured skull with a pneumatic drill. Finally, then, the image of the falling Spiegelman is emblematic both of the artist's inability to "distinguish my own neurotic depression from well-founded despair" (Spiegelman 2004: 8) and of his recognition of that inability. It is also Spiegelman's way of implicitly identifying himself not just with the "jumpers" of 9/11 but with the pantheon of golden-age comics characters who are depicted, in silhouette, on the back cover and inside covers of the book, in similar plunging postures to those of the falling self-portraits on page 6.[3]

In fact, the inclusion of these characters not just on the hard covers of the book but within its pages—in the form of a number of strips reproduced in a coda to Spiegelman's own comic—serves a dual purpose. On the one hand, they are a vehicle for what one might see as Spiegelman's project of self-mythologization: by juxtaposing his own work with theirs and, on the inside back cover, reproducing one of the self-portraits in freefall and inserting it among the other legendary silhouetted comics characters, he is implicitly situating himself (both as an artist and as a character) in the canonical tradition to which they belong. On the other hand, the fact that *In the Shadow of No Towers* finishes not with Spiegelman's work but with seven "plates" that form an anthology of sorts of comics art from the early part of the twentieth century arguably diminishes the status of what precedes it and undermines its urgency as a contemporary polemical and satirical response to the event that has arguably shaped twenty-first-century global political realities. Spiegelman's ostensible rationale for the inclusion of these comics is that they were "the only cultural artifacts that could . . . flood my eyes and brain with something other than images of burning towers" (Spiegelman 2004: 11) but to include them in the book, after the conclusion of his own comic, runs the risk of them displacing the images of the tower(s) not only in the artist's consciousness but in those of his readers. Although Mitchum Huehls argues that "these historical comics offer Spiegelman a safe temporality from which to approach the timely trauma of his immediate present" (Huehls 2008: 57), there is a sense in which *In the Shadow of No Towers*, for all its confrontational and provocative power, ends up retreating into nostalgia, taking refuge in the visions of what Spiegelman himself calls "the optimistic dawn of the 20th century" (Spiegelman 2004: 11).

This withdrawal from the events of 9/11 is echoed, albeit in very different form, in two other graphic novels that ostensibly take it as their subject: Rehr's *Tribeca Sunset* and Torres's *American Widow*. Like *In the Shadow of No Towers*, these books begin by engaging with the events of 9/11 and situate versions of their authors as victims, traumatized (and, in the case of Torres, bereaved) by the terrorist attacks, but in the end their 9/11 narratives are displaced, in Torres's *American Widow* by an extended account of Torres's struggle to get financial compensation for her loss and in *Tribeca Sunset* by a strange soap-opera style narrative revolving around a group of Bohemian friends in Manhattan, from which the author and his family disappear completely. In both cases, there are awkward, belated attempts visually to reinstate 9/11 as the subject of the narrative. In *American Widow*, this occurs most notably through the abrupt insertion of two pages of color photographs of the author's deceased husband, Luis Torres; these follow immediately a mostly blank page in the left-hand margin of which a single black silhouetted figure is visible, falling next to one of the towers (Torres 2008: 197–99). In *Tribeca Sunset*, the narrative is similarly interrupted without explanation by two pages of textless panels that juxtapose views of the Manhattan skyline, partly obscured by a snowstorm, with what appears to be a representation of an explosion that produces swirling debris which resembles the snowstorm (Rehr 2005: 94–95).

In psychoanalytical terms, this might be seen as the repression of the trauma of 9/11 (and the odd moments in which it is invoked again as the return of the repressed), but it might also be seen as the formal manifestation of an authorial anxiety about the "issues of self-representation" that Spiegelman identifies explicitly as a preoccupation of *In the Shadow of No Towers*, and of the dangers of becoming implicated in the mediation, simulation, and vicarious appropriation of trauma characteristic of much 9/11 discourse. Initial media coverage of the attacks on the towers was relentless, ubiquitous, graphic, and invasive, and at the same time selective, self-censoring, equivocal, and partial. Many of the comics dealing with 9/11 engage with this paradox by foregrounding the equivocal role of television in establishing the parameters of representation, to the extent that the television itself often displaces the events being broadcast on its screen as the central image of 9/11 narratives, and the focus of these stories becomes the act of witnessing the events being witnessed or even, in the case of footage of people filming the events, witnessing witnesses witnessing.[4] This distancing is reinforced by the fact that no 9/11 comic, as far as I am aware, attempts to represent events inside the towers—they are always represented from the outside. Paradoxically, however, this distancing, rather than constituting an acknowledgment that 9/11 is "unrepresentable" or "fantastic," domesticates the narrative of national trauma, relocating it in the private spaces—sitting rooms, bedrooms, and kitchens—of ordinary citizens. Furthermore, by representing themselves confronting the paradoxical nature of issues of representation and self-representation in their work—by representing their struggle to represent the "unrepresentable"—the best comics authors manage to make those things that are irrecoverable—the planes, the towers, and the dead—present in their very absence.

Notes

1 This image recalls the familiar visual tropes of crowds fleeing from alien invasions or rampaging monsters in the golden-age comics that Spiegelman pays tribute to in the second essay in the book ("*The Comic Supplement*") and in the appendix.

2 These include tiny and grotesquely large self-portraits, self-portraits as comics characters; bearded and clean-shaven self-portraits; self-portraits with a lampshade-head, a hand-holding-a-lit-cigarette head and a shoe-and-sock head; and as a cross-dressed cheerleader.

3 They also feature on the front cover of the book, this time in full color, in a rectangular box that is superimposed across an image of the towers as black shadows on a dark gray background and that reappears at the top of page 8. Some of these characters are also incorporated into the main narrative: the Katzenjammer Kids, renamed as the "tower twins" and sporting towers on their heads, appear on pages 2 and 5, and a section of page 10 is devoted to an "interview" with "Hapless Hooligan."

4 *In the Shadow of No Towers* opens with a sequence of panels showing a family (a man, a woman, a child, and a cat) watching television on the day before September 11; *American Widow* opens with an image of a burning tower on multiple television screens (Torres 2008: 184); and many of the contributions to the 9/11 comics anthologies depict characters—usually versions of the author—watching with incredulity as the towers burn. A common trope within these narratives is to show the horrified expressions of the viewers but for the television itself to be shown only from the back, so that precisely what they are looking at must be inferred (this is in fact what Spiegelman does in *In the Shadow of No Towers*).

Works cited

Baudrillard, Jean. "Simulacra and Simulation," 2011 [1981]. Available online: http://fields.ace.ed.ac.uk/disruptivetechnologies/wp-content/uploads/2011/10/Baudrillard Jean-Simulacra-And-Simulation2.pdf.

Baudrillard, Jean. "The Spirit of Terrorism," *Le Monde*, November 2, 2001. Translated by Rachel Bloul. Available online: http://www.egs.edu/faculty/jean-baudrillard/articles/the-spirit-of-terrorism/.

Cooper, Simon, and Paul Atkinson. "Graphic Implosion: Politics, Time, and Value in Post-9/11 Comics." *Literature After 9/11*, edited by Ann Keniston and Jeanne Follansbee Quinn, 60–81. New York: Routledge, 2008.

DeLillo, Don. *White Noise*. London: Picador, 1986 [1985].

DeLillo, Don. "In the Ruins of the Future." *The Guardian*, December 22, 2001. Available online: http://www.theguardian.com/books/2001/dec/22/fiction.dondelillo.

Duffy, Jo, Todd Nauck, and Jamie Mendoza. "Gemini Falling." In *9–11 September 11th 2001: The World's Finest Comic Book Writers and Artists Tell Stories to Remember*, 39. New York: DC Comics, 2002.

Dwyer, Kieron. Untitled art in *9–11 September 11th 2001: The World's Finest Comic Book Writers and Artists Tell Stories to Remember*, 14. New York, DC: Comics, 2002.

Eliopoulos, Chris. "Close to Home." In *9–11 Artists Respond Volume One*, 126–27. Milwaukee: Dark Horse Comics, 2002.

Gauthier, Tim. "9/11, Image Control, and the Graphic Narrative: Spiegelman, Rehr, Torres." *Journal of Postcolonial Writing* 46, no. 3 (2010): 369–80.

Glanzman, Sam. "There were Tears in her Eyes." In *9–11 September 11th 2001: The World's Finest Comic Book Writers and Artists Tell Stories to Remember*, 207–10. New York: DC Comics, 2002.

Glejzer, Richard. "Witnessing 9/11: Art Spiegelman and the Persistence of Trauma." In *Literature After 9/11*, edited by Ann Keniston and Jeanne Follansbee Quinn, 99–119. New York: Routledge, 2008.

Hall, Stefan. "9/11: A Graphic Depiction." *Phi Kappa Phi Forum* 91, no. 3 (2011): 18–19.

Hirsch, Marianne. "Family Pictures: *Maus*, Mourning, and Post-Memory Discourse." *Discourse* 15, no. 2 (1993): 3–29.

Huehls, Mitchum. "Foer, Spiegelman, and 9/11's Timely Traumas." In *Literature After 9/11*, edited by Ann Keniston and Jeanne Follansbee Quinn, 42–59. New York: Routledge, 2008.

Martin, Elaine. "'I' for Iconoclasm: Graphic Novels and the (re)presentation of Terrorism." *Critical Studies on Terrorism* 5, no. 3 (2012): 469–81.

Mason, Jeff, ed. *9–11: Emergency Relief*. Gainesville, FA: Alternative Comics Press, 2002.

Redfield, Marc. "Virtual Trauma: The Idiom of 9/11." *Diacritics* 37, no. 1 (2007): 55–80.

Rehr, Henrik. *Tribeca Sunset: A Story of 9/11*. New York: IBooks, 2005.

Spiegelman, Art. *In the Shadow of No Towers*. New York: Pantheon, 2004.

Torres, Alissa (illustrated by Sungyoon Choi). *American Widow*. New York: Villard, 2008.

Various artists. *9–11 Artists Respond Volume One*. Milwaukee: Dark Horse Comics, 2002.

Various artists. *9–11 September 11th 2001: The World's Finest Comic Book Writers and Artists Tell Stories to Remember*. New York: DC Comics, 2002.

Žižek, Slavoj. *Welcome to the Desert of the Real*. London: Verso, 2002.

4

Rebuilding after 9/11: The figure of the tower and poetics of the future

Aimee Pozorski[*]

> *Planes, people, towers—falling before our very eyes. On one bright morning in September, familiar images of travel banked suddenly, as through a heretofore unimagined opening, into another dimension as we watched. In a matter of minutes, soaring, once-symbolic towers were revealed in all their despairing literalness.*
>
> ~ WAYNE DODD, "The Third Tower" (2002)

In the wake of the 9/11 attacks, the figure of the falling tower seems to connote an impossible future. As early as 2002, poet Wayne Dodd, in William Heyen's *September 11, 2001: American Writers Respond* anthology, registers an uncertainty about poetry's potential to look forward, fixed, as we all were, to the image of the falling towers on September 11, 2001, and for many days after that.

Dodd suggests in the epigraph that the televised images of the falling towers transformed them from symbolic to merely literal, and therefore unpoetic, and yet we cannot talk about them without poetry. For Dodd, as well as for William Heyen, Bob Holman, E. Ann Kaplan, Kelly Levan, and Eric Pankey, the central image of the terrorist attacks of 9/11 is the fall of the Twin Towers, and despite Dodd's insistence that this image is to be taken literally, often in the literature, the image of the falling tower turns through a metonymic slip to the figure of a human falling. As Dodd continues, "And soon, around the wreckage of them, the walls of pathos, papered over with thousands of intimate photographs, looking disturbingly like the remains of a bedroom" (Dodd 2002: 103). Such an unimaginable fall "banks" (to borrow from Dodd) to the unknown: "an unimagined opening . . . another dimension" allegedly transforming the proudly symbolic tower into mere literal rubble, covered with actual photographs in what appears to be a disheveled bedroom: at once a most personal and intimate space and also the most symbolic of the future of a home.

But out of the wreckage of metaphor, came not the lacerating, anti-reparative art we have come to know as contemporary critics, but rather an art gesturing toward the future—a kind of art that emerged from Dodd's unimagined opening and called for something even more radical than reparation: it demanded a future. Something indeed must rise *In the Shadow of No Towers* (2004) as Art Spiegelman so eloquently illustrated. Heyen, the editor of *American Writers Respond*, himself betrayed insecurity about asking poets to write so soon after 9/11. He reflects in his preface: "Writing anything at all can seem like an obscene indulgence to us, and we remember Theodor Adorno's famous declaration that '*Nach Auschwitz, ein Gedicht zu schreiben ist barbarisc*' (to write a poem after Auschwitz is barbaric). His is the ultimate argument for silence, and much of my divided self nods assent to his injunction" (Heyen 2002: xi). But Adorno does not argue for silence, rather for the recognition of the ideological structures that bind poetry to catastrophe.

Adorno echoes Walter Benjamin's claim that "there is no document of civilization that is not at the same time a document of barbarism" (Benjamin 1940: 256–57). In this case, Adorno argues that the culture that produces lyric poetry is, at one and the same time, the culture that produced the Holocaust. And yet, art cannot of course be wholly understood in this way. For example, Cathy Caruth has theorized after 9/11 that trauma creates the possibility of something genuinely new. For her, language that "already lingers" on "the other side of the disaster" is, in effect, a language of futurity—a language that the post-9/11 poets seemed to reflect through their tower poetry from the beginning (Caruth 2014: 92). For Caruth, trauma leaves in its wake not simply full-scale destruction, what she calls catastrophe, but also language or creation that comes paradoxically, from the future—to use her language, from "the other side of disaster" (Caruth 2014: 92).

Both Adorno and Benjamin insist that we cannot just select the aspects of culture that we like, and pretend that they are unrelated to the horrors underneath. Without denying the force of their cultural critique, I argue through a reading of the figure of the tower in post-9/11 poetry how contemporary trauma theory invites us to think of catastrophic events differently. If, on the one hand, catastrophe is part and parcel of culture, then it also can become a way to open ourselves to the future and to the possibility of change.

All of these ideas are anticipated as early as Hannah Arendt's *Origins of Totalitarianism* (1973), where she argues that "there remains also the truth that every end in history necessarily contains a new beginning; this beginning is the promise, the only 'message' which the end can ever produce" (Arendt 1973: 478–79). Such a formulation seems surprising now, written in such close proximity with the annihilating histories of the Holocaust and the atomic bomb; however, even as early as 1951, Arendt's philosophy was pointing the way forward, to the promise of a future that paradoxically emerges from history's backward glance at the past.

Writing in 2015 about 9/11 poetics, I feel as though we have reached a turning point on the problem of 9/11 representation. We seem to have witnessed not only the fall of the towers but also a new mode in writing, one that once tended to see art as anti-reparative after the Holocaust but now sees a reparative gesture toward the future in its place.[1] The views (anti-reparative vs. reparative; commitment to the past vs. commitment to the future) seem inconsistent in many ways. But what I would offer here, to extend the conversation, considers a return to the value of a productive community of artists: artists creating together to find renewal in the ashes, an impulse generated as much by the need to create as it is generated by the national and international headlines of the twenty-first century.

Granted, these are very broad strokes I am making, perhaps narrowed significantly through my reading of the figure of the tower in post-9/11 poetry in an attempt to define a poetics of the future. This renewed emphasis on futurity is exemplified in Caruth, a key theoretician of trauma and literary reference, who conceives of the posttraumatic event differently in *Literature in the Ashes of History* (2014)—the title itself calling attention to rebuilding after the world we know has turned to ash. In the opening of the book, as in *Unclaimed Experience* (1996), Caruth focuses on Freud's 1920 *Beyond the Pleasure Principle*, where he "juxtaposes nightmares of war to the child's game." In this new work, however, Caruth underlines his "enigmatic move in the theory of trauma from the drive for death to the drive to life, from the reformulating of life around the witness to death to the possibility of witnessing and making history in creative acts of life" (Caruth 2014: 5).

In returning to *Beyond the Pleasure Principle* after the events of 9/11, Caruth's focus turns not to the problem of traumatic survival in the wake of war but rather to the possibilities that art brings, the act of "making history" through creativity, such as child's play, language, literature, and art. More striking still is the temporality of this creative making, as Caruth speculates that "stories of trauma cannot be limited to catastrophes they name, and the theory of catastrophic history may ultimately be written in a language that already lingers . . . after the end, in a time that comes to us from the other shore, from the other side of the disaster." In reading after 9/11 especially, I have seen this return in the form of figures of the Towers, but I have also seen an appeal toward creation in the future, a sentiment very different than the critical afterlife of Adorno's proclamation about the barbarism of poetry.

Perhaps, the fall of the Twin Towers and the urgency with which poets sought, symbolically, to rebuild comes out of what the towers stand for: American power, confidence, and indestructability. Although the poets, as countercultural figures in their own way, would reject the towers' alignment with American imperialism, they seem also to value the towers for what they say about American optimism and confidence, symbols of progress as revealed through the poets' own gestures toward a new poetic tradition. The towers, in other words, are almost hyperbolically Freudian symbols of prowess and ego—two qualities that appeal to twenty-first-century writers seeking to write their way to a new poetic mode: one that seeks to rebuild towers out of language but—after 9/11—the work they take up is collaborative, with a new emphasis on community and partnership. By looking closely at the visual towers composed of poetic lines offered by the People's Poetry Gathering, we begin to see the emergence of a poetics of the future. Guided by Michael Rothberg, I suggest that we ought to supplement a reading of 9/11 poetry via trauma theory with "a positive vision of social and political transformation" (Rothberg 2003: 156) in order to theorize the potential for poetic language in the wake of the 9/11 attacks. In response to the post–Second World War literary tradition that illuminates the destructive forces of history and the cyclical nature of the traumatic response, post-9/11 writers and their critics, such as Rothberg and Caruth, have recently begun to see the American literary tradition through a different lens, through the possibilities of the future.

Amir Eshel's *Futurity: Contemporary Literature and the Quest for the Past* (2013) explores works that make available the "open, future, possible" "in an era that has witnessed upheaval on an unprecedented scale and that doubts the very notion that we can affect tomorrow" (Eshel 2013: 4). Importantly, Eshel reads the figurative language of literary fiction as expressions of futurity, much as Dodd has done in the context of twenty-first-century poetry.

Like Eshel, Judith Butler invokes the possibilities of the future in her book *Undoing Gender* (2004), where she importantly links futurity with democracy. For Butler, however, this reclamation of the future despite the traumatic past is unsettling in the sense that it requires confidence in the face of the unforeseen. For Butler, we must "assume responsibility for a future"—a process characterized by "agonism" and "contestation." Butler writes: "To assume responsibility for a future is not to know its direction fully in advance, since the future, especially the future with and for others, requires a certain openness and unknowingness. It also implies that a certain agonism and contestation will and must be in play. They must be in play for politics to become democratic" (Butler 2004: 226). Butler incorporates an ethical position into her discussion of futurity, suggesting that the future we must claim, but nonetheless refrain from mastering, depends on the presence of others in a democracy that relies on the give and take of often-contentious dialogue.

To read canonical poems such as William Butler Yeats's *The Tower* (1928) or Hart Crane's *The Broken Tower* (1932) is to witness a twentieth-century-poem's foretelling of a twenty-first-century trauma. And yet, in some post-9/11 tower poems, it is impossible not to see possibility, to read reference not only to the past but to the future as well. Just as we have built *up* to reach a pinnacle of height, so too do the 9/11 poems build *with* language, constructing towers with nothing more and nothing less than words.

Influenced by the emergent poetics of the future, I am equally indebted to the poets and critics of 9/11 who have been among the first to see new hope in language alone and have introduced in the post-9/11 tower poems references to the future even as they call attention to the limitations of poetry itself. For example, in *Beyond Grief and Grievance*, (2011) Philip Metres reflects that

> when we read enough 9/11 poems, we become awash in falling people, planes described as birds, flaming towers of Babel, ash and angels, angels and ash. The mythic nature of this attack, this disaster—echoing everything from the tower of Babel to the fall of Icarus—is undeniable, and the acts of heroism and the brute loss of so many makes it difficult to find adequate words, even for our most accomplished poets. (Metres 2011: n. pag.)

Here, like Dodd, Metres locates in the events of 9/11 the uncanny moment when myth and figure resonate with a future to come. For many reasons, the fall of the towers, for example, feels like the most incommensurate trauma, one that had already named and imagined the worst possible fate of humanity.

And yet, as Metres continues "*September 11, 2001: American Writers Respond* (Etruscan Books, 2002) gathered poetry and reflections by poets and writers, offering an almost immediate but complex response to the attacks; the poems and letters to the editor William Heyen range from the reflective to the angry, from grief to grievance, from reactionary to radical" (Metres 2011: n. pag.). So here, too, we do see words, and therefore, an attempt to address the otherwise unimaginable: two of the tower poems (and one set of fragments) that I take up here appeared first in the Heyen collection, revealing that, as ever, the poets were at the *avant-garde* in offering, or attempting to offer, an adequate response. Likewise, poets can respond, indeed, they have the responsibility to respond, as according to Marjorie Perloff the poet's first obligation is to "keep the language efficient" by "refusing easy answers and invidious comparisons" (Perloff 2002: n. pag.).

Laurence Goldstein turns to the overdetermined nature of the poetic response to 9/11 in his essay, "The Response of American Poets to 9/11" (2009), where he argues, "Poets of today feel the lamentations and consolations of their predecessors weighing upon them and inspiring them, just as future poets, and readers, will look back to the elegists of this century's first decade for guidance amid the danger and rage to come" (Goldstein 2009: n. pag.). While Goldstein looks forward, he is not entirely hopeful, citing the "danger and rage to come" as guiding the next generation of poets. But he also refers back to the consolations of predecessors, many of whom also employed the figure of the tower to depict the emotional response of the day.

In seeking an exemplary case, Goldstein sees in William Heyen's *September 11, 2001* a model, if not for perfect poetry, then at least for the desire to try. Goldstein writes,

> A second anthology of writings in 2002 tested the pulse of the nation's authors: *September 11, 2001: American Writers Respond*, edited by William Heyen. Incorporating essays, poems, and memoirs, this assemblage is the most important literary document of the event so far. . . . Solicited authors were given a very brief lead time for composition, causing one invitee to tell me, "No matter what we say, we'll sound like idiots ten years from now." But writing under the pressure of the immediate trauma has its obvious value as well. (Goldstein 2009: n. pag.)

Acknowledging here the importance of writing, Goldstein offers a heartfelt, if self-deprecating, gesture of gratitude to Heyen for addressing other poets and challenging them to find the words. Goldstein reveals that he also has a poem in the collection, as it becomes increasingly clear here that it was important for him to be a part of that conversation very early on. Like Heyen, Peter Armenti also became an important leader or resource for collecting American poetic responses, as he compiled and maintained the Library of Congress Poetry of the September 11 archive, an online resource that features the groundbreaking People's Poetry Gathering Poem Towers, a collaborative, democratic long poem pastiche that, I would argue, is the most important example of a poetics of futurity to date.

Poets after 9/11 created their tower poems out of a challenge or pleas from colleagues: in the case of *American Writers Respond*, the call to pick up the pen came from William Heyen; for the Poetry Tower Project, it came from Bob Holman. In both cases, the poets revealed a kind of self-consciousness, writing so close to the event itself, but they all—especially in their poetry—reclaim the future in their references to the lost towers that can only be rebuilt through the poets' work.

In his editor's preface, William Heyen details what he wrote to the poets:

> I'm asking for intensive contributions of no longer than 4–5 pages. I'd prefer in this case that most responses be direct, in essay form, but would welcome a breakthrough poem, or a flash fiction that strikes through to psychic ground zero, or a sui generis piece that seems to catch and hold our quaking reality as does no other traditional mode of discourse. (Heyen 2002: xi)

He explains to his fellow poets that the terrorist attack of the 9/11 hijackers "demands from us a different retaliation, an intricate move toward world justice for each star or stripe on every Old Glory now or to come" (Heyen 2002: xii). The move forward, "toward world justice," was taken seriously by nearly every writer collected, as in many cases there is a social justice angle that grounds their poetry in a sense of urgency as well as a commitment to writing in a new mode—one that looks toward the future of America, as symbolized by the flag and, by extension, to a new tradition in American poetry.

Kelly Levan's poem resonates, through the movement of pebbles, with Samuel Beckett's *Molloy* (1951), a novel that opens with the apparently useless image of Molloy rotating rocks from pocket to pocket. Like the post–Second World War Beckett figure Molloy, one is not quite sure of the use of the pebbles otherwise. Yet, Levan writes in "To the Towers," of passing pebbles, one person to the next, rebuilding, stone by stone, heart by heart (Levan 2002: 342–43). The poem begins "If I knew/how to/hold each/pebble" (Levan 2002: 342). Levan draws on the pebble image as a symbol of empowerment and communal connection. Writing five quatrains composed of short, almost broken lines, the poem is an address to the fallen victims—both structural and human—ending with "heart." The tower in the poem, through address or *prosopopoeia*, is personified as a living object or memory. With an emphasis on the beating heart, the heart of the Towers, the hearts of the victims, and the heart of the City, Levan creates in her lyric a command to witness the life force of the towers themselves.

However, Levan turns the turning into a recuperative act, an act recuperated precisely through poetry, through the beating heart. In her follow-up remarks, she says,

> I would like to see the towers in pockets of people riding the subways and standing by bus stops. We carry them right now, every day, but I can't see the edges, poking out at acute angles. If we each kept a piece, we could reconstruct the buildings, spreading them out from shirt to shirt along the city, along the country. Nobody could break our mortar. (Levan 2002: 243)

Here is the linguistic equivalent of rebuilding, of passing between us piece by piece in an act of solidarity—our "mortar" being the impulse to exchange, to keep building up out of the ashes of history. Levan explains "I don't understand why Molloy needs to revolve his pebbles this way, but I wonder if we could do it, we Americans. I could take my piece of the towers and give it to you.... And this way, instead of a piece, we carry the towers, both of them, all of us. Shifting, all the time" (Levan 2002: 243). Unlike the unproductive shifting of Molloy's pebbles, we Americans might carry them, images of them, to revivify the towers—"both of them, all of us," Levan says, a collective of poets and witnesses to carry the burden of the towers in their rebuilding.

Dodd writes of the heart in "The Third Tower" as well, beginning with an epigraph: "*Hour after hour we watched them, day after day we watched them*," referring to the traumatic repetition of the flashing, burning image of the towers on our consciousness after 9/11 (Dodd 2002: 103). Here, the reader is left to wonder: what constitutes the third tower—the poem itself, the repetition of the image, always there in our heads and our hearts? The perpetual experience of always seeing them, always falling? The "them" also appears here on the very first line as a pronoun without an antecedent. What is "them"? Furthermore, even if you think the clue could be taken from the title, the plural of the pronoun "them" does not match the singular third tower of the title.

Later, we learn it is the twin towers falling, through a series of couplets as if to mirror the twin towers. The poem begins, "Falling forward, falling over,/falling out of" to denote the man and women falling, to call attention to how to difficult it is to imagine, and in this one turn, the towers become humans falling out of the towers (Dodd 2002: 103). The poem continues: "as the heart stops./Falling straight down" (Dodd 2002: 103). The word "stops" has the plosive "p" sound, the end stop, as the thing that stops is the heart not the fall. Here, as with the Levan poem, we see a metonymic shift or slip from the towers to the falling people or bodies, bodies falling: "endlessly/in darkness." "Endlessly" conveys the sense of traumatic repetition. The word here is also associated with darkness as expected, but then the next line gives no hope at all: "as well as light. Falling forever/out of the future" (Dodd 2002: 103). So here, for the poem, even in the light the towers are falling; collapsing; whereas ordinarily the image of light brings hope and clarity, in this poem the towers fall there too. Falling happens "out of the future," indicating a skewed sense of time; there will never not be a time when the towers are falling. The poem ends with "Falling into memory,/into absence . . ." calling to mind an absent presence, another paradox, a trace (Dodd 2002: 103). The last two lines, like the lines previous, are two-line couplets, creating the visual representation of the twin towers no longer there in Manhattan but only in memory.

In his reflection piece, Dodd writes, "The magnitude of these events was so great that we knew instinctively a fundamental change had occurred" (Dodd 2002: 104). The question, for Dodd, for all the poets in the Heyen collection, became what to do as a poet and a citizen in the wake or space of such a fundamental change, a question that would be ultimately answered in the People's Poetry Gathering, inspiring collective action through art.

Eric Pankey's reaction to the fall of the towers takes a much more ambivalent form. Most notably, he rejects the impulse to write a poem and offers instead only fragments that look back to the towers in ruins, fragments connected explicitly to the towers in ruins that T. S. Eliot depicts in *The Waste Land* (1922). To echo Eliot, Pankey titles his reflections, "Falling Towers: (Fragments September 11–October 1, 2001)" and begins:

These fragments I have shored against my ruins, T. S. Eliot writes in the final stanza of his poem, "*The Waste Land*," a heteroglossal, poly-vocalic, and wildly fragmented poem written in the wake of the first great war of the last century, a war precipitated, it could be argued, by a terrorist act against an empire. One wonders what lines will commemorate our contemporary loss, and one wonders if, as we read Eliot's wonder and dread at the devastation of great cities, of battered empires, we might not add under our breath the names of American cities: Falling towers/ Jerusalem, Athens, Alexandria/Vienna, London/Unreal. (Pankey 2002: 296)

The passage links the terrorism of 9/11 with the "terrorist" act of assassinating the Archduke Franz Ferdinand; even in commemorating the loss with his own intertextual fragments, Pankey asks who will commemorate it, ultimately wanting to add New York City to Eliot's list of falling towers—as if Eliot too predicted more falling towers to come. Eliot's poem reads thus:

> What is that sound high in the air
> Murmur of maternal lamentation
> Who are those hooded hordes swarming
> Over endless plains, stumbling in cracked earth
> Ringed by the flat horizon only
> What is the city over the mountains
> Cracks and reforms and bursts into the violet air
> Falling towers
> Jerusalem Athens Alexandria
> Vienna London
> Unreal. (Eliot 2001: 17–18)

As the Norton edition of *The Waste Land* notes, the stanza above refers to Eliot's reading in German of Herman Hesse's *In Sight of Chaos* (1922), where Hesse depicts "The Downfall of Europe" (North 2001: 61). Hesse's insight, as reflected through Eliot, seems true to this day, with a lingering dread, all these years on, about the falling towers in history. Eliot's uncanny phrases such as: "sound high in the air"; "murmur of maternal lamentation"; "hooded hordes swarming"; "city ... bursts into the violet air" evoke for the twenty-first-century reader the falling towers (in New York) and then ultimately the response: unreal.

The three tower poems in the post-9/11 collection I address here point to an insistence to go on, not only to find hope in poetry, but also to confront the vexed history of twentieth-century traumas behind it via Eliot (First World War) and Beckett (Second World War), among so many others. One of the ways out of this apparent stasis appears to be a commitment to rebuilding the towers out of the rubble, using not building materials—the rocks, the steel, for example—but rebuilding out of light and language, abstractions, and art: acts of creativity that point the way to the future.

For example, "Tribute in Light," which the Municipal Art Society of New York calls "one of the most powerful and healing works of public art ever produced," blue twin towers of light, visible within a 60-mile radius, shine from dusk on September 11 to the next day. According to the Municipal Art Society of New York,

> Comprising eighty-eight 7,000-watt xenon light bulbs positioned into two 48-foot squares that echo the shape and orientation of the Twin Towers, Tribute in Light is assembled each year on a roof near the World Trade Center site. The illuminated memorial reaches 4 miles into the sky and is the strongest shaft of light ever projected from earth into the night sky. (2015)

In the same vein, Bob Holman suggested rebuilding the towers, erecting them on the Internet with language, with poetic lines. In his remarks prefacing this project—remarks appropriately titled, "Tower of Words: The Place of Poetry in Crisis"—Holman writes,

> As a human, I watched the Towers implode from my office window on Duane Street, six blocks from ground zero. I thought, What to do? My response was to write a poem. And I wasn't alone. Towards the hole in the energy center, towards the sacred burial site of steel, concrete, and ash, words began to emerge, looking for meaning, mourning, attempting to understand. (Holman n. d.)

The answer, for Holman, could be a poem—a futuristic poem, a poem written in the spirit of the future—that he called upon other poets to write in a collective, communal exercise, a public exercise that would live on the web. He continues, "The impulse to build a Twin Towers of Words, to create a poem replicating/remembering what had been blasted by humanity's failings, a response of art, this came later. The word went out that a Tower was being built at the People's Poetry Gathering website (www.peoplespoetry.org)" (2002). Holman did the work of collecting, editing, and publishing, weaving the lines together in order to create a single poem—making the first poem 110 lines, one for each floor of the Towers.

The result is visually striking: two black tower-shaped rectangular towers that resemble Spiegelman's *New Yorker* towers, but covered in white lines of poetry; the work exists only online, as a digital collective exemplary of how twenty-first-century art evolved in the crisis of this twenty-first-century atrocity.[2] Out of the ruins grows not nature to show the life cycle, but rather digital poetry for a new age that simultaneously commemorates a time before.

The collectively written "Tower One" reflects, "We have become the heat-slick melt of infrastructure" (2002: 30). Somewhat fittingly, the author of the first line is given as unknown, calling to attention the fact that the rebuilding of the towers was a collective enterprise, that the ordeal they—we all—are building from is shared by the poets themselves. The "we" here also relies on the metonymic slip from tower to the people. The personification continues as the bedrock groans later in the poem:

Shhhhhh you can hear the twisted bedrock groaning.
I nominate the silence.
Then finding the lost words of poets
I tremble as I write.
My peace lies beside your piece. (Holman et al. 2002: 37–41)[3]

The "Shhhhhh you can hear" in line 37 functions as an important command to listen. At first, there is silence, but then the stanza returns to a focus on the power of poetry—poetry once lost but then found again in the bedrock. The persona's trembling comes from the power of the moment, but also perhaps an ambivalence or nervousness about trying to capture the lost towers. Within the collective voice of the five poets, we hear the voices running into one another, shifting as the foundation of the towers shift. We also see the self-consciousness about the act of writing a tower in the form of trembling, and ultimately the promise of creation that poetry brings through the use of homophones, piece, and peace, suggesting that writing leads to tranquility, that a piece of poetry, a piece of rubble can coexist with peace.

The poem continues with its emphasis on finding peace in the fragmented pieces, as in the line, authored by Paula Panzarella that reads as follows:

> Maybe if I fill up the hole in my stomach I can fill up the hole in the building and plug up the emptiness fill up the hole plug up my heart in my stomach the building fix and patch and fill in the emptiness fix the world my head my heart the building and stuff in and fill and patch my heart and fix the world and and and stuff and patch and fix and fill and fix . . . . (2002: 60)

In this wraparound line, the tower and the persona become one. The line runs on and on like the experience of running away from the fire, from the tower, from the responsibility to write it all. Furthermore, the repetition of the word "and," "and," "and," used to connect fragments recalls Eliot's attempt to shore himself against the ruins, to use art to fill up the empty hole. This single line also looks back to Beckett, as does Levan, in its allusion to the monologues found in such existential plays as *Waiting for Godot* (1953); however, an important difference in this line remains a sense of an emergent value for futurity, rather than just manic exhaustion, as seen in the will to "fix and fill and fix."

The poem continues to conflate the distant past with the near past, with both pasts connected via destruction and a traumatic legacy:

> Where the Twin Towers turn into the Coliseum
> Extras fall screaming murder murder murder
> Who died, who lived—thousands of lifelines,
> Of stirs & swipes, flagging down right and wrong
> Desperate for a piece of silence, the silence of peace. (Holman et al. 2002: 64–68)[4]

Here too, we see the homonym pairing piece and peace, which echoes lines 37–41. These lines refer back to the Roman history of the Coliseum, another moment when it is hard not to see literary representation as somehow predicting the future in its reference to the embodiment of the once great Roman Empire via the Coliseum, a site of public executions that now lies in ruins because of earthquakes and stone robbers. The references to "murder, murder, murder," drive home the extent to which murder underwrites history, but the word "fall" seems to take on historic specificity, referring back to the fall of the towers, the fall of people from the windows. The reference in line 67 to "stirs & swipes" seems at first glance to be typos for stars and stripes, but also speaks to the bastardization of the meaning of the flag, "flagging down right and wrong." Furthermore, what is called upon in the scene of murder is silence, peace—another cry for comfort following the fall.

The silence of peace is further threatened when the image of the jumpers returns and the poets write:

Its sense of security jumped out the window
Through golden grates and iron barricades
Sing! Don't argue
Chanting throats boil rage. (Holman et al. 2002: 99–102)[5]

Despite the repeated reference to the falling men and women, the stanza's focus remains the music of poetry with Heather Bourbeau's line: "Sing! Don't argue." On the one hand, the barricades and the rage seem to hold people back, but then there is the command to sing, to write poetry. The call to "sing," the line says, can overcome "chanting throats" that "boil rage."

"Tower One" ends with this self-referential celebration of poetry:

Tips my tongue that is loose
with words
words that cannot stop. (Holman et al. 2002: 110)

Susan Katz contributed line 110, a line that points to the qualities of language as reparative, unending, and restorative. In this line, I see the possibility for words to rebuild. In the form is the sense of this line, as it is composed of two and a half poetic feet alternating stresses: unstressed, stressed, unstressed, stressed, unstressed: "the words that cannot stop" echo interminably over and above the boiling rage of the previous lines.

However, the second Tower poem was created slightly differently; Bob Holman explains,

> The second tower was invitational—I sent out 130 invites, and most poets responded positively. . . . Poets were invited to place their lines wherever they wished, so the poem kept changing, evolving into itself. About halfway through—my hard drive crashed and I lost all the names—very embarrassing to have to ask which brilliant lines was whose. Robert Kelly wrote back, "Who cares? Aren't we all the poet? It sure is all the same crisis anyhow." (Holman n. d.)

Kelly's comment in this context calls attention to the radical nature of the project: a changing, evolving poem for the future, one that is truly collective in the sense that all the names were forgotten and retrieved; most interesting still is the idea "Aren't we all the poet? It sure is all the same crisis." The project emphasizes the process of poets working together, doing the actual work of rebuilding—one line, one floor at a time.

Bob Holman has the first line, shared with Eileen Myles: "In times of crisis, poets lose words. Find some" (Holman et al. 2002: 1). In this line, too, we see a command to find words. Having lost them is not enough: the real work begins in the search for a new language on the other side of disaster. Finding the language leads to a linguistic rebuilding of the towers only to see, momentarily, their perpetual loss:

> two horizontal towers were born, those fleeing fire and those
>   coming close. help help helping out!
> She cries, her hair a morning ruin: See our burnt balconies of air.
> We're breathing it in, all of them. (Holman et al. 2002: 22–24)[6]

The three collective lines say in both form and content that we are all in this together, breathing in history, taking in the same images, the same dust, the same ashes of those who fell and burned to their deaths. The call out for help is what lingers, as the collective voices of the poets make an appeal for help. Here, the phrase "helping out" takes the form of a present participle indicating the necessity of work in all future moments to come.

Later still, help returns in the form of words:

> The words irreversible, unmistakable, come to me. Invincible leaves.
> Words on page, mete out this woe; words on page undo sorrow.
> Bury your breath, then sing this woe a wing a minute these days
> Of black and white marks that express shades of grey in charred hearts.
> Forgetting names is when it hit me,
> A line that ends, ends at the sea. (Holman et al. 2002: 95–100)[7]

This stanza, like the previous, reflects a self-consciousness about words, but here, near the end of the poem, the self-consciousness is linked with positivity: the words come; they are "unmistakable." The reference to "leaves" refers simultaneously to the leaves of a fall September day; the leaves of pages; the leave-taking in departures. Poetry does this—only words on a page. The call to "sing," to write, to "undo sorrow" prescribes a never-ending remembering, a refusal to forget, as to end "at the sea" is always to wash back up.

The final couplet of the second tower poem reveals the return of the future:

> We are on the verge of imagining something else, aren't we? Can you feel the sentence forming?
> "Love should be put into action," screamed the dirty hermit of another poem. (Holman et al. 2002: 109–110)

These lines were written by Marie Howe and Adrienne Rich, respectively, with Rich echoing another poet, Elizabeth Bishop and her "*Chemin De Fer*" (1946), which is a French title meaning "railroad" or "the railway." In this way, the disembodied voice in the Bishop poem, matched only by the echo of the shotgun, is here given a voice in the collective poetic universe of the People's Poetry Gathering, as the action undertaken is rebuilding, not with brick and mortar but with words—and not on paper with pen but with digits in cyberspace, the public, and democratic space of the World Wide Web. The effect of this shift from disembodied voice to collective voices—from paper to digital format—renews a sense of strength in community, and privileges, in its very production, democracy over totalitarianism.

How to fill in the gap that the towers left in a democratic act of collaboration? The answer lies in words and images, art and poetry, which carry within them the potential for hope and change. It is only in the creative act, says Caruth—the writing to come out of the history of ashes—that transports us into the future. E. Ann Kaplan too arrives at some of these conclusions about art and futurity in her influential book, *Trauma Culture* (2005), where she writes,

> The gap where the Twin Towers had stood in the weeks that followed became a space full of horror but also of heroism. Their visual absence was traumatic: That is, it was impossible to comprehend that they were gone—that I no longer found the Towers in their place.... On the other hand, the "gap" was filled with other images.... *The New Yorker* created an unforgettable front page that was apparently totally black, but within whose dim darkness one could glimpse shadows or the ghosts of the Towers haunting the city. One or two art stores in Greenwich Village filled their windows with different sizes of beautiful framed color photographs of the Towers in the city landscape. (Kaplan 2005: 12–13)

As a New Yorker herself, Kaplan noticed specifically that art began to fill in the "gap," the art stores in New York City, the Spiegelman *New Yorker* cover, and—I would add—the Tower poetry after 9/11.

Where I might find a poetics of futurity, Kaplan sees traumatic repetition. She goes on to argue that

> the images were part of the traumatic symptom already evident in the media's constant repetition of the Towers being struck. Given trauma's peculiar visuality as a psychic disorder, this event seemed to feed trauma by being so highly visual in its happening. The images haunted one waking and dreaming. American culture was visually haunted by the repeated still unbelievable shots of a huge plane full of people plunging into a seemingly impenetrable tower, and bursting into fabulous orange flames. (Kaplan 2005: 13)

Using such language as "psychic disorder," "feed trauma," "images haunted," and "American culture was visually haunted," Kaplan seems to theorize the ways Tower imagery, in referring back to the past that will never be made right, haunts the visual, psychic, and artistic landscape of New York and America after 9/11.

But as this poetry reveals, we might also look into the burnished image of the burning tower that, in fact, feeds the future. There is the "peculiar visuality" associated with the burning but also the sound of the dirty hermit speaking through Elizabeth Bishop to Adrienne Rich through the editor Bob Holman, speaking in and through poetry to all of us about putting love into action, rebuilding after 9/11, rebuilding the future with poetic language and other kinds of creative acts. The twenty-first century in this way, instead of willing the future into existence as a projection of ourselves, has offered a poetics of the future to remake us in its more democratic image. We must, like the angel of history, have an eye on the past and simultaneously look ahead to the future; we must recognize that language can have material, cultural, and political effects, but only if we are willing to listen.

Notes

* I would like to thank Corina Lopes, Candace Barrington, Eric Leonidas, and Jason B. Jones for being such generous interlocutors during the writing of this essay. This essay would not be possible without them.

1 See for example, Jahan Ramazani's *Poetry of Mourning: The Modern Elegy from Hardy to Heaney*, which argues that the modern elegy "reopens the wounds of loss" (Ramazani 1994: 3).

2 The poems are archived here: https://web.archive.org/web/20120306144919/http://www.peoplespoetry.org/pg_spotlighttwr.html.

3 The authors of each line, respectively, are Gregory W. Farrell, Joe Dobkin, Susan Kats, Joe Dobkin/Bartolome de las Cases, and Ellen Feighny.

4 The authors of each line, respectively, are binda 23, Steve Zeitlin, and Susan Katz.

5 The authors of each line, respectively, are Heather Bourbeau, Joe Dobkin, Heather Bourbeau, and Gary Mex Gazner.

6 The authors of each line, respectively, are Cecilia Vicuña, Meena Alexander, and Martha Rhodes.

7 The authors of each line, respectively, are Mary Anne Caws, Maggie Balistreri, Bill Berkson, Gary Lenhart, Michael Gizzi, and Vincent Katz.

Works cited

Arendt, Hannah. *The Origins of Totalitarianism*. New York: Harcourt, Brace, Jovanovich, [1951] 1973.

Armenti, Peter. "Poetry of September 11" (2014). Available online: http://www.loc.gov/rr/program/bib/911poetry/.

Beckett, Samuel. *Molloy*. New York: Grove Press [1951] 1965.

Beckett, Samuel. *Waiting for Godot: A Tragicomedy in Two Acts*. New York: Grove Press, 1955.

Benjamin, Walter. "Theses on the Philosophy of History." In *Illuminations: Essays and Reflections*, edited by Hannah Arendt and translated by Harry Zohn, 256–57. New York: Schocken, [1940] 1969.

Butler, Judith. *Undoing Gender*. New York: Routledge, 2004.

Caruth, Cathy. *Literature in the Ashes of History*. Baltimore: Johns Hopkins University Press, 2014.

Caruth, Cathy. *Unclaimed Experience: Trauma, Narrative, and History*. Baltimore: Johns Hopkins University Press, 1996.

Crane, Hart. "The Broken Tower." In *The Complete Poems of Hart Crane*, edited by Marc Simon, 275–78. New York: Liveright ([1932] 2000).

Dodd, William. "The Third Tower." In *September 11, 2001: American Writers Respond*, edited by William Heyen, 103–04. Silver Spring: Etruscan Press, 2002.

Eliot, T. S. *The Waste Land*. *The Waste Land: A Norton Critical Edition*. Edited by Michael North, 3–26. New York: W. W. Norton & Company, [1922] 2004.

Eshel, Amir. *Futurity: Contemporary Literature and the Quest for the Past*. Chicago: University of Chicago Press, 2013.

Freud, Sigmund. *Beyond the Pleasure Principle*. New York: Norton [1920] 1990.

Goldstein, Lawrence. "The Response of American Poets to 9/11: A Provisional Report." *Michigan Quarterly Review* 38, no. 1 (2009). Available online: http://quod.lib.umich.edu/cgi/t/text/text-idx?cc=mqr;c=mqr;c=mqrarchive;idno=act2080.0048.108;g=mqrg;rgn=main;view=text;xc=1.

Heyen, William, ed. *September 11, 2001: American Writers Respond*. Wilkes-Barre, PA: Etruscan Press, 2002.

Holman, Bob. "Tower of Words: The Place of Poetry in Crisis." Available online: http://raceforthesky.org/pdf/Tower%20One.pdf.

Kaplan, E. Ann. *Trauma Culture*. New Brunswick: Rutgers University Press, 2005.

Levan, Kelly. "To the Towers." In *September 11, 2001: American Writers Respond*, edited by William Heyen, 242–43. Silver Spring: Etruscan Press, 2002.

Metres, Philip. "Beyond Grief and Grievance: The Poetry of 9/11 and Its Aftermath." (2011). Available online: http://www.poetryfoundation. org/article/242580.
Municipal Art Society of New York. "Tribute in Light." (2015). Available online: http://www.mas.org/programs/tributeinlight/.
Pankey, Eric. "Falling Towers." In *September 11, 2001: American Writers Respond*, edited by William Heyen, 296–98. Wilkes-Barre, PA: Etruscan Press, 2002.
Perloff, Marjorie. "Writing Poetry after 9/11." *American Letters & Commentary* (2002): 18–23. Available online: http://marjorieperloff. com/stein-duchamp-picasso/poetry-911/.
Ramazani, Jahan. *Poetry of Mourning: The Modern Elegy from Hardy to Heaney*. Chicago: University of Chicago Press, 1994.
Rothberg, Michael. "'There is No Poetry in This': Writing, Trauma and Home." In *Trauma at Home: After 9/11*, edited by Justine Greenberg, 147–57. Lincoln: University of Nebraska Press, 2003.
Spiegelman, Art. *In the Shadow of No Towers*. New York: Pantheon, 2004.
Yeats, W. B. "The Tower." *The Tower*. New York: Scribner, [1928] 2004.

5

Beyond belief: John Updike's *Terrorist*

Mark Eaton

In his poem *Icarus*, published just before 9/11, John Updike stages the following nervous encounter with a suspected terrorist on an airplane:

> O.K., you are sitting in an airplane and
> the person in the seat next to you is a sweaty, swarthy gentleman
>   of Middle Eastern origin
> whose carry-on luggage consists of a bulky black briefcase he
>   stashes,
> in compliance with airline regulations,
> underneath the seat ahead.
> He keeps looking at his watch and closing his eyes in prayer,
> resting his profusely dank forehead against the seatback ahead
>   of him,
> just above the black briefcase,
> which if you listen through the droning of the engines seems to
>   be ticking, ticking
> softly, softer than your heartbeat in your ears. (Updike 2001:
>   14–15)

The speaker invites readers to identify with his anxiety, making us complicit in a blatant act of racial profiling. If anything, the comedy here depends on the speaker's misplaced paranoia, for the guy sitting next to him turns out to be perfectly normal, of course, not a terrorist at all but a harmless, albeit not very sociable, lobbyist:

> I say to my companion, "Smooth flight so far."
> "So far."
> "That's quite a briefcase you've got there."
> He shrugs and says, "It contains my life's work."
> "And what is it, exactly, that you do?"
> "You could say I am a lobbyist."
> He does not want to talk.
> He wants to keep praying.
> His hands, with their silky beige backs and their nails cut close like a technician's,
> tremble and jump in handling the plastic glass of Sprite when it comes with its exploding bubbles. (Updike 2001: 14–15)

Somehow this joke at the speaker's expense, at his paranoia and prejudice, may not seem quite so funny after 9/11, when such suspicions became all too common, if not more justified. The poem takes on a somewhat ominous tone at the end, especially in light of what was to come: "Perhaps not this time, then./But the possibility of impossibility will keep drawing us back/to this scrape against the numbed sky" (Updike 2001: 15).

The poem was in one sense prescient, because it anticipated the hypervigilance of many passengers after 9/11, not to mention heightened security at airports. In a short essay that appeared in the first issue of *The New Yorker* published after 9/11, Updike invokes the increased sense of vulnerability to terrorist attacks following 9/11: "The sound of an airplane overhead still bears an unfamiliar menace, the thought of boarding an airplane with our old blasé blitheness keeps receding into the past" (Updike 2007: 118). What could be done to prevent such attacks in the future? His answer is hardly reassuring: "Determined men who have inwardly transposed their own lives to a martyr's afterlife can still inflict an amount of destruction that defies belief. War is conducted with a fury that requires abstraction—that turns a planeful of peaceful passengers, children included, into a missile the faceless enemy deserves" (Updike 2007: 118). Americans are accustomed to believe that "risk is the price of freedom," concludes Updike, but restrictions on freedom may well be the price we have to pay to combat terrorism (Updike 2007: 118).

In her book *The New Religious Intolerance: Overcoming the Politics of Fear in an Anxious Age* (2012), Martha C. Nussbaum observes similarly, "The 9/11 terrorist attacks ... have led to a certain amount of profiling when people are selected for full-body searches in airport screenings, as well as to 'no-fly' lists that bar people who are suspected terrorists" (Nussbaum 2012: 41). Nussbaum believes that such security measures are defensible, given the real terrorist threat: "They respond to a genuine problem, and even if the number of terrorist incidents is small, their catastrophic nature makes precaution reasonable when the only downside is longer wait lines and inconvenience" (Nussbaum 2012: 41). Of course, as the title of her book suggests, Nussbaum deems it "problematic" if not "deeply offensive" to "single out people on the basis of their religion and ethnicity," and so "the best course is very likely to search everyone, as is now done with body scanners" (Nussbaum 2012: 41). Updike wonders whether any such measures can stop those determined to commit acts of terror. "American freedom of motion, one of our prides, has taken a hit," writes Updike in his essay from the so-called black issue of *The New Yorker*, "Can we afford the openness that lets future kamikaze pilots, say, enroll in Florida flight schools?" (Updike 2007: 118).

As if taking up this question in earnest, Updike's short story "Varieties of Religious Experience," first published in *The Atlantic* in 2002, ventures inside a terrorist cell in Florida, where two would-be terrorists, Mohamed and Nawaf, are enrolled in a Florida flight school, while at night they frequent strip clubs, as if to assimilate into American culture more fully. "Their instructions were to blend in," the narrator tells us, so as to move about undetected, biding their time while "rehearsing once again the details of their enterprise, its many finely interlocked and synchronized parts, down to the last-minute cell-phone calls that gave the final go-ahead" to carry out their suicide mission (Updike 2002: 96). On several occasions, their plot is nearly discovered by nosy Floridians: "More than once small mishaps and moments of friction—a traffic ticket, an INS summons, an irritated slip of the tongue with an inquisitive neighbor seeking, in that doglike American way, to be friendly—had threatened to expose the whole elaborate structure; but the All-Merciful had extended His protecting hand" (Updike 2002: 98). Updike is fascinated with the irony of these two "masterminds of evil" taking full advantage of their anonymity to lay the groundwork "for the great deed that had been laid out like a precision drawing in an engineering class," which involves flying commercial airplanes into buildings:

> The greatness of the deed held him pressed upward like a species of nausea, straining his throat with a desire to cry out, to proclaim, as did the prophet whose name he bore, the magnificence, beyond all virtues and qualities imaginable on earth, of God and His justice. *For the unbelievers We have prepared fetters of chains, and a blazing Fire. Flames of fire shall be lashed at you, and melted brass.* (Updike 2002: 98, 103)

To capture the furious ideology behind such an undertaking, the author resorts to abstractions.

Updike would again take up the task of trying to understand the ideological roots and religious underpinnings of terrorism in his novel *Terrorist* (2006), which turned out to be the penultimate novel he wrote before his death in 2009. Despite the novel's implausible ending, *Terrorist* gives an all too plausible account of the radicalization of a young Muslim convert named Ahmad Ashmawy Mulloy, a high school student in New Jersey who comes under the influence of a radical imam at a local mosque, Shaikh Rashid. In light of recent examples of young men and women leaving the United States and attempting to join terrorist organizations abroad, Ahmad's nascent fanaticism is arguably less improbable than it may appear at first glance.[1] Updike portrays Ahmad's radicalization as a problem for the United States' much vaunted pluralism. By focusing on the appeal of religious fundamentalism for a young convert to radical Islam, this novel can help us understand the sort of cognitive dissonance that allows many believers to embrace strong religious identities in a so-called secular age. The events of 9/11 at once exacerbated fears about religious extremism and rendered one of the axioms of secularism—the notion that religion should have been more or less eradicated by now—totally untenable.[2] In fact, fundamentalism is less an historical anachronism than a complex, dialectical response to pluralism. But there can be no doubt that it represents one of the most pressing challenges of our time. How can we come to terms with and negotiate our differences in a world where pluralism and tolerance seem to be the necessary preconditions for peaceful coexistence? How do we, in effect, get beyond belief in order to live peacefully in a world of many faiths?

In *Terrorist*, Updike does not so much answer these questions as dramatize a scenario in which religious pluralism fails in the face of a terrorist threat. The author stages a conflict between a young Muslim convert and his agnostic teachers and peers that seems innocuous enough at first but quickly becomes alarming. In a passage of free indirect discourse on the first page of the novel, for instance, the narrator captures Ahmad's growing disdain for the obvious disaffection from religion all around him: "The teachers, weak Christians and nonobservant Jews, make a show of teaching virtue and righteous self-restraint, but their shifty eyes and hollow voices betray their lack of belief.... They lack true faith; they are not on the Straight Path; they are unclean" (Updike 2006: 3).

Eighteen-year-old Ahmad Ashmawy Mulloy is fully committed to the Straight Path. At a storefront mosque, he has been studying the Koran under the tutelage of Shaikh Rashid, who becomes a kind of "surrogate father" to him (Updike 2006: 13). Ahmad is an apt student:

> The student's faith exceeds the master's; it frightens Shaikh Rashid to be riding the winged white steed of Islam, its irresistible onrushing. He seeks to soften the Prophet's words, to make them blend with human reason, but they were not meant to blend: they invade our human softness like a sword. (Updike 2006: 7)

The narrator frames Ahmad's conversion here in terms of a familiar binary opposition between faith and reason. This novel complicates that binary, however, by showing how Ahmad manages to compartmentalize his faith, becoming a devoted follower of a supposedly irrational religion while remaining committed to reason in many other aspects of his life.

Such cognitive dissonance is evident in Ahmad's interactions with Jack Levy, his high school guidance counselor, who is characterized as a "disbelieving old Jew" deeply committed to "the religion-versus-faith divide" (Updike 2006: 27, 39). Like some kind of Philip Roth character, Jack Levy is married to a Lutheran, but if anything, his mixed marriage only reinforces his avowed agnosticism: "Religion meant nothing to him, and as they merged into a married entity it meant less and less to her" (Updike 2006: 30). When Jack Levy asks why he has switched from precollege courses to a vocational track, Ahmad explains that his religious leader Rashid had urged him to make the change because "the college track exposed me to corrupting influences" (Updike 2006: 38). The guidance counselor weakly suggests that "in a diverse and tolerant society like this one," it is important to "confront a variety of viewpoints" (Updike 2006: 39). Ahmad objects, "Such a relativistic approach trivializes religion, implying that it doesn't much matter. You believe this, I believe that, we all get along—that's the American way. . . . But the American way is the way of infidels" (Updike 2006: 39). Ahmad regards every alternative to Islam as "so many grotesquely mistaken and corrupt religions to lure millions down to hell forever" (Updike 2006: 17). He clings to an exclusivist view of religion that seems to preclude religious pluralism.

The contrast between Jack Levy and Ahmad Mulloy highlights different ways that people try to reconcile their personal beliefs with the fact of religious diversity, on the one hand, and the demands of religious pluralism and toleration, on the other. At the same time, *Terrorist* demonstrates how "confessional" believers—that is, those most strongly associated with a confessional faith and sectarian values—often base their group identity on opposition to a supposedly dominant secularism, which becomes a sort of foil and helps demarcate the boundaries between insiders and outsiders. In fact, fundamentalist groups tend to be heavily invested in a sense of being embattled against the reigning ideologies of the dominant culture, which suggests that these groups are driven by a toxic combination of ideology and religion.

While conducting research on the "pathways" to radicalization, sociologist Scott Atran and his colleagues have found that "what inspires the most lethal terrorists in the world today is not so much the Koran or religious teachings as a thrilling cause and call to action that promises glory and esteem in the eyes of friends" (Atran 2010: n. pag.). Atran has sought to replace the hypothetical "rational actor" of most economic and political theories with what he calls a "devoted actor" model: an individual who becomes "willing to protect morally important or sacred values through costly sacrifice and extreme actions, even being willing to kill and die, particularly when such values are embedded in or fused with group identity" in what amounts to his "imagined kin: brotherhoods, motherlands, fatherlands, homelands, and the like" (Atran and Ginges 2015:

69, 71). According to Atran, devoted actors think and behave much differently than rational actors do: they follow a "rule-bound logic" of morality and sacred values; they find violations of sacred values emotionally upsetting; they subscribe to a Manichean view of good and evil; they are immune to usual methods of moral persuasion and demonstrate a "backfire effect" when "outsiders" try to dissuade them from taking part in extreme actions; they are socially isolated from family; and solidarity with the sacred values of their group overrides the usual calculus of costs and consequences in favor of doing what is right no matter the risks (Atran and Ginges 2015: 70–71).

As a fictional experiment in tracking one character's radicalization and recruitment by a terrorist organization, Updike's novel *Terrorist* corroborates many aspects of this research. Confronted with all the usual temptations of a typical American high school, for instance, Ahmad tends to resist them on the basis not of morality so much as a fusion of his personal identity with the sacred values of a particular religion: "His religion keeps him from drugs and vice, though it also holds him rather aloof from his classmates" (Updike 2006: 8). Commitment to Islam entails not only ascetic self-denial but also social isolation. Ahmad's social isolation becomes evident in a telling turn of phrase regarding his mother: "Though they still live together, . . . [she] has little to do with the self he presents to the daytime world" (Updike 2006: 169). This passage might well describe the sort of dissembling or double life common among teenagers, of course, but the self that Ahmad presents to the world is nonconformist in the extreme:

> Ahmad feels his pride of isolation and willed identity to be threatened by the masses of ordinary, hard-pressed men and plain, practical women who are enrolled in Islam as a lazy matter of ethnic identity. Though he was not the only Muslim believer at Central High, there were no others quite like him—of mixed parentage and still fervent in the faith. (Updike 2006: 177)

As his devotion intensifies, so too does his alienation from family. The product of a mixed marriage—his mother is Irish, his father was an Egyptian exchange student who has long been out of the picture—Ahmad's relationship with his mother is increasingly distant and strained. Having "dropped out of the Catholic package when she was sixteen," Teresa Mulloy is not in a position to understand, much less sympathize with, her son's sudden interest in religion, for she is the type of lapsed Catholic "who never went to mass, and deplored the restraints of her own religion" (Updike 2006: 85, 99). A permissive parent, she lets Ahmad make his own decisions with respect to religion and everything else for that matter: "If he had turned against the God racket all the way, the way I did, I would have let that happen, too. Religion to me is all a matter of attitude" (Updike 2006: 91). Ahmad thinks of his mother, however, as "a victim of the American religion of freedom" (Updike 2006: 167). When Jack Levy meets with Teresa Mulloy about her son's disturbing and otherwise inexplicable change of attitude about his schooling—"Somebody's putting pressure on Ahmad, for whatever reason" (Updike 2006: 83)—they both agree that his recent obsession with Islam may have something to do with it. Just as Teresa is a lapsed Catholic, Jack is a secular Jew who cannot appreciate the appeal of Judaism, with its "long list of rules" (Updike 2006: 24). No doubt partly because of their shared disillusionment with religion, they tend to view Ahmad's conversion as a "self-elected religious affiliation," in effect blinding them to what matters most to him: an increasingly ominous identification with jihad (Updike 2006: 83).

The root meaning of jihad is an inner struggle on the part of Muslims to submit to the law, but the militant jihad promulgated by Al-Qaeda and the Islamic State or ISIS has come to mean something like "a holy war of Muslim martyrs against all infidels" (Buruma 2009: n. pag.). Ahmad himself initially defines jihad as "the struggle to become holy and closer to God" (Updike 2006: 108). Under the influence of Shaikh Rashid and his closest friend Charlie Chehab, Ahmad's understanding of jihad subtly and almost imperceptibly changes. At Rashid's suggestion, Ahmad gets a job working for Charlie's father Habib, who owns a furniture business named Excellency Home Furnishings. When the subject of the US detention center at Guantanamo Bay comes up in their conversation, Habib declares: "They are dangerous men. They wish to destroy America. . . . It is war for them. It is jihad" (Updike 2006: 149). Ahmad speaks up to defend jihad: "Jihad doesn't have to mean war. . . . It means striving, along a path of God. It can mean inner struggle" (Updike 2006: 149). It is Charlie who first introduces him to a more militant definition of jihad. Charlie insists that the "revolutions" now convulsing the Middle East "have much to teach our jihad," and he asks Ahmad, "You are with the jihad?" (Updike 2006: 183). Ahmad insists that he is: "Still, the jihad seems very distant" (Updike 2006: 183). But while driving around New Jersey delivering furniture on a hot July day, Charlie looks across the river to lower Manhattan and blurts out: "It's nice . . . to see those towers gone" (Updike 2006: 186–87). Ahmad shyly observes that some of the victims were Muslims, to which Charlie responds, "Ahmad, you must think of it as a war. War isn't tidy. There is collateral damage" (Updike 2006: 187). Charlie justifies the killing of civilians by resorting to a classic military euphemism, collateral damage. According to Louise Richardson, "The concept of jihad, as invoked by Islamic extremists, . . . is all about war. . . . Terrorists like to be considered soldiers at war because of the legitimacy they believe it brings their cause and for the status they believe it confers on them" (Richardson 2006: 176–77).

Not for the first time in the novel, Ahmad evinces a fascination with martyrdom that suggests his suitability for recruitment by Islamic extremists affiliated with the local mosque. "Already I have lived longer than many martyrs in Iran and Iraq," Ahmad informs Charlie at one point, as if "the God attached to him like an invisible twin, his other self, is a God not of enterprise but of submission, . . . as if in the delicious sleep of his devotion to Allah his future had been amputated" (Updike 2006: 175, 184). Taking advantage of an opening in their developing bond, which revolves around submission to whatever God requires of them, Charlie then asks him if he is willing to die for jihad, to which Ahmad tentatively responds, "If God wills it" (Updike 2006: 189).

The same sort of incremental radicalization can be seen in Ahmad's interactions with Shaikh Rashid, though the imam has surely targeted Ahmad for recruitment from the outset. "My teacher at the mosque says that all unbelievers are our enemies," Ahmad tells a fellow student at school. "The Prophet said that eventually all unbelievers must be destroyed" (Updike 2006: 68). Like Charlie Chehab, Rashid celebrates 9/11 as a day when "the twin towers of capitalist oppression were triumphantly brought down" (Updike 2006: 233). It turns out that Charlie has told him of Ahmad's affirmative response to his probing question about whether he is willing to give his life for jihad: "He informs me that you have expressed a willingness to die for jihad" (Updike 2006: 233). Suddenly, Rashid's influence looks considerably more sinister than it had appeared at first; his tutelage was, indeed, a form of grooming. Rashid assures Ahmad that he does not have to accept the assignment: "You do not have to do this. Your avowal to Charlie does not obligate you, if your heart quails" (Updike 2006: 237). Despite increased surveillance of mosques with suspected ties to terrorist organizations following 9/11, such groups apparently have little difficulty recruiting potential martyrs. Not long ago, the legal scholar Noah Feldman argued that "the declining popularity of revolutionary jihad" in many parts of the world gave him reason to hope for less religious extremism and violence in the future (Feldman 2003: 9). His optimism now seems premature, at best. As Shaikh Rashid informs Ahmad in the novel, "There are many others eager for a glorious name of eternal bliss. The jihad is overwhelmed by volunteers, even in this homeland of evil and irreligion" (Updike 2006: 237). Ahmad then agrees to take on the mission, and Updike seizes the opportunity to delve into the consciousness of a "devoted actor" in jihad:

> His self-sacrifice: it is becoming a part of him, a live, helpless thing like his heart. . . . His soul feels like one of those out-of-season flies that, trapped in winter in a warm room, buzz and insistently bump against the glass of a window saturated with the sunlight of an outdoors wherein they would quickly die. (Updike 2006: 236, 238)

This obvious allusion to an Emily Dickinson poem points to what literature can possibly add to our understanding of why terrorist organizations have been able to recruit suicide bombers. When Ahmad delivers an ottoman to a group of Middle Eastern men at the New Jersey shore, Charlie informs him that they are "true believers" because they are soldiers in the jihad (Updike 2006: 198). The passage suggests that Ahmad agrees to undertake the mission as an act of self-sacrifice in support of a religious war against infidels, or jihad: "The boy knows he is being manipulated, yet accedes to the manipulation, since it draws from him a sacred potential" (Updike 2006: 237).

Scholars have struggled to understand suicide bombings. In his book *Arguing About War* (2004), political theorist Michael Walzer defines terrorism as "the deliberate killing of innocent people, at random, in order to spread fear through a whole population and force the hand of its political leaders" (Walzer 2004: 130). But this definition, he admits, "best fits the terrorism of a national liberation or a revolutionary movement" (Walzer 2004: 130). Suicide bombings in contrast specifically target "noncombatants: not soldiers, not politicians, but ordinary people. And they aren't killed incidentally in the course of actions aimed elsewhere. They are killed intentionally" (Walzer 2004: 131). In the case of Islamic terrorism, such deliberate killings are even less random insofar as victims are being targeted for ostensibly religious reasons: "The enemy is the infidel" (Updike 2006: 133–34). And the sacrificial element of suicide bombings would seem to add yet another religious dimension to these horrific acts. In *On Suicide Bombing* (2007), religious studies scholar Talal Asad has argued that public fascination with and vilification of suicide bombers depends on ascribing a religious motive to them: "Thus although for the law it is the unlicensed act of killing civilians that defines the crime, for journalist and security experts it is his motive for doing this terrible thing that is of primary interest. And yet, because the actor dies in the event, his motives are not fully retrievable" (Asad 2007: 45, 47). Asad prefers to view suicide bombers as politically motivated, operating in a "developing political-ideological field" and driven by "daily humiliation" in their homelands to commit horrendous acts that are nonetheless properly seen as a form of political engagement: "The stress here should not be on violence as such but on spontaneous action when legal political means are blocked" (Asad 2007: 47). Indeed, suicide bombers are driven to martyrdom not by visions of virgins in Paradise but because it "offers them a secular form of immortality" (Asad 2007: 47). Louise Richardson agrees. "For all the religious rhetoric of bin Laden," she writes, "he has persistently articulated a set of political demands linked to American policy in the Middle East. In the wake of the attack, however, public discourse did not focus on these political demands but rather on the grandiose religious rhetoric" (Richardson 2006: 149). But it seems misguided to discount the religious or sacrificial elements of suicide bombings, just as it seems perilous to downplay the violence that results. In her book *Terror in the Name of God: Why Religious Militants Kill* (2003), Jessica Stern diagnoses the problem of "religious terrorism" as follows:

> Because the true faith is purportedly in jeopardy, emergency conditions prevail, and the killing of innocents becomes, in their

view, religiously and morally permissible. The point of religious terrorism is to purify the world of these corrupting influences. But what lies beneath these views? Over time, I began to see that these grievances often mask a deeper kind of angst and a deeper kind of fear. Fear of a godless universe, of chaos, of loose rules and loneliness. (Stern 2003: xix)

Similarly, sociologist Mark Juergensmeyer argues that religion serves to raise the stakes of their grievances, since terrorists tend to espouse a Manichean understanding of good and evil and apply moral absolutes to perceived conflicts.[3]

Updike's novel also gives us a glimpse into how religious, psychological, and sociopolitical motivations combine to create a potent cocktail of terror. In a sense, we might see fiction as a means of recovering the otherwise irretrievable motivations of suicide bombers. In particular, *Terrorist* supports the notion that terrorism might be motivated by angst and fear as well as by religious ideology. Updike offers a compelling psychological profile of his terrorist. Consider this passage just after Ahmad has agreed to commit a suicide bombing:

> A certain simplicity does lay hold of Ahmad in the troughs between surges of terror and then of exaltation, collapsing back into an impatience to be done with it. To have it behind him, whatever "him" will then be. He exists as a close neighbor to the unimaginable. The world in its sunstruck details, the minute scintillations of its interlocked workings, yawns all about him, a glistening bowl of busy emptiness, while within him a sodden black certainty weighs. He cannot forget the transformation awaiting him, behind, as it were, the snapped camera's shutter, even as his senses still receive their familiar bombardment of sights and sounds, scents and tastes. The luster of Paradise leads backward into his daily life.... Ahmad's every minute has taken on the intimate doubleness of prayer, the self-release of turning aside and addressing a self not his own but that of Another, a Being as close as the vein in his neck. (Updike 2006: 251–52)

For a writer who once declared "my only duty was to describe reality as it had come to me—and to give the mundane its beautiful due," this passage is doing something rather different (Updike 2003:

xvii). Far from giving the mundane its beautiful due, this passage registers a sort of "enraptured" focus on an ineffable, transcendent realm that infuses the character's mundane world with meaning. Updike burrows into the mind of a suicide bomber and forces his readers into a sort of complicity with an enchanted, if also perverted, worldview that might compel submission, or what the narrator calls the "slaglike dark weight nagging within him [that] skews his view of the world" (Updike 2006: 252). By illuminating such a skewed view of the world, the novel surely gives readers pause. Granted, this is a fictional example of how terrorism inspires a warped outlook on the world, not an account derived from fieldwork. Nonetheless, it alerts us to the fact that terrorism does not conform to the usual rational standards of political discourse. As Atran and Ginges point out, the most egregious acts of terror "defy the logic of *realpolitik*" (Atran and Ginges 2015: 82).

In the words of Shaikh Rashid, Ahmad's "glorious act" of self-sacrifice will be performed in service of "the cause of the true God, and God never deserts those who wage war on His behalf. *Allahu akbar!*" (Updike 2006: 269, 271). Ahmad draws on his faith to sustain him while performing his mission: "We must each meet death with what faith we have created within, and stored up against the Event" (Updike 2006: 272). There is an apocalyptic aspect to his mission: "Yes. Ahmad will be God's servant. Tomorrow. The day which is almost upon him" (Updike 2006: 274). No wonder he refers to Mohammed Atta and his coconspirators as "inspired martyrs" (Updike 2006: 275) for the cause. Ahmad wakes up the next day ready to join them in Paradise, and like them, he is almost preternaturally alert, focused on the task at hand:

> He moves swiftly, without running. He must not attract attention, he must slip through the city unseen. Later would come the headlines, the CNN reports filling the Middle East with jubilation, making the tyrants in their opulent Washington offices tremble. (Updike 2006: 281)

He is reminded of running the mile on a cinder track: "And until his body took over and his brain dissolved itself in adrenaline he was more nervous than he is now, because what he does not occurs within the palm of God's hand, His vast encompassing will" (Updike 2006: 282).

Ahmad's mission is to drive a truck full of explosives into the Lincoln Tunnel and detonate it, killing everyone inside, including himself. The day of his assignment finally arrives, about a week after the anniversary of 9/11, but as Ahmad approaches the parking lot where he is supposed to meet Charlie and pick up the truck of explosives, he suddenly intuits that "something has gone wrong; Charlie will not show up" (Updike 2006: 278). Indeed, Charlie does not show up, because he has been killed (beheaded, actually) by the terrorist plotters and dumped in the Meadows (Updike 2006: 290). We learn that he was a CIA undercover agent, which helps explain that character's inconsistencies at least. But the plan is not stymied: the truck with its twenty-five plastic containers of ammonium-nitrate fertilizer mixed with nitro-methane racing fuel is still there, waiting for Ahmad to drive it to the intended target. Mindful of his special role as "the final piece" of the terrorist plot, Ahmad proceeds to his destination, the Lincoln Tunnel: "He is not thinking normally, in this exalted yet thin atmosphere of last things. He must keep his head level by conceiving of himself as God's instrument, cool and hard and definite and thoughtless, as an instrument must be" (Updike 2006: 284–85).

Once he reaches the lowest part of the tunnel, Ahmad has a sudden change of heart, due in part to a very timely *deus-ex-machina* intervention by the fiercely atheist Jack Levy: "The unexpected sight stymies Ahmad. He fights to clear his racing mind" (Updike 2006: 287). For it turns out that Jack's sister-in-law Hermione conveniently works for Homeland Security and warns him of an imminent threat. Levy takes it upon himself to stop Ahmad before it's too late:

> Levy says, "I can't believe you're seriously intending to kill hundreds of innocent people."
> "Who says unbelief is innocent? Unbelievers say that. God says, in the Qur'an," *Be ruthless to unbelievers*. Burn them, crush them, because they have forgotten God. . . ."
> "So kill them now. That seems pretty severe."
> "It would to you, of course. You are a lapsed Jew, I believe. You believe nothing." (Updike 2006: 294)

By this point, some readers may feel that any suspense Updike had generated from the very possibility of a suicide bombing has been deflated, that something about the novel has suddenly gone terribly wrong. Here is Christopher Hitchens writing for *The Atlantic*:

> Never mind that the plot has been exposed by a cunning last-minute call from the frumpy Washington bureaucrat sister to the impossibly bulbous homebound New Jersey sister. And never mind that this exposure has *not* led the forces of Homeland Security to close the Lincoln Tunnel. No, stopping Ahmad comes down to the crushed, demoralized Jack Levy, who manages, with exquisite timing, to flag down Ahmad's truck and climb aboard and talk him out of it at the very last available cinematic second. (Hitchens 2006: n. pag.)

The narrator himself hints as much in this scene when he refers to Jack Levy's gesticulating and pleading as "presumably Jewish comedy" (Updike 2006: 294). As implausible as this ending is, though, I think *Terrorist* has important things to say about the pathways to religious extremism and violence that have continued to inspire young men like Ahmad, both in the United States and abroad. If the novel has much less to say about how terrorist attacks can be prevented, it still arguably presents a plausible scenario of radicalization that has played out many times since, as both European and American men have joined terrorist organizations or carried out terrorist acts. Even in the midst of an otherwise seemingly ridiculous conversation inside the truck, for instance, Updike rightly intuits that rational arguments are not likely to dissuade terrorists from their actions; on the contrary, Atran has observed a "backfire effect" that makes them unusually resistant to moral persuasion, which the narrator subtly hints in this scene: "Ahmad is beginning to take pleasure in not being moved by this intruder's arguments" (Updike 2006: 293). Still, it must be said that something like moral persuasion does appear to be effective in this instance, since the main reason for Ahmad's change of heart appears to be his recognition, at the end of their long conversation, that maybe God does not want him to go through with it, after all.

The novel is anticlimatic, not least because it resorts to cosmology, or the Big Bang, to explain Ahmad's last-minute decision not to depress the button and detonate his payload:

The pattern of the wall tiles and of the exhaust-darkened tiles of the ceiling—countless receding repetitions of squares like giant graph paper rolled into a third dimension—explodes outward in Ahmad's mind's eye in the gigantic fiat of Creation, one concentric wave after another, each pushing the other farther and farther out from the initial point of nothingness, God having willed the great transition from non-being to being. . . . He does not want us to desecrate His creation by willing death. He wills life. (Updike 2006: 306)

Somehow, Ahmad relents, "The moment for maximum damage has slipped by; the bend in the tunnel is slowly being pulled into a widening rectangle of daylight" (Updike 2006: 307). Terror averted.

In his essay "Religion in the Public Sphere" (2006), philosopher Jürgen Habermas characterizes fundamentalism as "a response to the challenge religious traditions have been facing in view of the fact of pluralism" (Habermas 2006: 13). Whether we can avoid "the polarization of world views" that occurs when we divide the world up "into fundamentalist and secular camps" will depend "on whether secular and religious citizens, each from their own respective angle, are prepared to embark on an interpretation of the relationship of faith and knowledge that first enables them to behave in a self-reflexive manner toward each other in the political public sphere" (Habermas 2006: 18, 20). In *Terrorist*, Updike posits fundamentalism as a litmus test for religious pluralism. If one response to secularization has been greater acceptance of pluralism, another response was insisting on one true faith. Fundamentalism amounts to an emphatic rejection of pluralism on the part of some believers whose disavowal of tolerance takes root in the same fertile ground that nourishes pluralism. Trying to understand what Islam means to Muslims living as religious minorities in the United States, he speculates at one point: "To these co-religionists, Islam is less a faith, a filigreed doorway to the supernatural, than a habit, a facet of their condition as an underclass, alien in a nation that persists in thinking of itself as light-skinned, English-speaking, and Christian" (Updike 2006: 244). Ahmad attests to the "courage and comfort" that "strong convictions" can bring (Updike 2006: 167). Jack Levy's wife Beth, however, observes that Islamic fundamentalists are "like Baptist fundamentalists, only worse, because they don't care if they die" (Updike 2006: 131). Yet, Updike understands that when push comes to shove, even the most staunch believers are perhaps less fundamentalist than we might think: "Even for a stout churchgoer like the Secretary, a will-of-God fatalism and a heavy bet on the next world have been left behind in the Dark Ages. Those who still hold to the bet have one thing going for them: they are eager to die" (Updike 2006: 48). Updike's secretary for Homeland Security, a character obviously based on John Ashcroft, is a believer, to be sure, but he is also a politician, and therefore his beliefs turn out to be rather tenuous compared to those of suicide bombers. Admittedly, some of these insights about religion may strike some readers as tendentious. All too often, the novel includes passages that appear to be designed less to advance the plot than to allow characters to voice their opinions about religion, the war on terror, and so on. But we cannot finally dismiss the seriousness with which Updike approaches these issues, and my approach to *Terrorist* has advocated a form of literary criticism that considers what literature can offer in the study of religious violence. What does fiction "know" about it that other forms do not?

As early as his memoir *Self-Consciousness* (1989), John Updike marveled at the astonishing growth of Islam, a religion that struck him as at once "gorgeously strange" and potentially threatening: "The world's outstanding believers these days are the Muslims: what forms has God taken in their heads—what does Allah mean to them as they surge forward in their Iranian human waves or Palestinian suicide missions?" (Updike 1989: 227). Ten years later, in his essay "The Future of Faith" (1999), which first appeared in *The New Yorker*, he was still worrying about it: "Islamic fundamentalism demonstrates a creed's power to induce censorship and repression and to inspire solidarity and martyrdom" (Updike 2007: 30). And in the poem "Icarus," as we have seen, Updike's speaker cannot help but project his own worries onto a fellow passenger in the seat next to him. In his only 9/11 novel, *Terrorist*, Updike investigated this power to inspire solidarity and martyrdom through imaginative literature. The result is a work of fiction that, however flawed in some respects, offers a frightening glimpse into the mind of terror.

Notes

1 Andrea Elliott, "The Jihadist Next Door," *The New York Times Magazine,* January 27, 2010. Available online: http://www.nytimes.com/2010/01/31/magazine/31Jihadist-t.html? pagewanted=all&_r=0; Charlie Webb, "Pennsylvania Woman Tied to Plot on Cartoonist," *The New York Times,* March 9, 2010. Available online: http://www.nytimes.com/2010/03/10/us/10pennsylvania.html; Scott Shane, "Ohio Man Trained in Syria Is Charged With Planning Terrorism in U.S.," *The New York Times,* April 16, 2015. Available online: http://www.nytimes.com/2015/04/17/us/ohio-man-trained-in-syria-is-charged-with-planning-terrorism-in-us.html; Scott Shane, "6 Minnesotans Held in Plot to Join ISIS," *The New York Times,* April 20, 2015. Available online: http://www.nytimes.com/2015/04/21/us/6-somali-americans-arrested-in-isis-recruiting-case.html.

2 Wendy Brown, *Regulating Aversion: Tolerance in the Age of Identity and Empire* (Princeton: Princeton University Press, 2006), 5–6.

3 See Mark Juergensmeyer, "Religion as a Cause of Terrorism," in *The Roots of Terrorism,* ed. Louise Richardson (New York: Routledge, 2013), 142. See also Mark Juergensmeyer, *Terror in the Mind of God: The Global Rise of Religious Violence* (Berkeley: University of California Press, 2003).

Works cited

Asad, Talal. *On Suicide Bombing.* New York: Columbia University Press, 2007.

Atran, Scott. "Pathways to and from Violent Extremism: The Case for Science-Based Research." *Edge.org,* March 9, 2010. Available online: https://edge.org/conversation/pathways-to-and-from-violent-extremism-the-case-for-science-based-field-research.

Atran, Scott, and Jeremy Ginges. "Devoted Actors and the Moral Foundations of Intractable Intergroup Conflict." In *The Moral Brain: A Multidisciplinary Perspective,* edited by Jean Decety and Thalia Wheatley, 69–86. Cambridge, MA: The MIT Press, 2015.

Brown, Wendy. *Regulating Aversion: Tolerance in the Age of Identity and Empire.* Princeton: Princeton University Press, 2006.

Buruma, Ian. "Living with Islam." *The New York Review of Books,* May 14, 2009. Available online: http://www.nybooks.com/articles/archives/2009/may/14/living-with-islam/.

Elliott, Andrea. "The Jihadist Next Door." *The New York Times Magazine*, January 27, 2010. Available online: http://www.nytimes.com/2010/01/31/magazine/31Jihadist-t.html?pagewanted=all&_r=0.
Feldman, Noah. *After Jihad: American and the Struggle for Islamic Democracy*. New York: Farrar, Straus and Giroux, 2003.
Habermas, Jürgen. "Religion in the Public Sphere." *European Journal of Philosophy* 14, no. 1 (2006): 1–25.
Hitchens, Christopher. "No Way." *The Atlantic*, June 1, 2006. Available online: http://www.theatlantic.com/magazine/archive/2006/06/no-way/304864/.
Juergensmeyer, Mark. "Religion as a Cause of Terrorism."In *The Roots of Terrorism*, edited by Louise Richardson, 133–44. New York: Routledge, 2013.
Juergensmeyer, Mark. *Terror in the Mind of God: The Global Rise of Religious Violence*. Berkeley: University of California Press, 2003.
Nussbaum, Martha C. *The New Religious Intolerance: Overcoming the Politics of Fear in an Anxious Age*. Cambridge, MA: Harvard University Press, 2012.
Richardson, Louise. *What Terrorists Want: Understanding the Enemy, Containing the Threat*. New York: Random House, 2006.
Shane, Scott. "Ohio Man Trained in Syria Is Charged With Planning Terrorism in U.S." *The New York Times*, April 16, 2015. Available online: http://www.nytimes.com/2015/04/17/us/ohio-man-trained-in-syria-is-charged-with-planning-terrorism-in-us.html.
Shane, Scott. "6 Minnesotans Held in Plot to Join ISIS." *The New York Times*, April 20, 2015. Available online: http://www.nytimes.com/2015/04/21/us/6-somali-americans-arrested-in-isis-recruiting-case.html.
Stern, Jessica. *Terror in the Name of God: Why Religious Militants Kill*. New York: Ecco, 2003.
Updike, John. *Americana: And Other Poems*. New York: Knopf, 2001.
Updike, John. *Due Considerations: Essays and Criticism*. New York: Knopf, 2007.
Updike, John. *Terrorist*. New York: Knopf, 2006.
Updike, John. "Varieties of Religious Experience." *The Atlantic Monthly* (November 2002): 92–103.
Walzer, Michael. *Arguing About War*. New Haven: Yale University Press, 2004.
Webb, Charlie. "Pennsylvania Woman Tied to Plot on Cartoonist." *The New York Times*, March 9, 2010. Available online: http://www.nytimes.com/2010/03/10/us/10pennsylvania.html.

6

Desperate domesticity? Translocating the political into the personal in Lynne Sharon Schwartz's *The Writing on the Wall* and Paul Auster's *Man in the Dark*

Sien Uytterschout and Kristiaan Versluys

> *I believe language to have been given us to make our meaning clear, and not to wrap it in dishonest doubt.*
> ~ CHARLOTTE BRONTË, Preface to *Wuthering Heights*, 1851

> *The quaint conceit of imagining what would have happened if some important or unimportant event had settled itself differently has become so fashionable that I am encouraged to enter upon an absurd speculation. What would have happened if Lee had not won the Battle of Gettysburg?*
> ~ WINSTON CHURCHILL, *The Great Republic: A History of America*, 2002

Introduction

In the preface to his short story anthology, *110 Stories. New York Writes After September 11* (2002), Ulrich Baer expresses his confidence in "New York's perpetual self-reconstitution through metaphor and language," a process that in the post-9/11 era especially "will prove as significant as the construction in concrete and steel." Instead of leaving meaning-making to opinion mongers and White House spokespersons, and allowing the events of 9/11 to be swallowed up and forever crystallized by such inadequate discourse, Baer calls for efforts that "turn the event into a story without glossing over its shocking singularity" (Baer 2002: 2). Strategies that will provide nothing but "simple answers, ready-made and precision-bombed solutions, and the arrogant and foolish certainty of having the correct response to a severe collective trauma" (Baer 2002: 2) must be countered by integrating that collective trauma into narrative, even if the results will unavoidably prove to be elliptic and skirting the limits of what language can express. If not, the inevitable alternative is a complete banishment of the events into the realm of the incomprehensible (Baer 2002: 1–2). This precarious balancing act between silence and speech, between a seemingly irresistible pull for quiet acquiescence and an equally strong desire to bear witness, we argue, is negotiated by Lynne Sharon Schwartz and Paul Auster in their respective works *The Writing on the Wall* (2005) and *Man in the Dark* (2008).

Schwartz's protagonist Renata, for instance, takes refuge in the semi-realistic dream world of uchronies, or what is referred to in one of the mottos to this chapter as "the quaint conceit of imagining what ... if" (Churchill 2002: 246). Long before the terrorist attacks of 9/11, Renata's story has been one of personal reckoning with the past, and a public refusal to confront the present. With her private loss compounded and reinvigorated by the public disaster of 9/11, Renata resorts to inventing "stories that imagine history taking a different course through some small but not inconceivable turn of events." Thus, Renata arms herself against the crushing weight of reality with a panoply of uchronistic thought experiments, ranging from the banal and the self-indulgent (Schwartz 2005: 147), to daydreams bordering on delusion, involving the miraculous reappearance of her long-lost niece, Gianna. These constructs cease to be harmless when they become more potent than physical reality.

In Paul Auster's *Man in the Dark*, septuagenarian August Brill, retired literary critic and chronic insomniac, imagines himself—or rather his persona Owen Brick—into a parallel world in which the Twin Towers still stand, and the war with Iraq never took place. Instead, America is at war with itself. As a consequence of the contested presidential elections of 2000, and at the instigation of the New York City mayoralty, sixteen states have seceded from the federation and joined the Independent States of America (Auster 2008: 62). Waking up in another America than the one in which he went to sleep, the nonplussed Owen Brick finds that he has been summoned to post-secession America by a shadowy consortium of Confederate authorities to assassinate the mastermind behind the war, a man named August Brill. Eventually, however, it is not Owen Brick who finishes off August Brill, but the other way around, and Brill's motives for spinning out this elaborate uchronistic fantasy, creating his own assassin, and thus potentially committing "suicide . . . in a roundabout way" (Auster 2008: 70–71), are laid bare. Imagining this alternative history permits Brill to defer touching upon the "real story": the personal calamities that he, his daughter Miriam and his granddaughter Katya are faced with. These little narratives of personal drama are ultimately overshadowed by the utterly horrifying event that is hinted at throughout, but only fully divulged at the very end of the novella: the televised abduction and gruesome execution of Katya's ex-boyfriend in Iraq. Putting the fictional Owen Brick out of his misery therefore testifies to Brill's resolve to leave his prolonged reverie behind him and address the horrors of "real" reality, horrors that can hardly be deemed less incredible and surreal than the chain of events in that other war-riddled America.

Our line of approach in this chapter is twofold. Both works, we argue *first*, offer an extended investigation into the ambivalence of language and narration by productively engaging with the question of whether or not narrative and linguistic power can "restore . . . the links between private memory and public history" (Keniston 2008: 9). The protagonists in each of the two works tell themselves stories—one more elaborate than the other—in an attempt to ward off, if not entirely rewrite, a painful past. While both authors acknowledge and tentatively endorse the potential therapeutic benefits of telling one's story, they make allowances for the possible dangers of narrative construction. "After all," as Ulrike

Tancke points out, "stories have the potential to be manipulative, to mould people and events according to the narrator's own desires" (Tancke 2009: 83). And as a strategy for overcoming trauma, creating narratives imbued with escapist motives is not without its pitfalls either. While doing so might grant the narrator temporary respite from past traumas, it might just as easily degenerate into a permanent refusal to acknowledge the posttraumatic present.

Mindful of the objections that have been raised by Michael Rothberg and Richard Gray, respectively denouncing the extant body of post-9/11 literature as a failure of the imagination (Rothberg 2009: 152) and a facile bid for domestication (Gray 2011: 134), this chapter, *second*, explores how public and private grief intersect, and how a certain amount of domestication—or as Gray puts it, an "assimilat[ion of] the unfamiliar into familiar structures" (Gray 2011: 134)—is unavoidable, if not indispensable when dealing with a massive trauma that was at once collective and personal. Indeed, if such familiarization through fiction can pierce through the mystification that has shrouded the events of 9/11, this contributes to the novel(la)'s strength. By refracting "the national impact into microcosmic tales by translocating the political into the personal spheres," Birgit Däwes convincingly proposes (Däwes 2011: 336), fiction can "offer in-depth explorations of the events' semantic repercussions, which ties them to the larger cultural formations in which they position themselves" (Däwes 2011: 338–39). Gray and Rothberg's harsh judgments can be mitigated, if not entirely countered, by the Lyotardian distinction between *grands récits* or grand narratives, and *petits récits* or little narratives. Distrustful of the former for their totalizing tendencies and their claim to possessing the ultimate truth, Lyotard gives preference to the diversification and subtlety of the latter (Lyotard 1997: 70). In this light, it makes sense to counterbalance the public grand narrative of 9/11 with a focus on more private and—if you will—*domesticated* little narratives. Ultimately, however, both remain two well-balanced sides of the same coin. By maintaining an intricate interplay between the grand narrative of 9/11 and the little narratives of their respective protagonists, and engaging in an incisive interrogation of the role of language in the post-9/11 context, the two novels withstand the accusations of familiarization and domestication leveled by Gray and Rothberg. Against the geopolitical canvas of post-9/11 reality, the different characters' intimate struggles to come to terms with their own personal history make for two works with "multiple thematic layers [and] symbolic complexity" (Däwes 2011: 302). It is this strategy of subtle intertexture that allows Auster and Schwartz to develop a counter-narrative in the spirit of the claims made by Ulrich Baer, while at the same time offering a way around the criticism leveled by Michael Rothberg and Richard Gray.

The Writing on the Wall: Wrong words and "Transformed Lives"

With a focus on Renata's quirky idiosyncrasies, marking her as an avid student of obscure languages and a collector of folders full of "Absurdities, Banalities, or Meaningless Words" (Schwartz 2005: 7), the novel's opening chapter in an oblique way already hints at its protagonist's conflicted past. More than the singularities of a hobbyist, Renata's impressive linguistic talents and her peculiar interest in what she calls "Transformed Lives" (Schwartz 2005: 10) are a meager disguise for her obsession with language and its limitations. Ever since tragedy struck her family when she was a teenager, Renata's lifelong quest has been one of finding "words commensurate with experience; the creation of metaphors to compensate for the failure of language faced with the exorbitance of the literal" (Miller 2002: 12). It is this never-ending quest that fuels Renata's outspoken obsession with "wrong words" (Schwartz 2005: 7). In addition to hoarding up snippets of language "mutilated and bent out of shape" (Schwartz 2005: 52), Renata also owns a scrapbook entitled "Transformed Lives or Everyone Wants to be Changed" (Schwartz 2005: 10), filled with stories of people whose lives have at some point undergone drastic change. These otherwise highly diverse accounts all have one thing in common. Ranging from a composer of classical music retraining to become a professional belly dancer (Schwartz 2005: 10–11), to a recently widowed woman taking up permanent residence on the *Queen Elizabeth 2* as a tribute to her late husband (Schwartz 2005: 115), and a photographer wanting to capture the lives of homeless people in New York and eventually coming "so close to his vision that he became part of his material" (Schwartz 2005: 57), the stories in Renata's collection nearly always document transformations resulting from a conscious decision. To Renata, who has had absolutely no control over the traumatic events that have unsettled her own life, this aspect of autonomy is particularly appealing. Her quest, in other words, is not solely one for linguistic mastery, but for self-determination *tout court*. Linguistic mastery, for her, is tantamount to regaining a modicum of control over her life story (Schwartz 2005: 11). But not all of the transformation stories in Renata's folder are testimonies of unqualified success. Accounts of positive change are eclipsed by more negative ones, some of which even have a distinctly dark and fatalistic ring to them. The photographer's total engrossment in his ambitious project, for instance, causing him to eventually turn into one of his photographic objects, is nothing if not cynical. Similarly, the widow's decision to spend the rest of her life on the *QE2* may at first sight seem a fitting, if slightly whimsical, commemoration of her husband. Upon closer inspection, however, it betrays a rather rigid and unproductive faithfulness to her grief. Again, it is the possibility of such an emotionally static life that finds favor with Renata, offering "the prospect of no powerful emotions ever again. She liked, or had persuaded herself that she liked, contemplating a peaceful stretch of blank years" (Schwartz 2005: 29).

Renata's alternating affinity with the transformation stories in her collection, now favoring the more optimistic and then reveling in the pessimistic ones, exemplifies her wavering success at negotiating her own troubled past. This already brittle bid for reconciliation of past and present is even further jeopardized by the events of 9/11 (Schwartz 2005: 103). The terrorist attacks work as a catalyst, or a "symbolic amplifier" (Däwes 2011: 303) for Renata's past traumas, that is, the tragic death under mysterious circumstances of her twin sister Claudia, and the subsequent disintegration of her entire family. As the only cognizant survivor of her family, Renata, as one reviewer remarks, has become a living repository (Upshaw 2005: C2). Not only is she a custodian of the foreign languages she studies, and a chronicler of her own traumatic family history, she has also become a "living archive" for her dead twin sister.[1] Renata's relentless self-loathing (Schwartz 2005: 123–24) following the family tragedy is momentarily stalled when, unexpectedly, she has to assume full responsibility for Claudia's child, a baby born out of a questionable liaison and given up for adoption just before Claudia's disappearance. The little girl, Gianna, becomes Renata's life-line, jostling her out of her emotional lethargy and forcing her back into at least a semblance of normality. That is, until Gianna disappears never to be heard of again: "Disappeared—kidnapped, lost, evaporated into thin air, transformed?" (Schwartz 2005: 217).

"Already they have words for it"

The Writing on the Wall, as Lynne Sharon Schwartz herself has pointed out, is primarily a book about the interconnection of public language and personal grief, confronting, among other things, the narrative and linguistic void that lies at the heart of Renata's personal life.[2] Despite Schwartz's self-proclaimed attempt at calling to account how the media (mis-)used language to label the events of 9/11 and their immediate aftermath, the novel, according to Michael Rothberg, utterly falls short of expectations. Although Rothberg grants that the novel's premise is rather promising in its attempt to establish modes of negotiation between private and public suffering, instead of giving impetus to "a possibly reinvigorated public sphere," he argues, it "retreats back into the reified world of domesticity" (Rothberg 2009: 154). Similar objections are raised by Richard Gray, who goes so far as to claim that the novel is "unusual only in making the turn towards the domestic so explicit and emphatic" (Gray 2011: 32). Both critics reproach Schwartz for a total lack of political and imaginative commitment. As inward-looking as it may seem, the novel's principle line of approach, with its emphasis on Renata's private struggles, exacerbated as they are by the more recent traumatic events of 9/11, enables Schwartz to critically engage with the media-dominated public domain. In so doing, Schwartz does notably more than simply "registering that *something* traumatic . . . has happened" (Gray 2011: 27 emphasis in original). Instead of finding fault with the novel's turn toward the domestic, or indeed, reading it as "a deliberate rejection of the public domain" (Gray 2011: 31), we argue that the novel is both ethically and politically engaged. Or in the words of David Cockley, "Schwartz questions the media foreclosure and approaches the mediated trauma [of 9/11] in a different way, by acknowledging how it takes away the voice of the victim" (Cockley 2009: 15).

As a reference librarian and an extraordinarily gifted linguist, Renata specializes in cataloguing near-extinct minority languages.

Continually pitting rich and exotic (and fictional) idioms against her native English, she holds the latter liable for its inadequacy in expressing the wide range of human emotions. Living by Socrates's motto that false words are not only evil in themselves, but also infect the soul with evil,[3] Renata has no patience with "language used mindlessly, in ignorance, language perverted to anti-language" (Schwartz 2005: 52). Renata's compulsive preoccupation with language testifies to more than an ordinary enthusiasm for her job. Philosophizing about why language functions as it does, and how it is deployed to shape experience, is Renata's *raison d'être*, and a means of outmaneuvering the traumatic past that threatens to catch up with her whenever she has an idle moment. When in the immediate aftermath of 9/11, the president's rhetoric of war infiltrates the public and the private sphere, and imposes itself as the dominant discourse, Renata's passion for language morphs into a full-blown obsession. "On top of everything," she muses, "another kind of butchery is in progress, not bloody but insidious, an assault on the common language" (Schwartz 2005: 78–79). But skeptical as Renata is, not even she can entirely escape the mesmerizing media spectacle and she falls for the fantasy that although "she didn't see it happen . . . she's seen it so many times since that it feels like she saw it" (Schwartz 2005: 45).

And yet, for all her marvelous linguistic acumen and strong convictions, Renata is nowhere near as articulate as she may seem at first sight. Provoked by the meiotic description of the events as "technical difficulties," Renata's wistful observation that "already they have words for it" (Schwartz 2005: 49), stands in stark contrast to her own inability to find words to match her experiences. Over the years, Renata has learned to silence herself. What is more (and possibly worse), she has allowed herself to be silenced by others. In so doing, she is at risk of succumbing to a complete loss of voice and of self, a process that the three main characters in Auster's *Man in the Dark* so tenaciously fight to resist. For a considerable time, Renata's professional and personal preoccupation with language and narration can tinsel over her fundamental inarticulateness. But the precarious balance between the therapeutic telling of one's story and a complete loss of self in a fantasy world decidedly tips downward toward the latter when Renata's long-term fascination with "what if"-stories induces her to take in an unknown girl she finds wandering the streets, a girl in whom she recognizes her long-lost niece, Gianna. The fairly harmless uchronistic fantasies Renata has entertained up until then at that point degenerate into dangerously real make-belief. Even after coming across Gianna's Missing poster, it still takes all of her friends' urgent insistence and power of persuasion for Renata to reluctantly give up the girl, and take her home to her (adoptive) parents. In the end, whether or not this uchronistic little narrative continues to exert a baleful influence on Renata's state of mind remains unclear.[4]

Little narratives

Invoking the interplay of what the French philosopher Jean-François Lyotard has termed *petits récits*, or little narratives, and *grands récits* or grand narratives, we argue that with *The Writing on the Wall*, Schwartz comes close to achieving an approach to the events of 9/11 that is at once politically engaged and imaginatively resourceful. This interaction is perceptible on two levels. On the novel's macrolevel, Renata's personal *petit récit* serves as a foil for the *grand récit* of 9/11. On the novel's microlevel, the variety of little narratives in Renata's "Transformed Lives" folder hold up a critical mirror to her personal grand narrative. It is by zooming in on Renata's little narrative in all its facets, and by contrasting it against the grand narrative of 9/11 that Schwartz is able, not only to provide a viable counter-narrative to "the all consuming [sic] nature of the spectacle," as David Cockley points out (Cockley 2009: 15), but also to offer an imaginative reconfiguration of what happened that day. Claiming that the novel is entirely apolitical, therefore, is to ignore its incisive indictment of the stolid 9/11 media discourse, and to deny the productive possibilities it offers when it allows the personal sphere to intersect with the public (Däwes 2011: 300–03).

These intricate interconnections between the private and the public, the grand récit of 9/11 and Renata's petit récit, allow Schwartz to salvage what might otherwise either be drowned out by the endlessly self-perpetuating media rhetoric or, in the case of her protagonist, lost in the interstices of the unsaid and the unsayable. Renata's entire adult life has been structured around the vacuum of meaning between what she has always intuited about the facts of Claudia's death and Gianna's disappearance, and what was never explicitly articulated by anyone, not least by herself. Past and present incidents threaten to engulf Renata in near-total voicelessness, a voicelessness that is to some extent self-imposed, and that she has learned to cultivate and cherish. But despite persistent efforts to the contrary, Renata cannot forever outrun her past by surrendering to silence. No matter how many inventively evasive (narrative) strategies she devises, the most painful and jarring residual traces of her past will continue to withstand attrition. With an emphasis on a single character's "inner library of traumas" and how that character struggles to "reorganize [her] past life to fit this new trauma in" (McGaffey 2005), Lynne Sharon Schwartz may very well have written a domesticated or overly familiarized account of the September 11 attacks. But it is precisely that familiarization that brings into relief the events' far-reaching political and cultural consequences.

Man in the Dark

In the course of one sleepless night, August Brill, narrator of the frame story and inventor of the novella's uchronistic inner story, relives a number of painful episodes from the past, and imaginatively re-enacts them by "mixing past and present, facts and fictions" (Simonetti 2011: 28) in the new and allohistorical reality he creates, involving an America that has not lived through 9/11 or the War on Terror, but that has become embroiled in civil war ever since the contested presidential elections in 2000. During his nightly ruminations Brill swerves between a desperate attempt not to think of "the horrifying story of that death, the images of that death, the pulverizing consequences of that death on my grieving granddaughter" (Auster 2008: 2) and what he knows is his moral responsibility, namely the obligation to speak the unspeakable (Hugonnier 2011: 278). Brill will ultimately divulge what "the horrifying story of that death" is at the novella's close. The character of Brill's initial vacillation, Birgit Däwes argues, is symbolic of "the dilemma of post-9/11 aesthetic representation at large" (Däwes 2011: 349), and is indicative of the author's active engagement with the "precarious balancing act between historical factuality and fictional representation" (Däwes 2011: 345). According to Dennis Barone, Brill's eventual determination to overcome his aporia thematically reflects "a new urgency" on the part of Auster, "a desire to express explicitly what has gone wrong with the political and public world, and to reconnect, at both the personal and national level, what has been ruptured" (n. pag.). Similarly, Stefania Ciocia and Jesús A. González observe in Auster's post-2001 works a preoccupation with "the importance and the power of narrative acts, the relationship between the personal and the public, the interplay between fiction and history, and the relevance of storytelling to the processing of traumatic or otherwise epochal events" (Ciocia 2011: 3). Since 9/11, they find, there has been a marked and, for Auster rather exceptionally explicit, "angered engagement with the politics of George W. Bush and the war on terror" (Varvogli 2011: 40).[5] This newfound "angered engagement" translates itself in *Man in the Dark* into the dystopian America August Brill creates. That this other America should be a complete dystopia, matching, if not surpassing the absurdities of post-9/11 American reality, is significant. Brill does not indulge in "any beautiful, tranquilizing lie, because it would not be persuasive," and because he realizes that "it is not by erasing the event nor by pretending it never happened that one can successfully cope with trauma" (Simonetti 2011: 28–29). It is this realization that in the end prompts Brill to live up to his responsibility, and to put a stop to his initial acts of deferment and emotional dithering.

In *Man in the Dark*, what threatens to engulf Brill and his loved ones is chronic and all-out melancholia. All three of them have creative minds, but one by one they have, over time, postponed or altogether ceased their artistic or expressive pursuits. While August has stopped working on his memoirs (Auster 2008: 13), his daughter Miriam is in perennial doubt about the quality of her work on a biography she is writing (Auster 2008: 179). Miriam's daughter Katya, in turn, has dropped out of film school (Auster 2008: 15). "It's a house of grieving, wounded souls," one character in the novella's inner story remarks, "and every night Brill lies awake in the dark trying not to think about his past, making up stories about other worlds" (Auster 2008: 17). Mourning the loss of his wife, Brill must not only learn to negotiate his own grief, but must at the same time find a way to balance it with his deep-felt concern for his daughter's and granddaughter's unhappiness. The behavior of both women betrays strategies of evasion akin to Brill's storytelling, but it is his granddaughter Katya, especially, who is in frantic search of ways to outsource the pain and guilt she nurtures over the death of her former boyfriend, Titus. Much like Renata's penchant for the little stories in her "Transformed Lives" folder, or the uchronies that involve her niece Gianna, Katya throws herself into obsessive movie-watching (Auster 2008: 13).

Seeing no immediate harm in it, Brill at first indulges, and even joins her in these daily screenings. After a while, though, he comes to understand that the movies are more than an innocent pastime. From that point onward, he makes it his duty to try to entice his granddaughter out of her emotional seclusion (Auster 2008: 15), attempts that Katya is just as determined to fend off (Auster 2008: 18). While astutely analyzing the theoretical aspects of the movies they watch, however, Katya unwittingly also diagnoses the mechanisms of her own deferral. Through these movies' little narratives, which invariably speak of hardship and poverty, but also—however tentatively—of hope, Katya is able to convey part of her own emotional hardship by circumlocution.[6] The movies—or rather Katya's readings of those movies—are a means for her to channel some of the excruciating guilt she feels.

America, but not America

Burdened with deep and complexly layered familial grief, Brill refuses to succumb to loss of voice and by extension, loss of self. Nor will he allow his daughter and granddaughter to surrender to the silence or—in the words of Judith Herman—the unspeakability of the trauma that binds them (Herman 1997: 1). Despite his own reluctance and strategies of deferral, Brill never once denies that the real stories—his own life story and the gruesome story of Titus's death—will have to be told. Brill, in other words, understands "the power of speaking the unspeakable and . . . the creative energy that is released when the barriers of denial and repression are lifted" (Herman 1997: 2). Although the contrived and uchronistic tale Brill concocts might at first sight appear to be nothing more than an elaborate ruse, a way of parrying unwanted memories, it is in fact a coded version of his own life, and of what happened to Titus in Iraq, while at the same time holding up a mirror to post-9/11 reality in general. Not insignificantly, the events indirectly leading up to the boy's death—the terrorist attacks of 9/11—have never taken place in Brill's alternative universe.

That is not to say that Brill's alternate world is one of prelapsarian harmony or utopian design run rampant.[7] Indeed, in Owen Brick's new reality, one atrocity has made way for another, and the far-reaching national and international ramifications of 9/11 have been exchanged for the ravages of a second American Civil War. In this alternate reality, one that has begun to bifurcate from canonical history ever since the contested presidential elections of 2000, three years of civil unrest eventually result in the secession of sixteen states and a declaration of war. When Brick is teleported into this unfamiliar America, the new "War between the States" has already been raging for an additional four years. Brick has been summoned, so he is informed, with the express purpose of putting an end to the war. Free passage back to his reality can only be obtained in exchange for Brick's carrying out a contract killing. The target is the man who, according to army intelligence, "owns the war [and] invented it. He sits in a room all day writing it down, and whatever he writes comes true. The intelligence reports say he's racked with guilt, but he can't stop himself" (Auster 2008: 10). It is at this point that, in true Austerian fashion, the two worlds of narrator and narratee converge, for the man Brick is ordered to assassinate is none other than August Brill.

More than just "another story about storytelling" (Turrentine 2008: T2), *Man in the Dark* becomes a parable for dealing with the events of 9/11 and their aftermath by *not* dealing with them. Or at least by not dealing with the events directly. Not even the typically Austerian narrative playfulness and wry authorial self-consciousness can smother the clearly audible—and one might add credible—cry of pain (Scurr 2008: n. pag.). The parallel world Brill devises in the course of his sleepless night is only a superficial and fairly harmless distraction. Before long, he sets fiction aside in order to confront reality. Once Brill arrives at the jarring truth of Titus's fate, it becomes evident that the tale about Owen Brick has merely served as a conduit, a way for Brill to redirect some of the gruesomeness of reality into fiction. The character of Owen Brick, therefore, is not so much his creator's puppet or empty mouthpiece as a tool skillfully plied by the master-narrator August Brill to eliminate whatever remaining inhibitions he might nourish toward divulging the family's—and the novella's—core trauma. Brick was never meant to literally kill August Brill. He serves as a (meta-)narrative device to prevent Brill from inventing more stories, and in so doing, force him to finally face the traumas of the distant and more recent past. The ruthless and very literal "character assassination" Brill has in store for his protagonist and alter ego marks the exact moment when he realizes that there is no longer any point in deferring the confrontation with the trauma that lies at the heart of his real life story. At the same time, Brick's meaningless death is meant to mirror the equally pointless and utterly gruesome death of Titus in Iraq (Simonetti 2011: 30).

A tale of two worlds

The other story that begs to be told is August Brill's own life story. Brill, like Renata in *The Writing on the Wall*, is the chronicler of his family history. But whereas Renata's role as a living repository has been thrust upon her by circumstances beyond her control, Brill— although gently prodded into action by his daughter Miriam— ultimately exercises conscious choice over his decision to start writing "the story of [his] life, the family history, a chronicle of a vanished world" (Auster 2008: 13). That is, until the death of his wife Sonia shatters his resolve. His remorse over past marital *faux pas*, in conjunction with the fresh grief of losing his spouse, fuels his desire to leave some of the more painful episodes in his married life untouched. These matrimonial troubles are part of the real story that Brill wishes to defer by inventing Owen Brick. For most of the night, he cannot help but feel that it is "still too early, and if I let myself go now, I'll end up brooding about [Sonia] for hours. Stick to the story. That's the only solution. Stick to the story, and then see what happens if I make it to the end" (Auster 2008: 22). Complete deferral, however, is out of the question since the character and story of Owen Brick contain a number of crossovers with the life of their creator, as well as with the fate of the unfortunate Titus Small. As narrator of the frame story and inventor of the inner tale, Brill straddles two worlds:

> The weird world, the battered world, the weird world rolling on as wars flame all around us: the chopped-off arms in Africa, the chopped-off heads in Iraq, and in my own head this other war, an imaginary war on home ground, America cracking apart, the noble experiment finally dead (Auster 2008: 49).

On one plane of meaning, Brill's uchrony functions as a transliteration of the emotionally straining familial battle that he, Miriam and Katya are fighting. At the same time, Auster has made *Man in the Dark* into a personal indictment of what has become of America under the Bush administration.[8] When Brill asserts that the noble experiment of America has finally foundered, his claim not only holds true for the country he invented but for the "real" America as well. Similarly, the country that the bewildered Owen Brick so forcefully renounces as his own on account of its having become utterly unrecognizable (Auster 2008: 36) bears reference not only to the chaos and Kafkaesque absurdities of post-secession America but also to the reality of post-9/11 America. The perambulatory conflict that on one side of the uchronistic barrier has led to the war on terror and the ensuing domestic dissension, has metamorphosed into all-out civil war on the other side. Its uchronistic premise notwithstanding, Brill's fictional and war-riddled America is not at all that far removed from its post-9/11 counterpart, and both versions become each other's uncanny double.

About two-thirds of the way into the novella, it becomes clear that what Brill has been doing up until this moment is setting the stage for the revelation that will follow. Having disposed of Owen Brick and extinguished his fictional parallel America, he exchanges his story of referred pain for a confrontation with the trauma proper. First, he unburdens himself to his granddaughter Katya, owning up to a series of unpleasant recollections of his infidelity to and subsequent separation from his wife (Auster 2008: 130–68). His candidness is rewarded when, however briefly, he succeeds in enticing Katya away from her constant self-punishment. When the plagued Katya finally drops off to sleep, and the horribly vivid details of Titus's death intrude upon his thoughts one more time, Brill no longer wills them away (Auster 2008: 175). Titus, it turns out, has been abducted and brutally murdered by a group of militant Islamists while on a mission for a contracting company based in Iraq. With Titus's abduction and execution, the real war that America is waging—the War on Terror—has penetrated the family's safe and secluded domestic space. This intrusion is then literally, and all the more brutally, driven home by the televised images of the boy's execution, and it irredeemably alters the family's reality.

Conclusion

The first epigraph captioning this chapter is a line taken from the Biographical Notice that Charlotte Brontë wrote for the 1851 edition of *Wuthering Heights*, written by her sister Emily. Addressing her sister's critics, among other things, Brontë also seeks to redress the misattribution of said novel's authorship to herself, passionately emphasizing her abhorrence of "deal[ing] in equivoque" of any kind (Bell 1851: x). In the preceding paragraph, Brontë also makes mention of *the writing on the wall*—not, we may safely assume, referencing Lynne Sharon Schwartz's 2005 novel, but certainly alluding to the same biblical passage from whence inspiration came for the latter novel's title and themes.[9] With her own allusion to *the writing on the wall*, Schwartz, for her part, although she does not go so far as to explicitly equate the extravagancies and excesses unfolding in Solomon's Temple with contemporary American policy makers, has nevertheless after careful weighing found something wanting in America's political and cultural reaction to the terrorist attacks of 9/11 (McGaffey 2005). In *The Writing on the Wall*, Schwartz draws a bead on the deliberate linguistic and discursive deceitfulness displayed by the government and media in the aftermath of the attacks. She does so by making one single character's personal traumas, traumas that predate the events of 9/11 by several decades, the focus of her novel. Much criticized on account of this supposedly familiarizing and domesticating line of approach, Schwartz's novel nevertheless manages to become an imaginatively and politically inspired counterpoint to the official discourse of—to once again recall the words of Ulrich Baer—"simple answers, ready-made and precision-bombed solutions, and the arrogant and foolish certainty of having the correct response to a severe and collective trauma" (Baer 2002: 2), without once walking into the same trap as the very discourse it sets out to debunk.

Schwartz takes a critical interest in the ways in which access to, and control over language play a role in the insidious dispersal of public and publicized grief into private suffering. Although Renata is to some extent able to see through the government's different stages of rhetorical strategizing (Schwartz 2005: 133), and although she privately fulminates against this profusion of what she would call "wrong words" (Schwartz 2005: 7), her instinctive impulse is not to engage in a more critical public dialogue, but to withdraw further into her long-smoldering uchronistic fantasies. Explicitly focusing on language and narration, and more particularly on the linguistic and narrative vacuum to which Renata, despite her multilingual talents, has fallen prey, Schwartz's novel draws attention to the mechanisms of overly mediated trauma and how it threatens to take away its victim's voice. But Schwartz's act of subversion does not stop here. On one level, Schwartz offers her character's *petit récit*—Renata's personal struggle with 9/11 and how it reawakens and exacerbates preexisting traumas—as a destabilizing contrast to the government's reifying official *grand récit*.

This is not to say that Schwartz simply and uncritically endorses her character's *petit récit*. Indeed, the manner in which Renata, who has had absolutely no control over the events that unsettled her life, seeks to compensate this powerlessness by aspiring to total linguistic mastery at times comes rather close to mirroring the administration's frantic "framings and reframing" of the events (Lakoff 2001: 4). Schwartz, in other words, not only challenges the reification of 9/11 by pitting Renata's *petit récit* against the obtuseness of the discursive framework developed by the Bush administration, she also questions and subtly subverts Renata's own coping mechanisms. Never once does Schwartz profess to give a definitive interpretation of the events of 9/11 and its aftermath, for the "meaning of 9/11 is neither self-evident nor contained in any single image or political account" (Keniston 2008: 11). Nor does she offer her readership any sense of closure when she leaves any potential resolution to Renata's past and present outside narrative consideration.

Like Lynne Sharon Schwartz, Paul Auster does not shrink from ventilating incisive criticism of post-2001 America, a country he himself has confessed to no longer recognizing as his own (Flood 2008: n. pag.), and which has in many ways become as utterly unrecognizable as the uchronistic story-within-a-story that August Brill invents in the course of one sleepless night. The fictional world Brill conjures up, although fairly innocuous in terms of deferment, represents a pertinent imaginative reworking of crucial episodes in Brill's private life, as well as intrusions of the (inter)national scene into the private sphere, most notably 9/11 and its devastating consequences. With its subtle interweaving of the narrator's world with that of the narratee, *Man in the Dark*, in its quest for narratable trauma, manages to strike a delicate balance between the therapeutic effects of storytelling and the dangers of loss of self in a self-constructed fantasy world. Amid all his fiction making, Brill never denies that the trauma proper must be addressed. Right from the start he shows the necessary resolve to leave his prolonged reverie behind him and address the horrors of reality. The same cannot be said of Renata, who, unlike Brill, has allowed her uchronistic fantasies and manifold obsessions to mold the greater part of her adult life into an ever-enduring traumatic present (Schwartz 2005: 98). After his nocturnal heart-to-heart with his granddaughter Katya in the closing pages of the novella, Brill comes to recognize his crucial role and responsibility in helping his daughter and granddaughter overcome their emotional and creative paralysis and takes the initiative in enticing them away from their mind-numbing passivity. In the end, Brill and his family are able to take a tentative first step toward recovery. "This expressive household," Dennis Barone writes, "survives because everyone in it speaks" (Barone 2008: n. pag).

The two works of fiction under discussion in this chapter are characterized by their negotiation with "the danger of incommensurability and the crucial work of literature—especially narrative—in bridging the private and the public realm" (Keniston 2008: 9). Schwartz's and Auster's decision to zoom in on "the microscopic space of the family" (Däwes 341) is not to be mistaken for a trivialization of the events, nor is it a mark of withdrawal from historical and political reality (as Gray and Rothberg have argued with specific reference to *The Writing on the Wall*). It is through their respective *petits récits*, in which the authors "break down the national impact into microscopic tales by translocating the political into the personal spheres" (Däwes 2011: 336), that Schwartz and Auster take aim at "the linguistic violence of government narratives" (Keniston 2008: 11) and on how those narratives have not only shaped post-9/11 American public reality but have also redefined private space and made us into "witnesses who see but are unable to feel or act" (Keniston 2008: 9). By highlighting these intricate interconnections between the personal and the public, and the national and the international, Schwartz and Auster do not so much focus their minds upon the events of 9/11 as they draw attention to the individual disorientation of their protagonists. Far from allowing the wider geopolitical canvas to go unacknowledged, however, the two works of fiction incisively comment on and throw that canvas into sharper relief. Apart from evidencing a deep authorial concern with the marked tendency in government communication to level out all incongruence in the 9/11 discourse, the presence of these *petits récits* also attests to the authors' heightened self-awareness and wariness of creating their own *grand récit*.

Notes

1 The term is Dominick LaCapra's (2001: 92).
2 cf. her television interview with Ben Cheever.
3 The quotation as it is attributed to Socrates in Plato's *Phaedo* goes, "You may be sure, dear Crito, [Socrates] said," "that inaccurate language is not only in itself a mistake: it implants evil in men's souls" (Plato 1955: 140).
4 David Cockley sees in Renata's eventual acquiescence "that [people] will have to live against a backdrop of violence while they live out their lives in peace" (Cockley 2009: 25) an indication that the recent national trauma of 9/11 has procured/facilitated an acceptance of, or a coming to terms with, her personal traumas. Birgit Däwes similarly subscribes to Renata's likely recovery, arguing that the mystery teenager is indeed Renata's long-lost niece and that Renata is now "ready for a new beginning" (Däwes 2011: 305). Unlike Cockley and Däwes, we beg to be more skeptical. The elements that for Däwes are reason enough to assume that the girl is really Gianna are circumstantial at best, and might just as easily be part of Renata's wishful thinking than of reality. In the interview with Ben Cheever, Schwartz refers to Renata "making the inner magical leap" to decide that the mute girl is in fact Gianna, but that her assumption is never unequivocally confirmed (McGaffey 2005). Any beneficial outcome is thus jeopardized by Renata's disinclination to fully relinquish the uchronistic fantasy of having recovered her niece.
5 See also Ciocia and González (2011: 4), Simonetti (2011: 15, 21), Varvogli (2011: 41), and Hugonnier (2011: 278), among others.
6 Among others, Katya's selection includes Jean Renoir's *Grand Illusion* (1937), Vittorio De Sica's *The Bicycle Thieves (1948)*, Satyajit Ray's *The World of Apu* (1959), and Yasujirô Ozu's *Tokyo Story* (1953).
7 With the notable exception of the rather naive basic principles that have been laid down for the new Independent States of America as they are described to Owen Brick: "Foreign policy: no meddling anywhere.... Domestic policy: universal health insurance, no more oil, no more cars or planes, a fourfold increase in teachers' salaries (to

attract the brightest students to the profession), strict gun control, free education and job training for the poor" (Auster 2008: 62–63).

8   Auster reveals as much in an interview with Christine Otten published in the book section of the Dutch newspaper *NRC Handelsblad* (2008). See also Alison Flood's interview with Paul Auster's that appeared in *The Guardian* (2008).

9   Brontë and Schwartz both allude to a passage in the Book of Daniel, to "the mob of Astrologers, Chaldeans, and Soothsayers gathered before 'the writing on the wall', and unable to read the characters or make known the interpretation" (Bell 1851: x).

Works cited

Auster, Paul. *Man in the Dark*. London: Faber and Faber, 2009.
Baer, Ulrich, ed. *110 Stories. New York Writes after September 11*. New York: New York University Press, 2002.
Barone, Dennis. "Seductive Notebooks. Paul Auster's 21st-Century Fiction." *Rain Taxi*. Online Edition Fall (2008). http://www.raintaxi.com/seductive-notebooks-paul-austers-21st-century-fiction/.
Bell, Currer. "Biographical Notice of Ellis and Acton Bell." In *Wuthering Heights and Agnes Grey by Ellis and Acton Bell*, edited by Currer Bell, v–xiv. Leipzig: Bernhard Tauchnitz, 1851.
Churchill, Winston. *The Great Republic: A History of America*. London: Cassell & Co, 2002.
Ciocia, Stefania, and Jesús A. González, eds. *The Invention of Illusions: International Perspectives on Paul Auster*. Newcastle upon Tyne: Cambridge Scholars Publishing, 2011.
Cockley, David. "Lynne Sharon Schwartz's *The Writing on the Wall*. Responding to the Media Spectacle." *Studies in American Jewish Literature* 28 (2009): 14–28.
Däwes, Birgit. *Ground Zero Fiction. History, Memory, and Representation in the American 9/11 Novel*. Heidelberg: Universitätsverlag Winter, 2011.
Flood, Alison. "Paul Auster Talks." Interview. *The Guardian*, October 29, 2008, sec. Books.
Gray, Richard. *After the Fall: American Literature since 9/11*. Chichester: Wiley-Blackwell, 2011.
Gray, Richard. "Open Doors, Closed Minds: American Prose Writing at a Time of Crisis." *American Literary History* 21, no. 1 (2009): 128–48.
Herman, Judith. *Trauma and Recovery*. New York: Basic Books, 1997.
Hugonnier, François. "Speaking the Unspeakable: Auster's Semiotic World." In *The Invention of Illusions: International Perspectives on*

Paul Auster, edited by Stefania Ciocia and Jesús A. González, 259–88. Newcastle upon Tyne: Cambridge Scholars Publishing, 2011.

Keniston, Ann, and Jeanne Follansbee Quinn, eds. *Literature after 9/11*. New York: Routledge, 2008.

LaCapra, Dominick. *Writing History, Writing Trauma*. Baltimore, MD: The Johns Hopkins University Press, 2001.

Lakoff, George. "Metaphors of Terror." *The Days After* (2001): 13 http://www.press.uchicago.edu/sites/daysafter/911lakoff.html.

Lynne Sharon Schwartz: The Writing on the Wall. Dir. McGaffey, Shane. Ben Cheever and Marlene Canapi. May 25, 2005.

Lyotard, Jean-François. *The Postmodern Condition: A Report on Knowledge*. Translated by Geoff Bennington and Brian Massumi. Theory and History of Literature. Manchester: Manchester University Press, 1997.

Miller, Nancy K., and Jason Tougaw, eds. *Extremities: Trauma, Testimony, and Community*. Urbana, IL: University of Illinois Press, 2002.

Otten, Christine. "Verhalen Maken De Mens." Interview. *NRC Handelsblad*, June 13, 2008.

Plato. "Phaedo." *Plato's Phaedo*. Edited by R. S. Bluck. London: Routledge, 1955.

Rothberg, Michael. "A Failure of the Imagination: Diagnosing the Post-9/11 Novel: A Response to Richard Gray." *American Literary History* 21, no. 1 (2009): 152–58.

Schwartz, Lynne Sharon. *The Writing on the Wall*. New York: Counterpoint, 2005.

Scurr, Ruth. "Man in the Dark by Paul Auster." Book Review. *The Telegraph*, September 5, 2008.

Simonetti, Paulo. "Loss, Ruins, War: Paul Auster's Response to 9/11 and The 'War on Terror'." In *The Invention of Illusions: International Perspectives on Paul Auster*, edited by Stefania Ciocia and Jesús A. González, 13–38. Newcastle upon Tyne: Cambridge Scholars Publishing, 2011.

Tancke, Ulrike. "Uses and Abuses of Trauma in Post-9/11 Fiction and Contemporary Culture." In *From Solidarity to Schisms. 9/11 and after in Fiction and Film from Outside the US*, edited by Cara Cilano, 75–93. Amsterdam: Rodopi, 2009.

Turrentine, Jeff. "Night Terrors." Book Review. *The Washington Post*, August 31 2008.

Upshaw, Reagan. "Her Self-Contained Life Blown Apart by Sept. 11." *The San Francisco Chronicle*, June 19, 2005: C2.

Varvogli, Aliki. "Paul Auster in the Twenty-First Century." In *The Invention of Illusions: International Perspectives on Paul Auster*, edited by Stefania Ciocia and Jesús A. González, 39–54. Newcastle upon Tyne: Cambridge Scholars Publishing, 2011.

7

"Anticipating the Fall": Art, memory, and historical reclamation in Colum McCann's *Let the Great World Spin*

Hamilton Carroll

The good high-wire walker strives to make his audience forget the dangers, to lure it away from thoughts of death by the beauty of what he does on the wire itself.
~ PAUL AUSTER, "*On the High Wire*" (1995)

Published in the United States in June 2009, Colum McCann's *Let the Great World Spin* was an instant critical success. In the year of its publication, the novel was awarded the National Book Award and, two years later, the prestigious International Dublin Literary Award. Taking its title from the Alfred, Lord Tennyson poem *Locksley Hall* (1835), *Let the Great World Spin* uses a series of ten interconnected narratives to construct an intimate history of New York at a very particular moment in time: early August, 1974. While the novel is focused very specifically on its time and place, it also makes a series of spatial and temporal shifts, most often in flashback and through the memories of its central protagonists, through which it both charts a longer history and brings the reader to the near present (in a final section set in 2006). The central event of the novel, which is drawn from real life, takes place on August 7, 1974 when French tightrope artist Philippe Petit joined the north and south towers of the as-yet-unfinished World Trade Center (WTC) with a steel cable and walked between them. Petit's spectacular act serves as the central spine of the novel—both structurally and thematically—and is the core around which its disparate narratives interconnect. The novel uses the intersection of Petit's wire walk and the lives of its central characters to examine a number of interconnected themes: the relationship between art and crime, between personal loss and national memory, history and its relationship to the event, and, finally, the recuperative capacities of art and literature.

McCann's novel further explores questions of cultural memory through a process of omission. For the novel does not mention the events of September 11, 2001 until its final chapter, set in 2006, when it links Philippe Petit's "small scrap of history" to the "larger one" of the as-yet-unnamed terrorist attacks of September 11 (McCann 2009: 325). This glancing mention is the novel's only reference to September 11, which never explicitly appears in its pages. As such, while that event is essential to the novel, it stands outside of it, annexed beyond the page. The destruction of the WTC in 2001 is held apart in the novel, caught between a past (1974) that appears to fully anticipate it and a future (2006), in which it has already been overshadowed by the US-led ground wars in Afghanistan and Iraq (both of which are named in the novel's final section).[1] Nevertheless, the attack on the WTC occupies a central place in McCann's novel and is the event through which—and toward which—its multiple narratives must travel.[2] Therefore, while *Let the Great World Spin* is not a novel *about* September 11, it is undoubtedly a novel *of* September 11, and it is that relationship I shall examine in this chapter, paying particular attention to the themes outlined above and to the novel's representations of the visual arts and performance. I argue that it is through its representations of art that the novel makes its most important interventions in the literary representations of the events of September 11, 2001 and their aftermath. Through its representations of wire walking, photography, painting, and literature, *Let the Great World Spin* meditates on the capacity of art to confront death.

"The art is the thing itself": Performance and death

The novel represents Philippe Petit's wire walk between the north and south towers of the unfinished WTC in two primary ways. First, in three short intersections, none more than eight pages in length, which bookend and divide the first two of the novel's four sections (which are called books); second, as a subject of discussion and of thought for a number of the novel's main characters. Each of the novel's primary fictional protagonists is affected by Petit's wire walk in some way and a number of them are brought together by the event. In the three intersections, which are told in the third person, Petit is the primary protagonist. He is never named in the novel, however, and is referred to as "he" throughout. The first intersection, which opens the novel, describes the moments leading up to the instance when Petit steps onto the wire at the beginning of his performance on the morning of August 7, 1974. It is narrated in the third person from the perspective of the crowd of onlookers who witness the event first hand. The second intersection divides the novel's first and second books and appears almost at the exact center of the novel. It describes Petit training for the walk and ends, like the first, at the moment when he steps out onto the wire. The third and final intersection, which comes at the end of the second book, describes Petit's life in New York before the walk and then gives the fullest description of the walk itself, concluding with its culmination as Petit is taken away from the scene in a police car. In their entirety, the three intersections (which total slightly fewer than twenty pages) give a relatively full account of Petit's wire walk, its preparation and planning, and present Petit himself to the reader as a fully fleshed out character with his own motivations and desires. As such, Petit's wire walk is more than just the node through which all of the other characters in the novel intersect; it is foundational to the novel's meaning and is the source of many of its thematic preoccupations: art and death, spectacle and war, and humanity and memory.

The three intersections provide the reader with a fictionalized recreation of Petit's wire walk. It is, though, a selective and partial account. There is no mention of any of the numerous accomplices who worked with Petit to stage the event, nor is there any attention paid to the collective nature of the endeavor. It is presented as a solo venture with Petit as its mastermind and only protagonist. As such, the novel's focus is on the nature of the act itself, on the virtuosity and artistry of the wire walk.[3] McCann devotes considerable attention to Petit's skills as a funambulist and a conjurer. His beguiling sleight of hand is described on a number of occasions and he is seen as an artist. What is placed on display in the novel is Petit's capacity for self-belief in the face of danger. If, as Paul Auster contends, "the good high-wire walker strives to make his audience forget the dangers, to lure it away from thoughts of death by the beauty of what he does on the wire itself," the power of this forgetting only exists because of the power of what is forgotten. As Auster further states, the act of high-wire walking presents to the audience "a life in its most naked delineation." This "naked delineation," however, is produced precisely because of the proximity to death and gains its power from it. "The art," Auster suggests, "is the thing itself." By this, he means that the raw reality of the proximity of the artist to death is so apparent that it "requires no explanation"; its meaning is there for all to see (Auster 1995: 91–92). If this is the case, Petit's wire walk is a work of art with no reference outside of itself; it is both unmediated and unmediating, speaking to nothing beside itself. And, in McCann's novel, Petit's performance is always represented in relationship to death and forms a significant part of the novel's meaning-making apparatus.

In addition to its representation in the novel's intersections, Petit's wire walk also appears within the bodies of the majority of the novel's ten primary chapters. Its first appearance comes in the second chapter of Book One, during a coffee morning hosted by Claire Soderberg, a wealthy Manhattanite whose son has been killed in the Vietnam War. The group of women that Claire is hosting in her Park Avenue apartment are all mothers of young men who have died in Vietnam. One of the women, Marcia, arrives at Claire's apartment flushed with excitement having just witnessed Petit's wire walk from the deck of the Staten Island ferry. Petit's walk is a subject of conversation throughout the course of the morning and is a repeated topic of thought for Claire. As such, it makes up the majority of the subject matter for this section of the novel, where it is repeatedly addressed in relation to the Vietnam War and the needless deaths of these women's young sons.

The inherent danger of the act that the crowd watches Petit perform on that August morning is thematized almost from the very beginning of McCann's novel and the subject of death is a constant theme. There is, in the first instance, a thematization of the fact that the spectacular nature of Petit's wire walk lies almost entirely in its inherent danger, what Auster calls its "naked delineation." In the novel's opening pages, the crowds watching the figure standing at the top of the south tower are caught in an anticipatory state, many of them waiting to witness death:

> None of them had yet made sense of the line strung at his feet from one tower to the other. Rather, it was the man-shape that held them there, their necks craned, torn between the promise of doom and the disappointment of the ordinary.
>
> It was the dilemma of the watchers: they did not want to wait around for nothing at all, some idiot standing on the precipice of the towers, but they didn't want to miss the moment either, if he slipped, or got arrested, or dove, arms stretched. (McCann 2009: 3)

What brings the watchers, who become a group as the event unfolds, together is the anticipation of something out of the ordinary, triumph or tragedy, either of which would suffice. The potential for death is made concrete twice in the opening pages through the use of two symbolic portents. In the first instance, the crowd watches as "a single pigeon swooped down from the top floor of the Federal Office Building, as if anticipating the fall" (McCann 2009: 5). In the second, a few pages later, the crowd's desire for spectacle is seemingly fulfilled as a sweatshirt accidentally dropped by Petit is mistaken for a falling body:

> Way above there was a movement. In the dark clothing his every twitch counted. He folded over, a half-thing, bent, as if examining his shoes, a pencil mark, most of which had been erased. The posture of a diver. And then they saw it. The watchers stood, silent. Even those who had wanted the man to jump felt the air knocked out. They drew back and moaned.

> A body was sailing out into the middle of the air.
> He was gone. He'd done it. Some blessed themselves. Closed their eyes. Waited for the thump. The body twirled and caught and flipped, thrown around by the wind.
> Then a shout sounded across the watchers, a woman's voice: God oh God, it's a shirt, it's just a shirt. (McCann 2009: 7)

It is at this moment that Petit steps out from the edge of the building and begins his spectacular walk, only for the narrative to be interrupted, put on hold for another ninety pages when it returns within one of the novel's main narrative sections (discussed above) and then, another fifty pages later, in the second of the novel's three intersections. By twice halting the narrative at the moment when Petit steps out onto the wire, McCann both elevates the act—by keeping the reader in a heightened state of expectation—and places it in an altered temporal state, always imminent, never quite fulfilled.[4] This doubled move gives these descriptions a powerful narrative force by reorienting the event in its relationship to the other strands of the novel's plot.

What the representation of Petit's walk does in the novel—as it does, albeit in different ways, in each of the post-9/11 texts in which it appears—is transform the potential for death into the possibility of life.[5] The gray pigeon and the black sweatshirt both serve as premonitions, reminders of what the final outcome of Petit's actions might be: a spectacular fall followed by a moment of death. What is actually produced is a moment of affirmation. The ultimate power of the performance lies in Petit's ability to move so far beyond the limits of danger that the event becomes transcendent, an act so superhuman that it humanizes. He did not merely cross the wire once, he spent almost thirty minutes on it, repeatedly crossing and re-crossing the span between the two towers, at times lying down and even running. "Dancing," as one of the policemen who witnessed the feat from the top of the south tower put it. The experience of watching a good wire walk, Auster contends, "reduces us all to our common humanity" (Auster 1995: 97). Its ultimate power, then, lies in the singular ability of an extraordinarily talented individual to bring a group of strangers together. In McCann's novel, Petit's singular act creates a community of watchers bound together by the act of witnessing. No longer a disparate group of individuals, journeying through the morning rush hour, but a crowd, an audience, a community; a multitude become singular, just as the two towers had become one. The crowd, hoping to see something spectacular and outside of the everyday, are rewarded with a feat of human endeavor that affirms life precisely because of its proximity to death. In *Let the Great World Spin*, art affirms life by allowing us to see beyond death. And this, on the most basic level, is what McCann's novel likewise aims to do: bring together a disparate group of people in their common humanity, witnesses all to a spectacular and life-affirming event.

"One small scrap of history": Photography and the fall

While the novel celebrates Petit's accomplishment in its own right, it also positions it as a portent of the ultimate fate of the twin towers some thirty years later, thereby yoking it to another spectacular act, the meaning of which lies in its relationship to death. In the first chapter of the novel's second book, entitled "Tag," a young would-be street photographer, Fernando, has been riding the gap between two subway cars on his way to work downtown. Hoping to capture some underground tagging on film, Fernando sees a group of cops running down along the platform of a downtown subway station. "Someone's gone and bought it" (McCann 2009: 174), he thinks at first but context allows the reader to realize that the policemen are heading above ground toward the WTC and Philippe Petit. The section ends a paragraph later with Fernando, camera in hand, following the cops in order to see what the commotion is all about. Some sixty pages later, inserted between the end of the second book and the final intersection on Petit, is a photograph of Petit walking across the wire (McCann 2009: 237). The photograph resonates powerfully because it depicts not only Petit but also, in its upper-left-hand corner, a small commercial airliner, which, as it is put later on in the novel, seems to be disappearing "into the edge of the building" (McCann 2009: 325). The building is, of course, the south tower of the WTC into which, thirty years later, another airplane actually would "disappear." While the photograph used here is a real-world artifact that was taken by the photographer Vic DeLuca, it is credited in the novel to the fictional character, Fernando (in the form of a copyright attribution given below the reproduction of the photograph). One of only a relatively small number of photographs that remain of Petit's walk, the image not only offers a visual record of Petit's feat but also conjures the specter of September 11 that haunts the novel.[6] The photograph is doubly interesting then in that, while it is a real-world artifact inserted into the novel, it is credited to a fictional character. As such, it brings the real world into the fictional realm of the novel in a striking and powerful way. But if that is what it does, the question remains as to why; what does the inclusion of this actual photograph do here? What does the visual record allow that the linguistic does not?[7]

A first answer to these questions lies in the perceived failure of language to properly or accurately record or portray the events of September 11. In the immediate aftermath of the attacks, a whole host of writers called into question the capacity of words, and of literary fiction more specifically, to do justice to such an overwhelmingly visual and spectacular event. Don DeLillo, for example, famously claimed "the event itself has no purchase on the mercies of analogy or simile" (DeLillo 2001: 39). Writing in a similar vein, Richard Powers stated, "There are no words. But there are only words." "No comparison can say what happened to us," he continues, "but we can start with the ruins of our similes, and let 'like' move us toward something larger, some understanding of what 'is'" (Powers 2001: 23). Jay McInerney suggested that "for a while, quite a while, fiction did seem inadequate to the moment." Despite this inadequacy, McInerney believes that "we desperately want to have a novelist ... process the experience for us" (McInerney 2005: 4). Like DeLillo, who finds the writer "desperate" (DeLillo 2001: 39), Powers and McInerney see a necessity in fiction that is coupled to a seeming inadequacy: we have what we have, we need it, but it is not enough.

There is, in such claims, a question of sufficiency. It is in such concerns that novels like McCann's find themselves and that explain, in part, the turn to the visual record that is so common in post-9/11 fiction. As an ostensibly unimpeachable representation of the real, the photograph shores up linguistic description. In McCann's novel, however, the facticity of the photograph is troubled by its direct attribution to a fictional character. The significance of this blurring of the photograph's representational limits is highlighted by McCann's decision not to represent Fernando either witnessing or taking photographs of Petit but to make that fact apparent to the reader sixty pages after Fernando is presented as a character within the narrative, and only through the inclusion of the photograph. It is important, moreover, that the photograph is placed outside the narrative, interstitially, and sandwiched between the end of one of the novel's books and another—itself interstitial—section (Petit's narrative), only to be described in the narrative proper some ninety pages later. The photograph is attributed to a character but has not yet appeared as a described object in the body of the novel; while it is itself a representational object, it is not yet an object of representation. As such, it floats free, not yet moored definitively to either its textual or paratextual references.

When the photograph does appear in the narrative itself, it is as a possession—a photograph owned by another character. In its representation in the final section of the novel, the photograph is no longer merely a visual representation of a historical event but has become a family heirloom and a nostalgic reminder of a prior time. As such, the photograph ties together the novel's twinned concerns with national memory and personal loss, yet remains neither entirely fact nor fiction. It inhabits, moreover, an equally uncertain temporality. When reproduced as a photograph, it is unmoored from any direct referentiality. The reader is given no context for it and, as such, has no way of positioning it in time. Does it refer to the chapter about Fernando? Or foreshadow the intersection about Petit that follows it? Is it a pictorial representation of the copy of the photograph that appears as an object at the end of the novel? None of this is entirely clear; the photograph is all of these things and none of them at the same time. That the photograph also references the events of September 11 only strengthens its power. It is a temporally unstable object with multiple reference points, not all of them are available to the reader at the place in which it is included in the novel.

As such, it is also important that the description of the photograph that opens the final chapter of the novel, which is set in 2006, places Petit in the present tense. "She often wonders what it is that holds the man so high in the air" (McCann 2009: 325), the chapter begins. The "she" in this sentence is Jaslyn Henderson, the daughter of one of the novel's other characters, an African-American prostitute who dies in a car accident on the day of Petit's wire walk. Raised with her sister by Gloria (one of the grieving Vietnam mothers and the protagonist of the novel's penultimate section), Jaslyn attended college at Yale and now works for a small foundation that provides tax preparation assistance for people displaced by hurricanes Katrina and Rita. When the photograph enters the narrative at this point, it is as a personal possession, found by Jaslyn at a San Francisco garage sale some years before and kept as a reminder of her mother. There is an important progression to be charted here: from fictional photographer to reproduced photograph (attributed to the fictional photographer) to representation of that photograph within the novel's narrative. The photograph is not attributed to Fernando here and, as such, its fictional taker—or his real counterpart, for that matter—drops away, and it is the photograph itself that becomes important.[8] Moreover, the photograph reminds Jaslyn of her mother despite the fact that it is a representation of an event related to her death only by the coincidence of time. For Jaslyn, the photograph is a representation of a thing that it does not represent. But, as I have already suggested, it is also this for the events of September 11, 2001 and, as such, the photograph is a referential object for an event that does not take place until a quarter of a century after it was taken.

While it is presented in these pages as a personal memento, the photograph provides the only direct—albeit oblique—link made in the novel between August 7, 1974 and September 11, 2001. It is in the representation of Jaslyn's thoughts about the photograph that the relationship between the novel's multiple and intertwined storylines and the events of September 11 are made clear:

> A man high in the air while a plane disappears, it seems, into the edge of the building. One small scrap of history meeting a larger one. As if the walking man were somehow anticipating what would come later. The intrusion of time and history. The collision point of stories. We wait for the explosion but it never occurs. The plane passes, the tightrope walker gets to the end of the wire. Things don't fall apart.
>
> It strikes her as an enduring moment, the man alone against scale, still capable of myth in the face of all other evidence. (McCann 2009: 325–26)

These sentences provide both a description of the photograph and an interpretation of it. The language is explicitly interpretative—"it seems," "as if"—and Jaslyn is the provider of these interpretations. This description, moreover, links history to the act of storytelling. As a "myth," Petit's wire walk substitutes for the act of terror, perpetrated almost thirty years later, that was the direct reason for the novel's creation. In the photograph, as he does in the novel, Petit inhabits the present tense. He is, like the photograph, a prophylactic against the fall. Holding the towers together, he also holds them up, still there and made new again; offered at the moment of their creation in order to memorialize the moment of their destruction. As a "small scrap of history," both Petit's walk and the photograph open up the WTC to the possibility not only of what McCann calls here "myth" but also of the transcendent possibilities of referentiality. Art precedes the fall.

"That moment of purity": Painting and catastrophe

If Petit's wire walk and its photographic representations are represented in the novel in relation to death and the possibilities of life, *Let the Great World Spin* is also concerned with the relationship between painting and catastrophe. This relationship is represented most fully in the chapter of the novel devoted to the story of Lara Liveman, a young artist and her husband, Blaine. Entitled "A Fear of Love" and told in the first person, the section provides a valuable discourse on the relationship between art and catastrophe that is so central to the novel. In an attempt not only to capture "the pulse of the trees . . ., the journey of grass, some dirt" (McCann 2009: 126) but also to kick their drug habits, the couple flee New York City and relocate to the countryside and attempt to live in the manner of the 1930s. In their turn away from the city, the focus on the urban that had marked their earlier art (and Blaine's short films in particular) is replaced by an attention to the natural world. A successful *avant-garde* filmmaker, Blaine "had decided it was time to go back to canvas, to paint in the style of Thomas Benton, or John Steuart Curry. He wanted that moment of purity, regionalism" (McCann 2009: 126). But it is also a turn away from the contemporary toward the past, a reactionary turn intended as a rejection of the postmodern in art and the sociopolitical upheavals of the Vietnam War and the

Watergate scandal that surround the young couple (but from which they keep a well-studied distance). The turn toward nature is a turn toward the past. It is a nostalgic turn and, as such, a retreat. But it is also a failure. Not only do Lara and Blaine return to the city, hoping to sell their new art (something that they fail to do), but they are also directly responsible for the car crash that kills John Corrigan and Jazzlyn Henderson, the two characters that are the primary subjects of the novel's first chapter. As the couple retreat in defeat from the city, still high from the drugs they consumed the night before, Blaine sideswipes Corrigan's van, forcing it off the road and into a fatal spin. The couple flee the scene and return to their upstate cabin. It is at this point that the relationship between art and catastrophe is represented in two interrelated ways.

In the first instance, Lara (who has fled the house seeking an escape both from Blaine and her own feelings of guilt) finds herself looking at an account of Petit's wire walk in the previous morning's newspaper. Reading in the account of the event Petit's claim that "if he saw oranges he wanted to juggle them, if he saw skyscrapers he wanted to walk between them," Lara "wondered what he might do if he walked into the diner and found the scattered pieces of me, lying around, too many of them to juggle" (McCann 2009: 131). In the second instance, the rain ruins the paintings that Lara and Blaine produced in the regionalist style of Benton and Curry when the couple accidentally leave them outside upon their return from the city. Rather than the catastrophe that Lara sees, Blaine sees in the ruined paintings a new form of art, what he calls a "comment on time" (McCann 2009: 133). "What happens," he asks Lara, "if we make a series of paintings and we leave them out in the weather?" (McCann 2009: 134). He answers his own question, enlivened by the possibilities:

> We allow the present to work on the past. We could do something radical here. Do the formal paintings in the style of the past and have the present destroy them. You let the weather become the imaginative force. The real world works on your art. So you give it a new ending. And then you reinterpret it. It's perfect, dig? (McCann 2009: 134)

There is a doubled relationship being represented here: between two artistic styles, on the one hand, and between different temporal moments, on the other. It is the transformative nature of time that is of most significance here. If you give something a different ending, Blaine says, it becomes new (McCann 2009: 132). And McCann's novel is itself a reworking of a prior artistic moment—a relationship between the past, present, and future in which the present works on the past, transforming it. But that is also what the terrorist attacks of September 11, 2001 did to Petit's wire walk in 1974: they gave it a new ending, transformed it, and reimagined it. After September 11, Petit's walk becomes something new entirely. If art represents the world, it is also transformed by it, gaining in the fullness of time meaning that the artist could never anticipate.

The relationship between art and the world that features so strongly in the novel's representation of the visual arts is also a prominent feature of its representations of Petit. In one example, which is discussed twice in the novel, the effect of the newly built WTC towers on the migratory patterns of birds is described. These moments are worth quoting in full because they are an important part of the novel's meaning-making apparatus, serving, as they do, to bring together a number of its central concerns. In the first instance, Claire ruminates on the negative effect that Marcia's description of Petit's walk has on her:

> This walking man, she can't shake him. The bubble of discontent in her mind. She is being ungenerous, she knows, but she just can't get rid of it. What if he hits somebody down below? She has heard that at night there are whole colonies of birds that fly into the WTC buildings, their glass reflection. The bash and fall. Will the walker thump with them?
> Snap to. Enough.
> Pull your mind together. Pick up all the feathers. Guide them gently back into the air. (McCann 2009: 105–06)

For Claire, Petit has placed not only himself in danger but also anyone below him. The walk is, therefore, an immoral act and one of reckless endangerment. Moreover, linking Petit's walk to the catastrophic effect the towers have on migratory birds raises the issue of unforeseen (or disregarded) consequences. Petit is making art but his actions also carry with them the possibility of danger; the WTC is advancing humankind but is also transforming the natural environment in unforeseen ways. But there is also a crucial relationship being drawn here between Petit's actions and Claire's mental state. She is "ungenerous" because she wishes to talk that morning about her dead son and not about Petit, who has so recklessly placed his own life in danger while the sons of Claire and the other women have been killed in Vietnam. His story has intruded into her son's, displacing it. For Claire to "pick up all the feathers" she will need to learn how to see things differently, to see the value in what Petit has done and not the risk. Petit's act serves as a spur to Claire's overcoming grief; as such, it is redemptive.

In the second instance in which the plight of migratory birds is discussed, it is Petit himself who is given cause to think about the relationship between the birds and his own actions:

> He was checking the perimeter of the south tower one dawn, marking out the schedules of delivery trucks, when he saw a woman in a green jumpsuit, bent down as if tying her shoelaces, over and over again, around the base of the towers. Little bursts of feathers came from the woman's hands. She was putting the dead birds in little ziploc bags. White-throated sparrows mostly, some songbirds too. They migrated late at night, when the air currents were calmest. Dazzled by the building lights, they crashed into the glass, or flew endlessly around the towers until exhaustion got them, their natural navigational abilities stunned. She handed him a feather from a black-throated warbler, and when he left the city again he brought it to the meadow and tacked that too just inside the cabin wall. Another reminder. (McCann 2009: 162)

As with Claire's ruminations, there is a clear link being drawn here between Petit's wire walk, death, and the unanticipated. For Petit, the black feather also serves as a reminder of the danger that he faces, that death—his own—is one possible outcome of his actions. For the reader, who is encountering the story of the birds for the second time, a strong link is being formed between the WTC towers and death—one that encompasses but also transcends Petit's actions. From the very beginning, these descriptions suggest, the WTC was a site of death and, no matter how small or inconsequential, there were always lives lost at the site. After September 11, of course, the image of flying objects colliding with the WTC takes on an entirely different resonance and, as with Vic DeLuca's photograph, this imagery provides a strong foreshadowing of what is to come, in world history if not in the novel. At the same time, the image of dead birds falling to the plaza below, what Claire thinks of as the "bash and fall," also evokes the memory of bodies falling from the towers on September 11. As such, and much like the description of the gray pigeon and the falling sweatshirt discussed earlier, it serves a mnemonic function, calling to mind that which has displaced it in the cultural imaginary of the United States. Petit's wire walk on August 7, 1974 is an example of the phenomenon of the "real world work[ing] on . . . art" that inspires Blaine; however, in this instance, it is not the natural progression of time and the elements but an act of terrorism that transforms the meaning of the work of art. But if Petit's performance is transformed by the act of terrorism that it so uncannily anticipates, that act is itself transformed for the relationship cuts in both directions. And it is in this doubling that the power of McCann's reclamation of Petit lies.

"An act of grace": Literature and redemption

If *Let the Great World Spin* devotes a great deal of attention to the visual and performing arts, it is also a deeply literary novel, concerned with the capacity of literature both to transcend and to make meaning of the "real world." Not only does the novel draw its title (and those of its interstitial sections and one of its chapters) from Tennyson's poem *Locksley Hall*, but also its pages are rife with quotations, paraphrases, and allusions from and to a plethora of literary works, from Shakespeare to Philip Larkin. Like the visual arts that I have already discussed, literature is understood in the novel to have recuperative properties. The novel's repeated allusions to Tennyson's poem are without a doubt its most direct engagement with the question of the West's relationship to Islam, which might contextualize the events of September 11. However, in the poem—as in the novel—this relationship is not explored in much depth, if at all. The poem provides the titles of the novel and two of the three intersections devoted to Philippe Petit, "*Let the Great World Spin Forever Down*" and "*The Ringing Grooves of Change*" (the first intersection is entitled "*Those Who Saw Him Hushed*," which is also the novel's first line). It also provides the title for the novel's final chapter, "*Roaring Seaward, and I Go.*" With the exception of the last, these titles both are taken from a single line in Tennyson's poem, "Let the great world spin for ever down the ringing grooves of change" (Tennyson 2006: 192). As such, it would be prudent not to make too much of them. However, they do suggest—as does the poem more broadly—themes that are central to the novel, most particularly the relationship between history and personal memory.

Consisting of ninety-seven rhyming couplets, "Locksley Hall" is a first-person account in which a young soldier traveling with a group of comrades is given the opportunity to reflect on his life when the men pass nearby Locksley Hall, the place where he spent part of his childhood. Born in "the Orient," the young man (who claims not to have known his mother) was orphaned as a boy after his father was killed in a battle. Taken in by his "selfish uncle," the youth falls in love with his cousin, Amy. Rebuffed, he escapes by joining the army. The poem describes the experiences of childhood and youth from the perspective of increased, if still youthful, experience. Railing against the travails of his young life, the protagonist fantasizes about returning to the "Orient" and fathering a new race of "iron-jointed" and "supple-sinewed" sons. By the poem's end, however, he has retreated from this dream and is content to side with the progress of European civilization over the atavistic paradise of the East. It is at this point that the line from which McCann's novel gets its title appears, followed by the lines, "Thro" the shadow of the globe we sweep into the younger day;/"Better fifty years of Europe than one cycle of Cathay" (Tennyson 2006: 192). These lines offer a standard, racist narrative that positions the West—enlightened, rational, and progressive—against the East, which is trapped in a childlike state of savagery. In the closing lines of the poem, the speaker finds himself able to move on with his life, having cast off the shadows of his past and imagines a thunderbolt striking Locksley Hall as he turns and walks away from it. Aside from the one or two slight thematic similarities, there is little in the poem's content to connect it with McCann's novel. McCann, himself, has stated:

> I had some difficulties finding the title, but then I came across the Tennyson quote: "Let the great world spin forever down the ringing grooves of change . . . ." And, as luck would have it,

Tennyson had been influenced by a series of sixth century pre-Islamic poems, the Mu'allaqat, which asks the question: "Is there any hope that this desolation can bring me solace?" And when I found that line, my heart skipped a beat or three, because it was exactly what I wanted. (Johnston 2009: n. pag.)

This description of McCann's reaction to finding the title for the novel suggests the novelist's desire to eradicate boundaries such as those drawn in Tennyson's poem. While the "desolation" contained in Tennyson's poem is related to the bitter experiences of one man's youth, the novel seeks to bind together a multitude of experiences, and thereby produce solace, what McCann calls, here and elsewhere, "grace." Elsewhere in the same interview, McCann states,

The book comes down to a very anonymous moment in the Bronx when two little kids are coming out of a very rough housing project, about to be taken away by the state, and they get rescued by an act of grace. That's it, not much maybe, but everything to me. And there's hardly a line in the novel about 9/11, but it's everywhere if the reader wants it to be. (Johnston 2009: n. pag.)

This "act of grace" is the decision of Gloria, one of the Vietnam mothers, to adopt Jaslyn and her sister. While the novel does not make it explicit, it does suggest that Claire—who is with Gloria when she sees the young girls being led away by social workers and decides to intervene—provides financial support throughout the girls' childhoods (and may, in fact, have funded Jaslyn's studies at Yale). In any case, she is certainly bonded with Gloria at this moment and is a significant figure in the girls' childhoods, coming to visit "in a chauffeured town car" (McCann 2009: 330). During one of these visits, Claire watches Jaslyn "run along with one foot on the pavement and the other on the road." "It took some gymnastics," McCann tells the reader, "she had to extend one leg and keep the other slightly bent, running at close to full pace." This image is then used to describe the relationship between Claire and Gloria, two women from strikingly different backgrounds who have joined together not only in their grief for their lost sons but also in the recuperative act of rescuing the girls from the state. "They looked so different, Claire in her neat skirt, Gloria in her flowered dress, as if they too were running on different levels of pavement, but in the same body, the two of them combined" (McCann 2009: 330). It is in this doubled description—Jaslyn as gymnast, Claire and Gloria as one—that the novel finds its "act of grace" and connects Petit's wire walk in 1974 to the post-9/11 world of 2006.

It is this idea of grace and community that is most important for McCann's novel, its capacity to affirm life in the face of death. As a series of ten interconnected narratives, each told from the perspective of a different character, *Let the Great World Spin* is most especially concerned with finding the thread that connects the disparate lives of each of its principal protagonists. It finds that connection in Petit's wire walk. Vastly different in their life experiences and expectations, social and economic fortunes, and racial and ethnic subjectivities, each of the novel's central characters is brought into contact with the others through Petit's wire walk. It is the central spine through which the tissue of each individual life is connected to each of the others. The novel is itself, then, a narrative actualization of the wire walk itself: a bringing together of different lives in order to assert their common humanity, an attempt to find grace in discord, the solace to be found in desolation. And it is in art—the performance, the photograph, the painting, and the novel alike—that *Let the Great World Spin* finds that ability. In spite of the misery and death contained within its pages—and the horrific central event it need not name—the novel is an attempt to move the reader away from the anticipation of the fall and toward the celebration of life.

Notes

1 The novel's references to the ground wars in Afghanistan and Iraq begin with a somewhat general reference to a "small mobile clinic set up for veterans home from the wars" (McCann 2009: 328) and then become more explicit, with references made to "another six dead in Iraq" (McCann 2009: 340), "the attacks on Afghanistan" (McCann 2009: 341), "a jet coming in with dead bodies from the Middle East" (McCann 2009: 341), and "the embassy in Baghdad" (McCann 2009: 343).
2 In this regard, it is important to note that in McCann's novel the simultaneous attack on the Pentagon and the hijacking and crash of

United 93 have—as they do in the broader public memory and most other fictional accounts—dropped out of the picture. The spectacular nature of the attack on the World Trade Center, and the extraordinary visual archive we have of "the most photographed day in history" (Tom Junod, "The Falling Man," *Esquire*, September 2003), have ensured that the World Trade Center and September 11 are synonymous for many people.

3 In its focus on Petit as a solo artist, McCann's novel tells a very different story than the one told by James Marsh's documentary *Man on Wire* (2008), which very explicitly casts the event as a heist. For more on Marsh's film, see my "September 11 as Heist," in the *Journal of American Studies* 45, no. 4 (2011): 835–51.

4 In *Falling Man* (2007), Don DeLillo similarly splits the events of September 11 by bookending his novel with a description of the collapse of the Twin Towers, thereby creating what he calls in the novel a "state of abeyance" into which he inserts his narrative (DeLillo 2007: 4). On DeLillo's novel and representation, see my "'Like Nothing in this Life'": September 11th and the Limits of Representation in Don DeLillo's *Falling Man*', *Studies in American Fiction* 40, no. 1 (Spring 2013): 107–30.

5 While never entirely forgotten, Petit's wire walk certainly gained a renewed significance in the aftermath of September 11th and was the subject of a variety of other cultural texts. Petit's own account of the walk, *To Reach the Clouds* was published in 2003. Mordicai Gerstein's Caldecott Medal winning children's story, *The Man Who Walked Between the Towers*, also was published in 2003. James Marsh's documentary, *Man on Wire*, mentioned above, was released in 2008. Finally, at the time of writing, Robert Zemeckis's fictional account of Petit's wire walk, starring Joseph Gordon-Levitt as Petit and entitled *The Walk*, was due for release in October 2015.

6 Petit's own account of the event, *To Reach the Clouds*, contains a relatively wide range of photographs and other documents. There is no film footage of Petit's walk. While film was planned, in the excitement of the day the accomplice who was supposed to operate the camera forgot and the only visual record exists in the form of still photographs. See Philippe Petit, *To Reach the Clouds*. London: Faber and Faber, 2003.

7 In order to answer these questions, it is important to note that McCann is not the only author to insert photography into the pages of a post-9/11 novel. Perhaps most famously, Jonathan Safran Foer's *Extremely Loud and Incredibly Close* (2005) includes a number of photographs of bodies falling from the World Trade Center

in its pages and, at its end, a "flip book" constructed through the manipulation of an image of a falling body. While it does not include any actual images, Don DeLillo's *Falling Man* (2007) does give an extended description of perhaps the most famous photograph taken on September 11, Richard Drew's "the falling man" (from which the novel gets its title).

8 There is, of course, a question here about whether or not the reader recognizes that Fernando is given a copyright attribution here, and about what difference that makes to the photograph's meaning.

Works cited

Auster, Paul. "On the High Wire." In *The Red Notebook*, 88–98. London: Faber and Faber, 1995.
Carroll, Hamilton. "'Like Nothing in this Life': September 11 and the Limits of Representation in Don DeLillo's *Falling Man*." *Studies in American Fiction* 40, no.1 (Spring 2013): 107–30.
Carroll, Hamilton. "September 11 as Heist." *Journal of American Studies* 45, no. 4 (2011): 835–51.
DeLillo, Don. *Falling Man*. London: Picador, 2007.
DeLillo, Don. "In the Ruins of the Future." *Harper's* (December 2001): 33–40.
Foer, Jonathan Safran. *Extremely Loud and Incredibly Close*. London: Penguin, 2005.
Johnston, Brett Anthony. "Interview with Colum McCann." Available online: http://www.nationalbook.org/nba2009_f_mccann_interv.html.
McCann, Colum. *Let the Great World Spin*. London: Bloomsbury, 2009.
McInerney, Jay. "The Uses of Invention." *The Guardian*, September 17, 2005. Available online: http://www.theguardian.com/books/2005/sep/17/fiction.vsnaipaul.
Petit, Philippe. *To Reach the Clouds*. London: Faber and Faber, 2003.
Powers, Richard. "The Way We Live Now: 9–23-01: Close Reading: Elements of Tragedy; The Simile." *The New York Times*, September 23, 2001. Available online: http://www.nytimes.com/2001/09/23/magazine/the-way-we-live-now-9-23-01-close-reading-elements-of-tragedy-the-simile.html.
Tennyson, Alfred Lord. "Locksley Hall." In *Tennyson: A Selected Edition*, edited by Christopher Ricks, 183–93. London: Pearson Education, 2006.

8

Jonathan Franzen's *Freedom* and "the great national tragedy"

Paul Jenner

How might we understand Jonathan Franzen's *Freedom* (2010) as a post-9/11 novel, in a substantive rather than a trivially chronological sense? Although it does not focus on the terrorist attacks directly, *Freedom* does explore the aftermath of "the great national tragedy" (Franzen 2010: 28) of 9/11, as it intersects with the attempts of its characters to, in one of the novel's refrains, figure out how to live. Considerable discursive attention is given to the national mood and social ontology of Bush-era America; of the "Siamese-twin fundamentalisms of Bush and bin Laden" the novel's emphasis is very much upon the Bush administration's "years of high-tech lying and manipulation" (Franzen 2010: 332–33). *Freedom* implies that, as Franzen puts the matter elsewhere, "the worse damage to the country was being done not by the pathogen but by the immune system's massive overresponse to it" (Franzen 2012: 152), or by what one of the novel's characters refers to as "Bush II, the worst regime of all" (Franzen 2010: 205).

For Joey Berglund, young Republican-leaning son of Walter, the immediate effect of 9/11 is to induce an uncharacteristically "clueless" act (Franzen 2010: 248). In his second week at university,

Joey leaves his roommate Jonathan watching news coverage of the terrorist attacks on television and rushes to an economics lecture—only to find, unsurprisingly, a near empty lecture hall. If this misjudgment awakens in Joey the sense that "a really serious glitch had occurred," the glitch involves his own personal narrative as much as any broader narrative of national identity, interrupting as it does numerous exceptionalist assurances heretofore that "his life was destined to be a lucky one" (Franzen 2010: 247). This clueless act prepares the ground for "his intensely *personal* resentment of the terrorist attacks," engendering a sense of anger whose "specific object refused to come into focus": not quite bin Laden, but instead "something deeper, something not political, something structurally malicious, like a bump in a sidewalk that trips you on your face when you're innocently out walking" (Franzen 2010: 248).

The difficulty of bringing political concerns "into focus" experientially, their inseparability from personal concerns that are no less easy to focus, and no less bumpy, becomes a key preoccupation of the novel. Clashing with his liberal leftist father Walter, for instance, Joey finds himself "experiencing a hurt that felt structural, as if he and his dad had each chosen their politics for the sole purpose of hating the other" (Franzen 2010: 428). How much weight should be given to this experience? It might be considered that this moment rather inverts the task of novelistic realism, disclosing the structuring effect of the personal upon the political rather than vice versa. The "as if" here will become important, signaling as it does the novel's wish to implicate personal and familial relationships with the political without ceding a sense, not of their autonomy exactly, but of their own density and logic. *Freedom* is somewhat invested in the idea of "something deeper, something not political," rather than regarding such depths as illusory.

Joey's dislocation, the suspension of his feelings of entitlement and potency, begins to be remedied only as he fastens his sense of self to the flawed justificatory narratives woven around the invasion of Iraq. Watching the assault on Baghdad on Fox News, he "feels his long-standing resentment of 9/11 beginning to dissolve. The country was finally moving on, finally taking history in its hands again, and this was somehow of a piece with the deference and gratitude that Blake and Carol showed him," impressed as they are by his involvement with the think tanks responsible for planning the post-invasion reconstruction of Iraq (Franzen 2010: 420).

This involvement is aligned in the narrative with Joey's romantic pursuit of his roommate's sister, Jenna (a name he associates, excitedly, with the Bush daughters), with a further estrangement from his father, and with his ongoing attempt to fashion a hard self in contrast to a liberal softness linked in his mind to his father and to masturbation: "Jenna excited him the way large sums of money did. He knew perfectly well that Jenna was bad news. Indeed, what excited him was wondering if he might become bad enough news himself to get her" (Franzen 2010: 411).

As the political narratives justifying the invasion are discredited and cynically revised—from an emphasis on removing weapons of mass destruction to a deep if newfound concern for the liberty of the Iraqi people—and as Joey begins to feel sickened by the ethically flawed profiteering of reconstruction, another self begins to emerge. As Jenna had early intuited, in any case, Joey was "way too nice" (Franzen 2010: 295) for the predatory financial world he aspired to enter. His ethical epiphany is accompanied by the (somehow touchingly reluctant) recognition of the depth of his commitment to his girlfriend and future wife Connie, "his caughtness in a story larger than himself" (Franzen 2010: 431), but this newly felt story is personal rather than political. Somewhat inconveniently and, in literary critical terms, unfashionably, Franzen has Joey discover something approaching a core self or personality: "This wasn't the person he'd thought he was, or would have chosen to be if he'd been free to choose, but there was something comforting and liberating about being an actual definite someone, rather than a collection of potentially contradictory someones" (Franzen 2010: 459). Joey is thereby exempted, mercifully, from the thankless task of "Performing Identity in a Multivalent World," the satirical title Franzen gives to an academic colloquium attended by Patty and Jessica. For Joey, "The world immediately seemed to slow down and steady itself, as if it, too, were settling into a new necessity" (Franzen 2010: 459), an experience (including the "as if") that captures something of the tone and aspiration of Franzen's novel.

Freedom gives more attention to the impact of 9/11 on Joey than to any of its other characters. His involvement as a college student with national defense contractors, however, selling obviously inadequate spare vehicle parts to the military, has been seen as straining credibility, threatening to undo the novel's realism. Áine Mahon notes that "the unlikeliness of a university student being trusted with a military commission amounting to tens of thousands of dollars"—an opinion shared by Walter—and finds this representative "of the occasional strain on Franzen's socially realist ambitions" (Mahon 2014: 99). The strain is understandable. Mark Greif is in agreement that the book's "memorializing" of the reconstruction of Iraq makes *Freedom* "temporarily, absurd," but finds this to be less a failure of the novel than of the period it sets on record. For Greif, Joey's scheme is realistic precisely *because* it is "cartoonish," capturing the brazen "infamy" of the profiteering at work in the reconstruction of Iraq, a disaster which "interrupts the novel, rather than elevating it," since it has little do with novelistic nuance (Greif 2010: 129).

Joey is not the only character in the novel to feel ethically compromised or complicit, not the only misplaced self. *Freedom* is much interested in the politics of popular music and the aestheticization of everyday life, from the mindless banality of mainstream rock (as rendered by Walter, "Gotta be free, so free, yeah, yeah, yeah. Can't live without my freedom, yeah, yeah" (Franzen 2010: 154)) to the twee sincerity of an indie scene "in harmony with consuming" (Franzen 2010: 392) and the reactionary political implications of the iPod. As a founder member of punk band The Traumatics, it might be expected that Richard Katz would be all too familiar with a wilfully self-sabotaging logic of futility and impurity—hard to sell out from within a punk form which already foregrounds its own complicity as a constitutive part of its anger. The commercial success of his alternative country album *Nameless Lake*, however, is distasteful to Katz, leading as it does to such "traumatic events" as "(1) receiving a Grammy nomination, (2) hearing his music played on National Public Radio, and (3) deducing, from December sales figures, that *Nameless Lake* had made the perfect little Christmas gift to leave beneath tastefully trimmed trees in several hundred thousand NPR-listening households" (Franzen 2010: 204). The freedom afforded by this success leaves Katz close to suicide, "his psychic gills straining futilely to extract dark sustenance from an atmosphere of plenitude and approval" (Franzen 2010: 205).

According to Patty Berglund's account, which forms a substantial part of the narrative, this mainstream success, however distasteful to Katz, leaves Walter with feelings of rejection and hurt that lead him to belittle his own accomplishments working for a nature conservancy. These feelings underwrite what Patty presents as an act of competition, on Walter's part, as he starts to work from within a mainstream establishment in ways that are similarly (but far more) problematic in their complicity: "Within weeks of the release of *Nameless Lake*, he was flying to Houston for his first interview with the megamillionaire Vin Haven. . . . It was obvious to Patty, if not to Walter himself, that his resolve to go to Washington and create the Cerulean Mountain Trust and become a more ambitious international player was fuelled by competition" (Franzen 2010: 198). Katz, indeed, does experience "envy" of Walter for his "taking on Bush's cronies and trying to beat them at their own game" (Franzen 2010: 231); undoubtedly, though, this is also an authorial settling of scores on Patty's part: acutely conscious of her own tendency to compete, she feels that Walter is less frank about his own competitiveness. Walter's attempt to do environmental good by working with rather than against the coal industry leaves him no less compromised than Joey, and he shifts his political energies instead to an anti-population growth agenda, an agenda that, albeit in different ways, proves no less problematic.

The *interminably* problematic or fraught character of Walter's political convictions is symptomatic of the novel's response to the alarmist response of the Bush administration to 9/11. It is a response at once confident and uncertain—a composite that is evident in the novel's very form. Around a third of *Freedom* consists of an autobiographical document, "Mistakes Were Made," written by Patty at the suggestion of her St. Paul therapist. Patty describes the document to Joey in flippant terms as "a little creative-writing project, for my own amusement" (Franzen 2010: 260); it certainly proves "compelling and transformative" (Franzen 2010: 487) for Walter, first in a negative sense, as he learns of Patty's affair with Richard; second, in a more positive sense, as the "Conclusion" to her project, "A Sort of Letter" to Walter, sparked by Katz's suggestion that she tell Walter "a story," helps to write into being their eventual reconciliation. As Greif argues, just as a significant portion of the novel is presented as psychotherapy, *Freedom* itself can be regarded as "a work of therapy on deep unarticulated crises of America, but a cure at odds with the 'culture of therapy' that is just supposed to make you happy" (Greif 2010: 130). Distinguishing between an Americanized and a Viennese Freud, the former "acknowledging hidden impulses and undoing neuroses by talk," the latter drawing attention to the inescapably problematic nature of desire which holds "danger in both directions—towards restraint and freedom" (Greif 2010: 129), Greif contends that neither Freud wins out in Franzen's novel. For Walter and Patty, for instance, sexual expression is at once necessary and inadequate for happiness. Patty's therapeutic narrative is productive of sorrowful wisdom rather than happiness, involving as it does reconciliation to reality rather than fantasy (whether personal or national).

Writing of Franzen's previous novel, *The Corrections*, and grouping it together with contemporary novels comparable in their conspicuous deployment of a recognizably realist mode, Richard Gray has suggested that "to label these novels realistic, because of their attention to the empirical details of a particular society and individual psychology, is to say what is probably the least interesting thing about them" (Gray 2011: 67). Critical discussion of *Freedom*, however, has found Franzen's realism to be of considerable interest. In some quarters, the novel's reception has been marked by a certain sense of gratitude. This gratitude was in part directed to its ability to voice and entangle the empirical details and psychological vicissitudes of its contemporary moment; *The New York Times* review, for instance, enthused that Franzen "seems to gather up every fresh datum of our shared millennial life"—a gathering up that might contribute to or conjure the sense of an otherwise fractured life *as* shared (Tanenhaus: 2010). The idea, moreover, that the white middle-aged subject has only to voice its discontents for a sense of reality to be restored is one that *Freedom* feels at once drawn to and repelled by. Interestingly, Franzen himself has cautioned against what he dubbed the literary critical "Fallacy of Capture," "as if a novel were primarily an ethnographic recording" (Franzen [2002] 2004: 259). The caution was meant to trouble the premise that a certain kind of formal innovation is required in order to represent newness. It is not the case for Franzen, for instance, that "our situation as suburbanized, gasoline-dependent, TV watching Americans is still so new and urgent as to preempt old-fashioned storytelling" (Franzen [2002] 2004: 259)—particularly since the experimental strategies of postmodernism, for instance, are now somewhat old-fashioned themselves. Nonetheless, the caution holds for realist novels too and, as if in awareness of the fallacy of capture, the same reviewer also lamented that *Freedom* "abounds in journalistic detail, some of it slapdash" (Tanenhaus: 2010). It might be added that the novel's adherence to a certain kind of accessible realism or "old-fashioned storytelling" not only leaves it vulnerable to middlebrow touches but also renders its more literary moments interestingly isolated and conspicuous. This is true, for instance, of the novel's description of Joey as "alone with his body; and since, weirdly, he *was* his body, this meant he was entirely alone" (Franzen 2010: 414), with its echoes of David Foster Wallace's syllogistic style.

The gratitude characterizing *Freedom*'s reception welcomed its apparent demonstration, as if in reassurance, that a certain type of realist novel might still be possible, and might speak of and to its moment in ways that unsettle as well as comfort and stabilize. Franzen's own critically informed essays in part prepared the ground for this emphasis on realism. His apparent privileging of "contract" over "status" novels, for instance, privileging readerly pleasure over writerly experimentation, can be taken to imply an allegiance to a familiar realism as against more avant-garde modernist and postmodernist literary modes, however much we might then want to blur such labels (Franzen [2002] 2004: 240). If Franzen's work is difficult, then, as he puts it in another context, this difficulty is less a matter of formal difficulty than "the difficulty of life itself" (Franzen [2002] 2004: 269). The novelist and critic Benjamin Kunkel has associated Franzen's novelistic practice with what he refers to as a

> new *self-conscious* traditionalism, a preference among many sophisticated writers and critics for what are felt to be tried-and-true ways of doing things. For the novel, this means endorsing a relatively high degree of sentimentality, as against the chilly affect of someone like DeLillo or Bret Easton Ellis; a "well rounded" approach to characterization, as against a previously avant-garde commitment to the evasiveness or speciousness of robust personal identity; and an acceptance of all the artificial contrivance involved in the plotting associated with Dickens, say. (Kunkel 2000: n. pag.)

Freedom may fairly safely be identified as an instance of what Kunkel tentatively terms the "*perennial novel*." If such novels give an impression of "glacial stability" in the face of a rapidly changing culture, however, that impression may be misleading, since this very stability may be taken to indicate the fundamental *openness* of the novel as a form "to new historical content—new ways of talking, eating, and dressing, along with new technologies, manners and beliefs" (Kunkel 2000: n. pag.). Gray has argued that "some kind of alteration of imaginative structures is required to register the contemporary crisis" of 9/11 (Gray 2011: 29–30). Kunkel implies that, in principle, the perennial novel as a form may still register crises through its openness to new historical content. This openness need not be understood, moreover, in terms of uncritical passivity; if the realist novel lends stability to the world it describes, this might be taken as a condition of critique against a reification of the social world. Franzen has described *Freedom* as an explicitly political novel, sharply critical, for instance, of the new ways of talking and technologies of Bush-era America. *Freedom* is "open" to these developments, in the sense that it meditates upon their nature in resistant, uncertain ways; if such resistance is then subject to the twin threats of irony, on the one hand, and snowballing, destabilizing "omnidirectional anger" on the other (Franzen 2010: 313), this is suggestive less of an absence of conviction and more of the self-questioning burdens of liberal subjectivity.

Gratitude for the achievement of a realist novel, further, is internally related to gratitude for the continued viability of the novel as such, lent salience by a sense that the culture at large has become inimical to the *good* of the novel. Franzen has written of how his "impulse to defend the novel . . . is stronger than ever":

> *Freedom* was conceived and eventually written in a decade where language was under as concerted an assault as we've seen in my lifetime. The propaganda of the Bush administration, its appropriation of words like *freedom* for cynical short-term gain, was a clear and present danger. This was also the decade that brought us YouTube and universal cell-phone ownership and Facebook and Twitter. Which is to say: brought us a whole new world of busyness and distraction. So the defense of the novel moved to different fronts. Let's take one of those buzzwords, *freedom*, and try to restore it to its problematic glory. Let's redouble our efforts to write a book with a narrative strong enough to pull you into a place where you can feel and think in ways that are difficult when you're distracted and busy and electronically bombarded. (Burn 2010: n. pag.)

If the perennial novel, as realized by Franzen, can resist this assault on language, it does so not by contrast with a discourse of purity but with a discourse whose authenticity is secured precisely through the transparency of its contested and uncertain nature, its "problematic glory." At the same time, the novel form—its "way of talking"—is presented here in more confident terms as in some way resistant to a state of distraction and busyness associated with new technologies, as providing or restoring a location allowing for forms of feeling and thought that are otherwise endangered—it is hard not to draw a link here between Franzen's concern for the novel and Walter's conservationist concerns. The novelist and critic David Shields provides such a link, contending that Franzen's traditionalism is self-conscious in the sense of mannered, the forms of feeling and thought it elicits essentially those of "nostalgic entertainment" (O'Hagan 2010: n. pag.). Shields might agree that *Freedom*'s affective and cognitive properties differentiate it from a distracted culture, only now in the negative sense that its "antediluvian" mode "fails to convey what it feels like to live in the 21st century" (O'Hagan 2010: n. pag.). It might be felt that Shields's intervention in itself is somewhat nostalgic, reprising as it does debates between realism and postmodernism, a reprisal that functions to reinforce rather than question the novel's relevance.

If, as Kunkel reminds us, Franzen's traditionalism is wholly *self-conscious*, then perhaps the forms of thinking and feeling elicited by *Freedom* should not be understood as automatically conferring anything other than problematic glories. What kind of self-consciousness is at stake here? Drawing on Stephen Burn's account of Franzen's work as in dialogue with postmodernism, Mahon contends that *Freedom* is self-conscious in the sense of self-reflexive. Mahon thereby troubles Richard Rorty's opposition between cynical-experimental and patriotic narratives, finding *Freedom* to be both at once (Mahon 2014: *passim*). Margaret Hunt Gram, meanwhile, argues that the political questions taken up by *Freedom* are variously occluded and stifled both by the mechanisms of realism and by Franzen's investment in a reader-centered, contract model of novelistic production: "In the world of *Freedom*, growth capitalism's ecological and material depredations . . . are allowed to become visible only insofar as their visibility promises not to threaten the novel's own market value. They can show only so much of themselves as *Freedom*'s imagined readers will fail to notice" (Hunt Gram 2015: 309–10).

Near the end of *Freedom*, Walter Berglund's Canterbridge Estates neighbors are said to detect a "political trembling in his voice" (Franzen 2010: 576). This is a trembling that *Freedom* in some way shares. Resisting her hopes that he reconcile with his wife Patty, Walter acknowledges to their daughter Jessica, "I know you want a happy ending" (Franzen 2010: 508). Franzen's novel *does* supply its readers with something approaching this happy ending, in that Walter and Patty reconcile, and its characters attain chastened insight (although the matter of Jessica's happiness is somewhat in question, given that she is dedicated like her father to a "declining and unprofitable enterprise," albeit now "literary publishing" (Franzen 2010: 567) rather than conservation). This personal happiness is hard won precisely because it is suspended within broader social, cultural, and political questions that remain entirely fraught. As such, the novel's happy ending, while unquestionably sincere and, as it were, earned also feels provisional, tentative, and self-conscious. *Freedom* does not allow itself a fantasy of negation, but it does work to refuse the false choice between "the dream of limitless freedom" and "misanthropy and rage" (Franzen 2010: 473).

We can usefully distinguish between the politics *in* and the politics *of* a novel. What happens if we take this distinction to *Freedom*? Provocatively, Jon Baskin has suggested that Franzen's novels "are political in the sense that they contain characters who remain passionate about politics. But to the extent that they emphasize the negative emotional consequences (and causes) of political conviction, they are anti-political" (Baskin 2012: n. pag.). "Anti-political," of course, might mean a number of different things here; it might be taken to suggest the possibility of a contestation and redrawing of the political rather than its renunciation or abandonment. The moral to be drawn from this association, within Franzen's fiction, between negative affect and the political, remains wholly open. Neither *Freedom* nor its characters, for instance, could sensibly be held to be in retreat from the political—although it is something one can feel about the novel, and something its characters might wish for; both might rather be said to withstand the political, as they withstand the emotional. Something of this is captured in the tone of Franzen's essay, "Inauguration Day, January 2001" (2002), a brief, second person account of his bus trip with young socialists and fellow travellers to Washington in order to protest Bush's inauguration. Having worn an appropriate "costume" for the occasion, the "you" of Franzen's narrative returns home to find "a wholly different kind of costume hanging in your closet; and in the shower you're naked and alone" (Franzen [2002] 2004: 306). Selfhood here becomes a difficult remainder of the political.

Baskin's claim that "negative emotional consequences" are presented by Franzen as not just effects but *causes* of political conviction is troubling; it might (though need not) be taken in a reductive sense, as the suggestion that political convictions are merely affective residues. Certainly, as Baskin suggests, the intimate connection between political belief and emotional suffering is under sustained scrutiny in *Freedom*. When he joins Walter in Washington to discuss his friend's antigrowth initiative, Katz is surprised less by the fact that his friend has become something of a political crank, since this was more or less predictable, and more "by what an *angry* crank Walter had become" (Franzen 2010: 232). Spending a summer at his Mother's lake house ("secondhand paperback copy of *Walden* and Super-8 movie camera" in hand (Franzen 2010: 483)), Walter's solitude is brought to a halt by the arrival of his less transcendentally inclined brother, Mitch, who has friends and is not much interested in learning how to be alone:

> He could hear the noise from half a mile away. Cock-rock guitar soloing, blunt drunken shouting, the dog baying, firecrackers, a motorcycle engine spluttering and screaming. . . . He locked himself in the bedroom and lay in bed and let himself be tortured by the noise. Why couldn't they be *quiet*? Why this need to sonically assault a world in which *some people* appreciated silence? The din went on and on. It produced a fever to which everyone else was apparently immune. A fever of self-pitying alienation. Which, as it raged in Walter that night, scarred him permanently with hatred of the bellowing vox populi, and also, curiously, with an aversion to the outdoor world. He'd come open-hearted to nature, and nature, in its weakness, which was like his mother's weakness, had let him down. Had allowed itself so easily to be overrun by noisy idiots. He loved nature, but only abstractly. . . . Even when he left 3M to do conservation work, his primary interest in working for the Conservancy, and later for the Trust, was to safeguard pockets of nature from loutish

country people like his brother. The love he felt for the creatures whose habitat he was protecting was founded on projection: on identification with their own wish to be left alone by noisy human beings. (Franzen 2010: 486)

These are adolescent thoughts but thereby formative; the suggestion here as elsewhere in *Freedom* is that, put bluntly, Walter's political convictions are abstractions bound up with misanthropy. What follows from this? If Walter's "neurotic anger" (Franzen 2010: 521) and alienation inform his political sensibility, that need not discredit that sensibility outright as if in contamination; if negative affect is the mode within which the political appears, it may after all—to overwork the novel's Thoreauvian pun—be preferable to "see more of bitternness and less of nothing" (Franzen 2010: 484), a matter of finding an "enduringly discontented situation to struggle against and fashion an existence within" (Franzen 2010: 529).

Walter's lifelong dislike of the noisy vox populi is apparent in his work with Vin Haven for the Cerulean Mountain Trust, as his initial encounters with local environmental groups wholly hostile to mountain top removal lead him to the realization that "he simply couldn't afford to take his full case to the public. The clock was ticking; there was no time for the slow work of educating the public and shaping its opinion" (Franzen 2010: 340). Far better, as he tells Katz, "to turn to a few billionaires [such as Vin Haven] than to educate American voters who are perfectly happy with their cable and their Xboxes and their broadband" (Franzen 2010: 226). A significant difficulty with Walter's strategy and sentiment here, of course, is its uncomfortable if partial echo of elements of neoconservative thought, in particular the notion of the "noble lie" as voiced in the novel by Jenna's father: the Straussian suggestion, couched in Platonic terms, that the "blurry shadows" cast on the cave wall by the media should be manipulated in the name of a "greater truth" (Franzen 2010: 284).

Freedom suggests that the overcoming of isolating anger is both the condition of a livable life and the one thing needed in a broader cultural and political terrain marked by enmity and rage. Organizing "Free Space" events with Lalitha, Walter is troubled to find himself "immersed in the rage that was gripping the country that summer" (Franzen 2010: 525). If conservative rage is "mysterious" to Walter given that the Republicans "controlled all three branches of federal government" (Franzen 2010: 525), he is no less alarmed by the way that this "conservative rage had engendered a left-wing counter-rage that practically scorched off his eyebrows at the Free Space events in Los Angeles and San Francisco. . . . That 9/11 had been orchestrated by Halliburton and the Saudi royal family was a near-universal article of faith" (Franzen 2010: 525). Speaking at his Free Space antigrowth event, Walter finds himself applauded by his youthful audience only to the extent that he echoes his earlier "meltdown" and provides "intemperate" and "incendiary words"—words that *Freedom* might nonetheless fully mean, of course (Franzen 2010: 525). His less glamorous leftist liberal emphasis that they should 'be disciplined in their message . . . stick to the facts about overpopulation . . . stake out the biggest possible tent" is met with either silence or a chanting of Walter's antihumanist environmentalist outburst, "Cancer on the Planet!" (Franzen 2010: 525). The oppressive thought, for Walter, is that "the country's ugly rage was no more than an amplified echo of his own anger" (Franzen 2010: 525).

While several of *Freedom*'s characters, by the novel's close, have as it were become characters by negotiating hard emotional truths that have in some way driven their political standpoints, thereby attaining a degree of calm, the political trembling that may be taken to characterize the novel still remains. This trembling is not exactly a form of political uncertainty, since the novel's political diagnosis of Bush-era America is hardly characterized by hesitancy. The novel's trembling, rather, relates to the efficacy of its liberal voice as represented by Walter. Indeed, the novel can be viewed as something of a case study in the felt difficulty of articulating a liberal position; the overlap in *Freedom* between political conviction and emotional strife emerges as a symptom of this difficulty. The first we hear of him in the novel, his old neighbors in St. Paul are struggling to reconcile unflattering descriptions of Walter—"'arrogant,' 'high-handed,' 'ethically compromised'"—in a report on his work for the Trust in *The New York Times* with their memories of a smiling, modest man "greener than Greenpeace" (Franzen 2010: 3). This reconciliation is well under way by the close of the novel's first paragraph, disclosing as it does the collective neighborly judgment that "there had always been something not quite right about the Berglunds" (Franzen 2010: 3). The rest of the novel might be understood as a working through of this suggestion.

The opening section of *Freedom*, "Good Neighbours," rehearses the history of the Berglund family home in Ramsey Hill, St. Paul, from their arrival as "young pioneers" of urban gentrification in the early 1980s to the sale of the house soon after 9/11, as the Berglunds move to Washington for Walter's work with the Trust (Franzen 2010: 3). The Berglunds' liberalism is explored in some detail. They are presented as socioculturally archetypal, at the vanguard of urban gentrification, thereby forced to relearn life skills that a previous generation "had fled to the suburbs specifically to forget," such as "How to respond when a poor person of color accused you of destroying her neighborhood?" (Franzen 2010: 4). Greif suggests that *Freedom* "takes up a form of American liberalism that doesn't yet have a name: *liberalism as niceness*," tracing "the agony of liberalism-as-niceness in an era that publicly rejected it" (Greif 2010: 124). Some of Patty's neighbors question the character of her good neighborliness, or niceness, finding her habitual self-deprecation to be a form of condescension, for instance, since designed to put less accomplished homemakers at ease. When the sixteen-year-old Joey, as Walter puts it, "fires" his parents and moves next door with the Monaghans, "everybody had the sense, fairly or not, that Walter—his niceness—was somehow to blame" (Franzen 2010: 27). Memorably, Seth Paulsen deems the Berglunds to be "the super-guilty sort of liberals who needed to forgive everybody so their own good fortune could be forgiven; who lacked the courage of their own privilege" (Franzen 2010: 7). Seth's wife Merrie, however, refuses to see Patty's good neighborliness as in any way progressive, deeming it instead "regressive housewifely bullshit": "Frankly, if you were to scratch below the nicey-nice surface you might be surprised to find something rather hard and Reaganite in Patty" (Franzen 2010: 8).

The attractiveness of the Republican Party to Joey is also presented in terms of a disputation of the nature of liberal niceness. Again, the political is bound up with the personal and emotional: anger at his mother's unfairness and condescension to his girlfriend, Connie (daughter of "the only non-gentrifier left" (Franzen 2010: 7) on the Berglunds' block) leads "in a roundabout way" to his sense of allegiance with "the party of angry anti-snobbism": "What Joey liked about the Republicans was that they didn't *disdain* people the way liberal Democrats did. . . .

They were simply sick of the kind of unexamined condescension with which his mother treated the Monaghans" (Franzen 2010: 417). *Freedom* is much interested in the functioning and significance of this "roundabout way," of the entwining and co-articulation of the personal and the political. As Marco Roth notes, *Freedom* "holds the forces that govern our messy human lives and the forces that govern messy human societies in equal and unresolvable tension, without reducing one to the terms of the other. . . . This sustained irresolution drives the novel" (Roth 2010: 123). This is part of what makes Franzen's mode of perennial fiction both difficult and self-conscious—its return to character and emotion after the flat and affectless tendencies of postmodern fiction is less comforting than might at first appear, since these characters are in any case neither untroubled nor autonomous agents. The novel's tentative resolution, precisely because, like the novel as a whole, it expresses political discord in domestic, familial terms but refuses to fully reduce it to those terms, leaves both the novel and its characters irredeemably caught up in "the insane making, velocitous world" (Franzen 2010: 341). The roundabout relationship between the political and the personal is expressed by the novel's tendency to picture the personal as structuring the political no less than vice versa: it *feels* to Joey as if he and his father have chosen their political allegiances in order to disagree with one another, but it can never quite be as simple as that. Walter's sadness is at once "a world sadness, a life sadness" (Franzen 2010: 513).

A further way in which the novel is self-conscious is that it refuses what Franzen takes to be one of the presuppositions of realism, "that the author has access to truth." As Franzen puts the matter, realist fiction

> implies a superiority of the author to his or her comically blundering characters. . . . In *Freedom*, the recurrent metaphor is sleepwalking. Not that you're deceiving yourself—you're simply asleep, not paying attention, you're in some sort of dream state. *The Corrections* was preoccupied with the unreal, wilfully self-deceptive worlds we make for ourselves to live in. . . . And the realist writer can play a useful and entertaining role in violently breaking the spell. But something about the position this puts the

writer in, as a possessor of truth, as an epistemological enforcer, has come to make me uncomfortable. I've become more interested in joining the characters in their dream, and experiencing it with them, and less interested in the mere fact that it's a dream. (Burn 2010: n. pag.)

If *Freedom*'s characters are still figuring out how to live, then, this is not entirely a case of their stumbling toward a truth or truths already evident to the author or the reader. Walter's political trembling, for instance, matches that of the novel, since both express the difficulty of being liberal in a period fairly dominated by conservative voices. It is telling that in one of the novel's key scenes—Walter's Whitmanville rant, which captures the capaciousness of *Walt* Whitman's poetry but delivers only discord rather than democratic unity—Walter seems to morph into an *entertainer* of sorts, "wresting the mike from its holder and dancing away with it" (Franzen 2010: 514), an entertainer who repels his immediate audience only to find internet fame. The way that Walter's jeremiad assumes something of a giddy, comic mode here is reminiscent, in a sense, of the role of television programs such as *The Daily Show* during Bush-era America: offering a haven for liberal thought and leftist satire but combining certainty with a form of powerlessness, marked and potentially limited by what Franzen refers to in his "Inauguration Day" essay as the pleasure of being "in violent agreement" (Franzen 2002: 306).

Just how much of a crank *is* Walter, and to what extent does *Freedom* join him in his dream—how much of crank does the novel take him to be? For a time, before his work with the Cerulean Mountain Trust, he is kept awake at night by worries over fragmentation:

> It's the same problem everywhere. It's like the internet, or cable TV—there's never any center, there's no communal agreement, there's just a trillion bits of distracting noise. We can never sit down and have any kind of sustained conversation, it's all just cheap trash and shitty development. All the real things, the authentic things, the honest things are dying off. Intellectually and culturally, we just bounce around like random billiard balls, reacting to the latest random stimuli. (Franzen 2010: 232)

It is hard not to align this sentiment not only with Franzen's own jeremiads but also with his subsequent, self-aware recalibration of the scope and tone of their argument ("I used to be a very angry and theory-minded person. I used to consider it apocalyptically worrisome that Americans watch a lot of TV and don't read much Henry James" (Franzen 2002: 4)). Katz's deflationary, comic rejoinder to Walter's worries over fragmentation ("'There's some pretty good porn on the internet'") does little to settle the question of Walter's crankiness, because it feels too much like a gesture of embarrassment on the novel's part and somehow more stilted than the over-earnestness it might otherwise interrupt (Franzen 2010: 232). In his ongoing attempt to figure out "how to live," Walter feels the absence of a "controlling narrative" (Franzen 2010: 338). *Freedom* is open both about its wish to provide such a narrative and about its inability to do so: the novel's question—how to live?—captures the difficulty of giving existential content to liberal procedural norms.

Works cited

Baskin, John. "Coming to Terms." *The Point*. 2012. Available online: http://thepointmag.com/2012/criticism/coming-to-terms.

Burn, Stephen J. "The Art of Fiction 207: Jonathan Franzen."
The Paris Review 195 (2010): 38–79. Available online: http://www.theparisreview.org/interviews/6054/the-art-of-fiction-no-207-jonathan-franzen.

Franzen, Jonathan. *Farther Away*. New York: Farrar, Straus and Giroux, 2012.

Franzen, Jonathan. *Freedom*. London: Fourth Estate, [2011] 2010.

Franzen, Jonathan. *How To Be Alone*. London: Harper Perennial, [2002] 2004.

Gram, Margaret Hunt. "*Freedom*'s Limits: Jonathan Franzen, the Realist Novel, and the Problem of Growth." *American Literary History* 26, no. 2 (2011): 295–316.

Gray, Richard. *After the Fall: American Literature Since 9/11*. Oxford: Wiley-Blackwell, 2011.

Greif, Mark. "Liberalism as Niceness." *n+1* 10 (2010): 124–29.

Kunkel, Benjamin. "Letter to Norway: A Report on the American Fiction of the Last Decade." *n+1* (August 2010). Available online: https://nplusonemag.com/online-only/online-only/letter-to-norway/.

Mahon, Áine. "Achieving Their Country: Richard Rorty and Jonathan Franzen." *Philosophy and Literature* 38, no. 1 (2014): 90–109.
O'Hagan, Andrew. "*Reality Hunger* by David Shields." *The Observer*, February 28, 2010. Available online: http://www.theguardian.com/books/2010/feb/28/reality- hunger-book-review.
Roth, Marco. "Freedom's End." *n+1* 10 (2010): 121–24.
Tanenhaus, Sam. "Peace and War." *The New York Times*, August 19, 2010. Available online: http://www.nytimes.com/2010/08/29/books/review/Tanenhaus-t.html?_r=0.

9

The architecture of memory and memorialization in Amy Waldman's *The Submission*

Catherine Morley

Published to a fanfare of plaudits and positive reviews, Amy Waldman's *The Submission* (2011) opens on the premise of a competition for the design of a public memorial on the site of Ground Zero.[1] The competition, in which the entrants' identities are anonymized, is judged by a series of New York dignitaries, politicos, and artists, as well as a representative of the families who lost loved ones in the World Trade Center (WTC) attacks. The reader is immediately thrust into the deliberations of the judges, who have narrowed their shortlist down to two entries: "The Void" and "The Garden." Each design is strongly backed by a female judge, and the opening section of the book pivots on the debate between Ariana Montagu, a celebrated sculptor, and Claire Burwell, a beautiful, determined 9/11 widow.

Ariana lobbies for "The Void," a modernist design of black rectangular granite, towering twelve stories high over an oval pool that would reflect the names of the dead carved into the granite above. She describes the proposed memorial as "visceral, angry, dark, raw.... You can't tell if that slab is rising or falling, which is honest—it speaks exactly to this moment in history. It's created destruction, which robs the real destruction of its power, dialectically speaking" (Waldman 2011: 5). Championing "The Garden," meanwhile, Claire argues that "The Void" is too dark for the families of the victims, who seek a space that will allow them to mourn but also to heal, as well as a place to commemorate their dead. Claire is drawn to the solace of the four geometrically aligned verdant quadrants, with their grid of living and steel trees. The enclosing wall of the garden would bear the names of the victims, "patterned to mimic the geometric cladding of the destroyed buildings," while "the steel trees reincarnated the buildings even more literally: they would be made from their salvaged scraps" (Waldman 2011: 4).

The tension between the women as they debate the merits of each design encapsulates one of the central themes of the novel, namely the requirements and intentions of the artist (or in this case, the architect) and the needs of those whose grief and loss the artistic edifice is meant to assuage. As Claire talks of the need for beauty, citing George Herbert's "The Flower" (1633), a poem of contemplation and spiritual rejuvenation, she pleads for the memorial to have an emotional dimension—a plea her antagonist is quick to rebut. "A memorial," says Ariana coldly, "isn't a graveyard. It's a national symbol, an historic signifier, a way to make sure anyone who visits—no matter how attenuated their link in time or geography to the attack—understands how it felt, what it meant" (Waldman 2011: 5). The verbal sparring between the two jurors illuminates the dialectics at the heart of memorial construction and the very real debate over the efficacy and validity of public memorials. When Ariana talks about the replacement of one destruction by another, for example, she echoes the words of Horst Hoheisel in 1995 during a competition for a German national memorial to the Jews murdered in the Holocaust. Hoheisel proposed to blow up the Brandenburg Gate, and grind the remains into dust to be sprinkled over the site and then covered over with granite plates. As James E. Young observes, "Rather than commemorating the destruction of a people with the construction of yet another edifice, Hoheisel would mark one destruction with another destruction" (Young 2001: 1). And while Hoheisel's proposal was unique to the very particular context of memorialization within Germany, it has an obvious resonance within the American context, and within the context of the debate between Ariana and Claire that Waldman sets up. How, after all, does the memorial mourn and serve the victims and their families, while at the same time ensuring that the healing process engendered by the memorial does not expunge public memory? For Ariana, a monument that engenders healing runs the risk of displacing public memory, and she sees it as appealing to those who value the fuzziness of impressionism. She sees the modernist brutality of "The Void" as a necessary and unwavering reminder of the brutality of the day, its very "rawness" a reminder of an unsutured wound. For Claire, however, the very monumentalism of "The Void" seems merely an attempt to replicate what has been destroyed in the attacks, an attempt to force the viewer to perceive the memorial in a directed, rather than a personal and reflective, way. "The Garden," as opposed to "The Void," does not impose a particular memory upon the viewer but rather allows viewers to contemplate their own memories and, in the case of the victims' families, their own private traumas. Claire sees the garden as accommodating the agency and individualism of the visitor, but is put off by what she sees as the coercive monumentalism of "The Void."

Waldman's debate between Ariana and Claire recalls what James E. Young, a Judaic Studies scholar and former member of the National 9/11 Memorial at Ground Zero Committee, which selected the Israeli architect Michael Arad's "Reflecting Absence," sees as the inherent difficulty of memorialization and the erection of monuments. There is, he has written, "a fundamental tension between the families' need for closure and the contemporary artist's need to articulate unredeemable loss" (Young 2012: n. pag.). Indeed, in setting out the requirements of public memorialization alongside those of private individuals, Waldman seems to be addressing a central question in post-9/11 art and literature, namely how the artist or writer reconciles the representation of the individual and the collective. In other words, how might a writer depict the small everyday dramas and traumas of personal individuals alongside the wider sociopolitical portrait? It is surely no coincidence, then, that, in citing the influences upon her work, Waldman has singled out Jonathan Franzen and Richard Price for the ways in which they work "very deeply with character, but the intersection of that with politics and social issues" (Brown 2011: n. pag.).

That Waldman engages with the discourse of architectural memorialization is evident not only in this opening debate between the judges of the memorial design competition but also in the compositional structure of the novel, which accommodates the personal stories of various individuals while at the same time offering a wider, panoramic portrait of post-9/11 social discord. In her counterfactual history of the Ground Zero memorial, Waldman offers a novel that straddles the small domestic stories of personal trauma, for instance, through the experiences of Sean (the brother of one of the victims) and Claire, and the wider political debates about the global ramifications of the 9/11 terrorist attacks, through the lives of the Bangladeshi widow Asma Anwar and the designer of "The Garden," Mohammed Khan. This is embodied in the very shape of the novel, smaller spaces enclosed within a larger frame, which is self-consciously modeled upon the shape of the fictional garden design. And this in turn is self-consciously modeled upon European gardens of Islamic inspiration: the gardens of the Alhambra in Granada, the gardens of Seville and Cordoba, or the Catalonian gardens of Fernando Caruncho.[2] In fact, Waldman deliberately draws the reader's attention to these international and trans-temporal influences through her *New York Times* architecture critic's assessment of "the geometry, the walls, the four quadrants, the water, even the pavilion" as paralleling "gardens that had been built across the Islamic world, from Spain to Iran to India to Afghanistan, over a dozen or more centuries" (Waldman 2011: 115). In shaping the garden thus, Waldman is linking the proposed New York space with a wider transnational history, presenting it as a potential space that is both local and global. But she is also deliberately drawing the reader's attention to the intersecting lines of the design—lines paralleled in her own fictional creation, which offers geometrically proportioned portraits of individuals of different national, social, and ethnic backgrounds.

The narrative abounds with architectural references, both in its form and in its content, offering precisely the kind of synergy of structure and meaning toward which most architectural and sculptural memorials aspire. Richard Serra, Henry Moore, and Capability Brown, for instance, are given passing nods. Perhaps most significantly, the name of the architect who designed the Vietnam Veterans Memorial, Maya Lin, is frequently invoked throughout the novel. As an undergraduate student at the Yale School of Architecture (the same institute from which Waldman's fictional architect has graduated), Lin anonymously entered and won a competition to design the memorial. The combination of the revelation of her design—a haunting v-shaped granite wall stretching from the Washington Monument to the Lincoln Memorial and bearing the names of the lost combatants—her relative inexperience and, most tellingly, her Asian American ethnicity brought a torrent of objections. Perhaps most notable was the voice of Tom Carhart, writing in *The New York Times*, who described the design as a "black gash of shame and sorrow hacked into the national visage that is the Mall" (Carhart 1981: 23). In her recollections of the press coverage following her selection, Lin notes,

> I remember at the very first press conference a reporter asking me if I did not find it ironic that the memorial was for the Vietnam War and that I was of Asian descent. I was so righteous in my response that my race was completely irrelevant. It took me almost nine months to ask the VVMF, in charge of building the memorial, if my race was at all an issue. It had never occurred to me that it would be, and I think they had taken all the measures they could to shield me from such comments about a "gook" designing the memorial. (Lin 2000: n. pag.)

Lin's experiences are, to some extent, replicated in *The Submission* through the character of Khan, the up-and-coming architect behind the garden design. Waldman has admitted that she drew on Lin's experiences for the premise of the novel, reimagining the scenario for the Ground Zero memorial.[3] Indeed, in conversations between Khan and the jury chairman, Paul Rubin, Lin is held up as an exemplar for her grace in submitting to the demand for the erection of "The Three Soldiers" statue following the negative reactions to her original design and James G. Watt's withholding of a building permit for her unadulterated granite wall design. However, unlike Lin, Khan is not shielded from the public backlash against a Muslim designing a 9/11 memorial. His unveiling unleashes a gush of public fury, spearheaded by Sean Gallagher and his irrepressible cheerleader Debbie Dawson. It is interesting that Lin, in her recollections, cites the role of the press in her public vilification, for Waldman makes the press, personified in the figure of Alyssa Spier, a crucially important factor in the hounding of Khan. In many ways, Spier is the architect of Khan's undoing—the chief manipulator of the major characters in the novel. Again, there is perhaps a certain self-consciousness here in the casting of Spier, since Waldman herself was a *Times* reporter for eight years and covered 9/11 and its aftermath, perhaps most notably in her contributions to the "Portraits of Grief" series (which are rendered in the novel as "Relatives' Rumination").[4] Not for nothing, then, does the critic Emily Witt describe the novel as a "synthesis of [Waldman's] firsthand experience as a reporter" (Witt 2011: n. pag). While there is undoubtedly an element of truth in this description, it seems to me that in the character of Spier Waldman is also offering another example of the impulse to make shapes or patterns (in this instance, destructive ones) out of human experience. It is interesting that Spier works in print media and is elated when her investigative work leads to her own "column," each of which we see her labor over and fabricate. She jokingly remarks to the news anchor Bill O'Reilly that Muslims may be a "fifth column" (Waldman 2011: 156). In a separate but analogous instance, Paul Rubin uses columns in making sense of the pros and cons for Khan's memorial. For Rubin, the columns are a rationalization tool in contemplating his neutralization of Spier and his possible elimination of Khan.

In a novel of grids, lines, and quadrants, the geometrical allusion, just like Spier and Rubin's manipulation of individuals in their columns, is, of course, deliberate. Mo's design is seemingly very simple: four quadrants locked within an outlying square. Yet, the simplicity of the design gives rise to ambiguity when individuals and groups feel their losses and grief manipulated by the architect. In a further instance of the manipulative tendencies of the press, the backlash against Mo is prompted by an architectural feature in *The Times*'s Art section, which notes that the geometry of Khan's design is indebted to "one of the many rich art forms produced by the Islamic world" and suggestively notes that "some might say the designer is mocking us or playing with his religious heritage" (Waldman 2011: 115). Within moments, Fox News anchors describe the memorial design as a "martyr's paradise" while the next day's *Wall Street Journal* describes the garden as "an assault on America's Judeo-Christian heritage" and a "covert attempt at Islamization." Meanwhile, Debbie Dawson's Save America from Islam (SAFI) views the proposed garden as "a code to jihadis . . . it's the Trojan horse" (Waldman 2011: 216–17).

At the heart of all of this is the American public's fear of and vulnerability to manipulation, which very obviously undermines the memorial's purpose as a space in which to freely grieve and remember. And it is this notion of the manipulation and coercion of personal memory that lies at the heart of *The Submission*. This, after all, is what draws Claire to what she sees as the liberating garden design, rather than the directive monolith that constitutes "The Void." And it is this, too, that drives her unease with her son's documentary at the end of the novel: "The camera," she thinks, "strips the eye of its freedom, holds viewers hostage to its choices" (Waldman 2011: 297). Similarly, the SAFI firebrands fear that the monument manipulates and encroaches upon their way of life, their values, and their history. Yet, they themselves are guilty of manipulation and coercion for their own ends in deploying emotive images, language, and tactics (even those of Martin Luther King) in their attempts to put a stop to the implementation of Khan's garden design. The Debbie Dawson figure is especially mendacious in her vitriolic language and manipulation of the media in her provocative, slogan-emblazoned, tight T-shirts. But individuals on all sides of the debate are portrayed as manipulative, from the emotional tactics used by Claire to push through her preferred design to the spatial manipulation techniques used by the antiterrorist agents who interview Mo in the wake of the 9/11 attacks. Such manipulation is not, of course, always necessarily negative, though when characters in the novel rail against their manipulation by others, they do not mean it as a compliment. At a deeper level, though, the theme of manipulation works to draw the reader's attention to the desire to makes shapes and patterns out of that which is often askew. It is a way of ordering the seeming chaos of a crisis, the anarchy of a multifarious culture.

As I have suggested, the novel itself is complicit in this manipulation of facts, events, and characters, through the shaping of the narrative. Any novel, and perhaps especially a counterfactual novel such as *The Submission*, which deliberately plots and alters the facts of history, is after all a kind of deception. It is a carefully wrought fiction that masquerades as a version of reality, manipulated by a guiding author. Split into four sections, each flagged with an accompanying number of cypress trees to delineate the beginning of a new section, *The Submission* closes with a coda set twenty years or so in the future in Mumbai, where the controversial garden design has been realized for a wealthy Muslim sultan or emir. In the space, which was to be carved the names of the 9/11 dead, is a passage of Arabic scripture from the Quran, which Khan refuses to translate for the young documentary maker William Burwell. The closing coda is the larger square, marked by a single large cypress tree, which encloses the four sections and the raft of disparate characters contained therein. What Waldman presents, therefore, in terms of the shape of the novel, is a grid: a space of enclosed orthogonal lines. Similarly, Khan refers to his garden as a grid:

> The Garden has order, which its geometry manifests, for a reason, which is that it's an answer to the disorder that was inflicted on us. It's not meant to look like nature. Or like confusion, which is what the attack left behind. If anything it's mean to evoke the layout of the city it will sit in. . . .
> A grid subdividing endlessly can be a form of infinity. (Waldman 2011: 138–39)

Later still, when speaking to Claire about the design, Khan sketches what at first looks like a cross, and when turned diagonally an X, and around this a square which Claire describes as a "a checkerboard" and then "maybe Manhattan," to which he replies,

> It's all of those things, or maybe none of them. It's lines on a plane, just like the Garden. . . . Lines on a place. Geometry doesn't belong to a single culture. The grid is the quintessential modernist form. (Waldman 2011: 269)

Khan's sense of the necessary imposition of order is manifest at various levels throughout the text, in his experiences of the cities of Kabul, Mumbai, and New York. The Afghan capital, for example, is presented as not unlike those famous pictures of the early development of twentieth-century New York, with workmen perched aloft girders and ascending precarious-looking scaffolding. Here, in his conversations first with Rubin and later with Claire, Khan likens his design to the gridiron shape of the city, a shape developed from the Jeffersonian model of the checkerboard city, which was designed to halt the spread of disease and to reserve particular geographical areas for specific mercantile functions. Indeed, the gridiron model was to be the embodiment of regularity and rationality, and what fascinates Waldman is clearly the dark and complex irony that it is this overtly rational design which provokes such an irrational reaction. After all, this is what she did herself in her work on the "Portraits of Grief" series, which in their visual composition of subdivided columns on the pages of *The New*

York Times formed a kind of encapsulating grid for the disorder of complex lives.[5]

Waldman's deployment of the grid structure in the composition of the fictional garden, and as a way of shaping her own narrative, is not only a means of containing the messy lives and polyphonic voices of her New Yorkers. The grid introduces graduated increments of distance, which give the perception of depth in a piece of art or architecture. It is interesting that *The Submission* is frequently described as a piece of realist fiction, because the vertical and horizontal planes of a grid, the intersecting orthogonal lines, facilitate the depth and distance required for optical verisimilitude.[6] And certainly, the novel offers that sense of depth as it moves up and down the various social hierarchies, the various quadrants subdividing into the narratives of different characters. The grid structure introduces an element of spatiality to the novel—a book which in many ways, after all, is concerned with the manipulation of space. The 9/11 attacks might be viewed in part as a devastating alternation of public space; the proposed memorial, by contrast, is a proposal to reclaim and reengineer that same public space. Indeed, when detained and interrogated at Los Angeles International Airport shortly after the terrorist attacks, Mo observes,

> In architecture, space was a material to be shaped, even created. . . . When they left the room he surveyed it. They had used a partition with the texture of a gray, moldy bulletin board to shrink the room's dimensions and maximize its oppressiveness. The room wasn't windowless after all; the partition blocked the natural light to create the ambience of a cell. Someone among them had understood the manipulation of space. (Waldman 2011: 27)

The interview room, with its grubby dividing wall, is deliberately claustrophobic, but it is also another example of the ever-decreasing rectilinear lines throughout the novel, which include Paul and Alyssa's columns, Claire's jackknife incisions in the waters of her pool, the lengths she swims, the photographs and notices which form "the quilt of the missing," the God Box that houses the Muslim American Coordinating Committee (MACC) and an array of other religious organizations, Khan's miniature doodle of his garden, the miniature glass-encased garden presented to Claire on her birthday, William's childish drawings of "The Garden," and the gingerbread reconstruction of the vanished towers presented to the judges in the Gracie Mansion parlor during their deliberations on the memorial (Waldman 2011: 29). And though not quite a grid, as such, the specially commissioned multiple sets of Burwell *matryoshka* dolls present a similar *mise-en-abyme* impression as the rectilinear spaces. The effect of all of these decreasing planes is the illusion of texture and depth in the narrative, but there is also a self-reflexivity in their deployment, as the author calls attention to the lines of her composition.

Rosalind Krauss's work on grids in twentieth-century art and symbolist painting is especially interesting in this regard, and offers some insights into Khan's ideas about the possibilities for infinity in his garden design. For Krauss, the grid "states the autonomy of the realm of art." She goes on to observe that the grid structure is "flattened, geometricized, ordered, it is antinatural, antireal," and concludes that "the grid is the means of crowding out the dimensions of the real and replacing them with the lateral spread of a single surface" (Krauss 1979: 50). As this suggests, Krauss's argument about the structure and role of the grid when imposed upon or within a work of art gives rise to a tension between the grid as a device facilitating depth, and the grid as an entity which draws attention to the structured nature of the artwork. Thus, we return to Waldman's declared intention to portray the multifaceted elements of individual and collective lives.[7] The deployment of the grid, in a way, signals a self-conscious acknowledgment of the impossibility of delivering such an objective. At all times, the grid reminds the viewer of its very structured nature, and so, in dividing the novel into the sectional quadrants, Waldman seems to be directing the reader's attention to the artificiality of her design.

One can look at the grid, either Khan's or Waldman's, as performing two functions. In the first instance, it offers the perception of depth (a grid within a grid within a grid *ad infinitum*); yet, on the other hand, it also reminds us of its own artificiality—indeed, the artificial nature of any artwork. Again, Krauss is interesting on this point. The grid, she writes, "separates the work of art from the world, from ambient space and from other objects. The grid is an introjection of the boundaries of the world into the interior of the work; it is a mapping of the space inside the frame on to itself" (Krauss 1979: 61). What is also interesting about this consideration of the grid is that it introduces an element of interplay between illusions of reality and assertions of artificiality. So embodied in the very grid form is a kind of power play between two oppositional forces. At a thematic level, one might see this power play as being acted out between SAFI or the Memorial Defense Committee (MDC) and MACC, between Khan and Rubin, Claire and Sean, and so on. The net result is again a balanced synergy of form and content, the kind of result Khan envisages when he plans his design to manipulate the "new gap in space" where the self-consciously monumental towers once stood (Waldman 2011: 29).

Ultimately, alas, the grid structure, in drawing attention to its own artificiality and construction (it is interesting to note that Mo considers it a modernist design, which he thought would appeal to Ariana Montagu), does not engender the healing and redemption required by the 9/11 families, and following the assassination of Asma Anwar, Khan withdraws his design. And thus, we return to the question of the efficacy and use of memorials. While "The Garden" is defeated, the memorial maintains a space within the novel. In trying to explain the loss of their father to her children and assuage her son's anxiety that his lost father was actually trying to make his way home, Claire sets the children on an expedition, first gathering stones and then creating a trail of miniature cairns across the city leading to the family garden, "just like the bread crumbs in Hansel and Gretel," as she puts it (Waldman 2011: 83). The allusion to the fairytale of Hansel and Gretel, the story of siblings who lose a parent and are cast into the woods by a selfish stepmother, offers a reassuring frame for the children. After all, when Hansel and Gretel have outwitted the witch of the gingerbread house (perhaps a passing allusion to the gingerbread towers constructed by Jorge in an earlier scene in the novel), they are carried home to find their father awaiting them.

But it is the story itself, as well as the memorializing cairn, that helps the children to overcome their grief and nightmares. There is once again, I would suggest, a certain self-reflexivity in Waldman's bringing together a story, a German folktale in this instance, and the miniature memorial structure in this way. The memorial alone, over which William cries due to its smallness, "disappointing—against the city's vertical thrust"—seems insufficient to the children's needs (Waldman 2011: 84). By contrast, the cairn, combined with the story, which links the children's experience with that of others across geographical space and time, offers something approaching emotional recovery and acceptance. When the children arrive at their home and set to work on the final cairn, Claire observes that they "rearranged the stones as if they were perfecting a haiku" (Waldman 2011: 85). The haiku, a juxtaposition of two images or ideas, almost geometrical in its syllabic composition, in its very essence combines the healing qualities of the memorial with the unifying qualities of narrative and of literature. For instance, the allusion to Hansel and Gretel recurs in Asma's narrative when the bag of rice she purchases from her local store splits and forms a trail of rice from store to her home. Once again, the effect is to link the individual story and trauma of the Burwells to that of Asma and her baby son, who have also lost a husband and a father.

Spread across the city, the Burwells' cairns are redolent of Horst Hoheisel's "Denk-Stein-Sammlung" (Thought Stones Collection) project of 1988–95, in which the architect visited the schools of Kassel with a stone, a book and a piece of paper. The book was entitled *Namen and Schicksale der Juden Kassels, 1933–45* (The Names and Fates of Kassel's Jews), and was, in composition and shape, not unlike the "Portraits of Grief" thumbnail sketches of the 9/11 victims.[8] As part of his project, Hoheisel used the book to tell Kassel's schoolchildren about its vanished Jewish community and to assign each child a life to research and on which to write a short narrative piece. These short life stories were then wrapped around cobblestones and deposited in the archival baskets within each school. When the baskets were filled, they were replaced and refilled and the stones were taken to Kassel's railway station, where they were laid in a permanent installation, a memorial cairn, which commemorates the dead but also symbolizes the next generation's education about the devastating realities of the Holocaust.[9] Hoheisel's memorial cairn at Kassel does not allow the community to forget its history, thereby offering a positive response to the difficulty articulated in the debates between Ariana and Claire. Here, therefore, is a memorial that allows people to mourn the victims of disaster, while still ensuring that the healing process does not obliterate or falsify public memory. Crucially, the memorial cairn also allowed each child, each writer, to bring part of themselves to the memorial through the creative act of writing. So the words and the stone combine to form one of the most common forms of memorialization, the memorial stone or headstone, but as part of a collaborative and evolving project rather than an individual and static one. As such, it constitutes what Young describes as counter-monuments or indeed counter-memorials: "Memorial spaces conceived to challenge the very premise of the monument" (Young 1999: 3).

This sense of the evolving cairn memorial is at the very heart of *The Submission*. Shortly after the trip downtown with the children, Claire arrives home to find an altered cairn structure outside the family home:

> She saw, in the milky light cast by house and moon, a box of Raisin Bran . . . a pile of books pillaged from Cal's study; a stray tennis racket; his $2,000 wedding tuxedo—all of it arranged around the cairn. A child's necromancy: William believing he could coax the stones to life, or his father home. (Waldman 2011: 91)

The altered cairn, which notably adds books, stories, to the piles of stones, gestures to the past, to the present and the future. The tennis racket reminds the reader of Claire's earlier recollection of the moment when Cal had stopped her as she left a tennis court and told her he would marry her, which of course leads to the wedding tuxedo. The Raisin Bran, which Claire describes as "Daddy's favorite" in an effort to entice her children to eat it, is a daily reminder of their father, a kind of everyday nourishing of his memory. Claire imagines her son is trying to lure his father back to life, but his alteration of the structure demonstrates his evolving grief. And the cairn evolves again, crossing geographical space and time, to find its way into Mohammad Khan's garden in its final incarnation in Mumbai. Twenty years after the submission debacle, and two years after the Museum of New Architecture in New York has mounted a retrospective of Khan's career, *Mohammad Khan: American Architect*, William Burwell and his girlfriend find themselves in "The Garden" interviewing Khan for a documentary project about the memorial competition. For the critic Rebecca Walkowitz, the documentary works as a living memorial, "in which subjects watch and respond to each other's interviews" (Walkowitz 2011: n. pag.). And indeed, the structure of the documentary offers a microcosmic version of the novel. By revisiting some of the main participants in the earlier events and asking them to reflect upon their decisions and opinions, it elicits the kind of individual participation and reflection that Hoheisel engineered in the execution of his evolving cairn. On witnessing the footage of the garden, the dying Claire momentarily feels closer to her dead husband than at any point in the previous twenty years. Ultimately, though, the garden does not bring the pleasure and redemption she yearns for. She is puzzled by Khan's instruction that she "use her imagination," unaware of Khan's mother's words that "all the best gardens are imaginary" (Waldman 2011: 293). Instead, Claire finds solace in the hastily erected cairn deposited by her son:

> The screen showed, in close-up, a few small rocks stacked in a corner of the garden....
> "The cairns, Mom. You remember."
> That day flooded back, the shade of every stone, the shape of every mound they left for Cal to find his way, even as she had lost hers.
> In Khan's garden, her son had laid his hand. With a pile of stones, he had written a name. (Waldman 2011: 299)

The stone cairn, a symbolic laying of hands, is a healing gesture that delivers to Claire the healing she has sought in a memorial. Created by the next generation, it revives the past, grants a kind of absolution, and lays an inscription to her loss. And in this way, William's cairn is a kind of counter-memorial to "The Garden": a private and individualized memorial space that negates the grand geometry and self-conscious precision of the gridded garden.

In the final words of her novel, "With a pile of stones, he had written a name," Waldman not only neatly juxtaposes two images, but offers a kind of geometrically imperfect haiku. But then the cairn itself, too, is a geometrically imperfect memorial. These final words bring the reader back to the act of writing, and the possibilities of textual inscription. The self-consciousness of *The Submission* testifies to Waldman's sense of her novel as a kind of tribute to the lives she could not accommodate in her journalistic work: her own memorial, of sorts. For Waldman, the evolving, unfolding, and textured nature of narrative offers a form commensurate with the lived experience of loss, grief, and memory. Picked up, put down, revisited, absorbed, and forgotten, the narrative invites us to participate in the propagation of meaning and, in this instance, in the process of memorialization. Its abiding message echoes Khan's refusal to divulge the meaning and origins of his garden: "Use your imagination" (Waldman 2011: 298).

Notes

1. The novel won the American Book Award, was shortlisted for *The Guardian* First Book Award, won the Janet Heidinger Kafka Prize, and was a finalist for the Hemingway Foundation/PEN First Fiction Award. Michael Prodger and Michiko Kakutani praised the novel as a model of the post-9/11 novel. Kakutani observed that Waldman had responded to Tom Wolfe's call for a new social realism, having "created a choral novel with a big historical; backdrop and pointillist emotional detail, a novel that gives the reader a visceral understanding of how New York City and the country at large reacted to 9/11, and how that terrible day affected some Americans' attitudes toward Muslims and immigrants." See Kakutani, "The Right Architect with the Wrong Name," *The New York Times*, August 16, 2011, C1.
2. See the official website for *The Submission*, which offers a series of quotations and images that inspired aspects of the novel: http://www.thesubmissionnovel.com/.
3. See Jeffrey Brown, "Conversation with Amy Waldman, Author of *The Submission*," http://www.pbs.org/newshour/art/conversation-amy-waldman-author-of-the- submission/.
4. Indeed, David Simpson has observed that the "Portraits of Grief" pieces "seem regimented, even militarized, made to march to the beat of a single drum." See David Simpson, *9/11: The Culture of Commemoration* (Chicago: University of Chicago Press, 2006), 23.
5. Waldman herself has freely admitted her ambivalence about the "Portraits of Grief" series, noting that the word limit made it difficult to relay the complex lives of the victims: "The project made me ask, how do you avoid reducing the dead to thumbnail profiles?" See "Amy Waldman on 9/11 Literature: Five Books," http://fivebooks.com/interviews/amy-waldman-on-911-literature.
6. For the realist aspects of the novel, see, for example, Michiko Kakutani's review cited above.
7. See Jeffrey Brown's PBS interview, "Conversation with Amy Waldman, Author of *The Submission*," in which Waldman talks about the greater possibilities of fiction compared with journalism, and about her desire to explore a larger picture: "This decade that we've lived through, all of those elements [politics, the media, class] are very present in the debates around Islam, the War on Terror, how we react to 9/11, all

of it, even looking at the family members from 9/11. They are such a diverse group, and we talk about them as a monolith, but in terms of class, politics everything, they are so diverse, and so I wanted to capture that."

8 For a PDF version of the book, see https://kobra.bibliothek. uni-kassel.de/bitstream/urn:nbn:de:hebis:34-2013121644679/1/ SchicksaleDerJudenKassels.pdf. It is worth noting its rectilinear column construction.

9 For a detailed discussion of Hoheisel's notion of the counter-monument and his work in Kassel, see John E. Young, *The Texture of Memory: Holocaust Memorials and Meaning* (New Haven: Yale University, 1993).

Works cited

Brown, Jeffrey. "Conversation with Amy Waldman, Author of *The Submission*." Available online: http://www.pbs.org/newshour/art/conversation-amy-waldman-author-of-the- submission/.

Carhart, Tom. "Insulting Vietnam Vets." *The New York Times*, October 24, 1981: 23.

Kakutani, Michiko. "The Right Architect with the Wrong Name." *The New York Times*, August 16, 2011: C1.

Krauss, Rosalind. "Grids." *October 9* (October 1979): 50–64.

Lin, Maya. *Boundaries*. New York: Simon and Schuster, 2000.

Simpson, David. *9/11: The Culture of Commemoration*. Chicago: University of Chicago Press, 2006.

Waldman, Amy. *The Submission*. London: Heinemann, 2011.

Walkowitz, Rebecca L. "Building Character." *Public Culture*, March 12, 2011. Available online: http://www.publicculture.org/news/view/public-books-rebecca-l-walkowitz-on-the-submission.

Young, James E. "Memory and Countermemory: The End of the Monument in Germany." *Harvard Design Magazine* 9 (Fall 1999): 1–10.

Young, James E. "Counterfactual 9/11 Storm Hits NYC." *Public Culture*, March 12, 2012. Available online: http://www.publicculture.org/news/view/public-books-james-e-young-on-the-submission.

Young, James E. *The Texture of Memory: Holocaust Memorials and Meaning*. New Haven: Yale University, 1993.

INDEX

110 Stories: New York Writes After 9/11 126
"24-Hour *Psycho*" 43
28 Days Later 7
9-11: Artists Respond 6, 62, 71
9/11 Emergency Relief 15, 62
9/11 Memorial Museum 51
The 9/11 Report: A Graphic Adaptation 62
9/11 September 11th 2001: The World's Finest Comic Book Writers and Artists Tell Stories to Remember 62, 71

abjection 25–7
Abu Ghraib 55
Adorno, Theodor 84–5, 86
After 9/11: America's War on Terror 63
After London 9, 11
Aldiss, Brian 7
Al-Queda 112
Americana 43
American Widow 78
Amis, Martin 13
Anderson, Benedict 55
Angel of History 49–50, 52, 54
Anker, Elizabeth S. 42, 46–7
Arad, Michael 187
Arendt, Hannah 45, 85
Armenti, Peter 89
Asad, Talal 115
Ashcroft, John 121

Athens 9–10
Atkinson, Paul 63
Atran, Scott 110–11, 117, 119
Atta, Mohammad 46, 117
Auschwitz 72–5, 84
Auster, Paul 4, 17, 125–43, 147, 150, 152

Babylon 9–10, 13
Baer, Ulrich 3–4, 126, 129, 140
Barone, Dennis 134–5, 142
Baskin, Jon 176–7
Baudrillard, Jean 15, 64–6
Beckett, Samuel 90, 94, 96
Bellow, Saul 14
Benjamin, Walter 15, 46, 49–50, 52–5, 84–5
Benton, Thomas 157, 158
Beyond the Pleasure Principle 86
Bin Laden, Osama 73, 167, 168
Bishop, Elizabeth 99, 101
The Body Artist 43, 45
Bourbeau, Heather 97
Boxall, Peter 43, 45–6
Brandenburg Gate 186
Brontë, Charlotte 125, 140
Brown, Capability 188
Burn, Stephen 175
Bush, George 73–4, 135, 167
Butler, Judith 87

Call of Duty 5
Carhart, Tom 189
Caruth, Cathy 84–6, 87, 100

Castor and Pollux 71
Chaucer, Geoffrey 16
Churchill, Winston 125, 126
Ciocia, Stefania 135
Cockley, David 131, 133
Codde, Philippe 29
Cohen, Samuel 56
Colón, Ernie 62
Conrad, Josef 14
Constantinople 9–10
Cooper, Simon 63
The Corrections 172, 181
Cosmopolis 43, 45
counterhistory 36, 37
counter-memorial 197, 198
counter-monument 197
counter-narrative 14, 23, 44, 46, 47, 55
Crane, Hart 13, 88
Crane, Stephen 14
Curry, John Steuart 157, 158

The Daily Show 182
Däwes, Birgit 128, 129, 130, 134
The Day of the Triffids 7–8
The Death and Life of Great American Cities 9
Debord, Guy 52
DeLillo, Don 8, 12, 15, 41–57, 64–6, 154, 173
DeLuca, Vic 153, 160
"Denk-Stein-Sammlung" 196
Derrida, Jacques 33
Dickens, Charles 173
Dickinson, Emily 114
Dodd, Wayne 83–4, 87, 88, 91–2
Dos Passos, John 9–10
Dreiser, Theodore 14
Drew, Richard 45
Dubus, Andre 41
Duffy, Jo 71

Dugdale, John 13
Duvall, John 37, 42
Dwyer, Keiron 71

Eliot, T. S. 16, 92–4, 96
Ellis, Bret Easton 173
End Zone 43
Engle, Karen 70
Eshel, Amir 87
Extremely Loud and Incredibly Close 13, 21–37

Facebook 174
Fahrenheit 911 62
Falling Man 15, 41–57
Fallout: New Vegas 5
Fallout 3 4–5, 9
Faulkner, William 14
Feldman, Noah 114
Fischl, Eric 45
Franzen, Jonathan 17–18, 167–83, 187
Franz Ferdinand 93
Freedom 17–18, 167–83
Freud, Sigmund 16, 25, 29, 86, 171–2
Fukuyama, Francis 43
"The Future of Faith" 121

Gauthier, Tim 63–4, 70
"Gemini Falling" 71
Gilgamesh 12
Ginges, Jeremy 117
Giuliani, Rudi 51–2
Glanzman, Sam 13, 16, 72–4
Glejzer, Richard 69, 77
Goldstein, Laurence 89
González, Jesús A. 135
grands récits 128, 133–43
Gray, Richard 41–2, 128–9, 131, 142, 172, 173
Great Flood 12
Greengrass, Paul 62

Greif, Mark   170, 171–2, 180
Ground Zero   32, 55, 66, 185, 188, 189
Guantanamo Bay   56, 112

Habermas, Jürgen   120
Halaby, Laila   41
Hall, Stefan   63
Hamid, Mohsin   41
Harutoonian, Harry   56
Hemingway, Ernest   37
Herbert, George   186
Herman, Judith   136
Hesse, Herman   93
Heyen, William   83–4, 88, 89, 90, 92
Hillcoat, John   2
Hiroshima   73–4
Hirsch, Marianne   75
Hitchens, Christopher   119
Hoheisel, Horst   186, 196, 197
Holman, Bob   84, 90, 94–9, 101
Holocaust   24, 27, 36, 74–5, 85, 186, 196
Homeland Security   56, 118, 119, 121
Hornung, Alfred   22
Howe, Marie   99
Huehls, Mitchum   78
Hunt Gram, Margaret   175
Huntington, Samuel   56

"Icarus"   16, 105–7, 121
In Sight of Chaos   93
International Dublin Literary Award   147
"In the Ruins of the Future"   43, 55, 57
In the Shadow of No Towers   15–16, 61–79, 84, 94
Islam   16, 108–12, 120–1, 161, 200
Islamic State (ISIS)   112

Jacobs, Jane   9
Jacobson, Sid   62
Jeffries, Richard   9
jihad   112–13, 114
Juergensmeyer, Mark   116

Kalfus, Ken   4
Kaplan, Ann E.   84, 100–1
Katz, Susan   97
Kelly, Robert   98
Kennon, Kevin   51
Kipling, Rudyard   10–11
Kirkham, Robert   5–6
Klee, Paul   49, 52
Krauss, Rosalind   194
Kristeva, Julia   25
Kunkel, Benjamin   173–4

Lang, Karen   45
Larkin, Philip   17, 161
Law of Ruins   48–9, 51
Let the Great World Spin   17, 147–64
Levan, Kelly   84, 90–1, 96
Lewis, Charles   23, 27–8
Liberalism   179–83
Libra   43
Lin, Maya   188–9
Lindbergh, Charles   22, 26
Literature in the Ashes of History   86
Locksley Hall   147, 161, 162–3
Lyotard, Jean-François   128, 133

McCann, Colum   17, 147–64
McCarthy, Cormac   1–6, 14, 15, 41, 57
McCrum, Robert   4
McEwan, Ian   4, 8
McInerney, Jay   3, 4, 13–14, 154
Mahon, Áine   169–70, 175
Mailer, Norman   3
Manhattan Transfer   9–10

INDEX

Man in the Dark   17, 125–43
Marzec, Robert   37
Maslowski, Maciej   43, 45–6
Maus   16, 62, 73–7
memorial   185–98
Mendoza, Jamie   71
Messud, Claire   4, 41, 56
Metres, Philip   88
The Mikado   41, 49
Millet, Lydia   56
Mitchell, David   24
Molloy   90, 91
Moore, Henry   188
Moore, Lorrie   41
Moore, Michael   62
Morandi, Georgio   42, 50
Mrs Dalloway   37
Municipal Art Society of New York   94
Myles, Eileen   98

Nahum   11
National 9/11 Memorial at Ground Zero   187
National Book Award   147
Nauck, Todd   71
Ninevah   9–10, 11
Nussbaum, Martha C.   107

Obama, Barack   56
O'Brien, Tim   14
O'Neill, Joseph   56
Origins of Totalitarianism   85

Packard, Vance   48
painting   157–61
Pankey, Eric   84, 92–3
Panzerella, Pauka   95
Parrish, Tim   27
Paz, Sharon   45
Pease, Donald   56
Penhall, Joe   2
Pentagon, the   42, 67

People's Poetry Gathering   87, 89, 92, 95, 99
Perloff, Marjorie   89
Petit, Philippe   17, 148–57, 157, 159, 160, 161, 164
petits récits   128, 133–43
photography   153–7
The Plot Against America   13, 21–37
Poetry Tower Project   90
Point Omega   43
"Portraits of Grief"   190, 192–3, 196
postmemory   75
postmodernism   172, 175
Powers, Ricjard   154
prosthesis (as trope)   23, 21–37
Pynchon, Thomas   42

Recessional   10–11
Redfield, Marc   62, 64, 66–7, 70
"Reflecting Absence"   187
Rehr, Henrick   61, 71, 78–9
Rich, Adrienne   99, 101
Richardson, Louise   113, 115
The Road   1–6, 11–12, 14, 18, 57
Rome   9–10
Rorty, Richard   175
Rosenthal, Michael   53, 54
Roth, Henry   14
Roth, Marco   181
Roth, Philip   13, 15, 21–37, 41
Rothberg, Michael   24, 87, 128–9, 131, 142
Rowe, John Carlos   57
Ruskin, John   49

Saal, Ilka   36–7
Safran Foer, Jonathan   13, 15, 21–37
Schwartz, Lynne Sharon   12–13, 17, 125–43
Self-Consciousness   121

Senefelder, Aloin 54
September 11, 2001: American Writers Respond 83, 84, 88, 89, 90
September 11th Fund 6
Serra, Richard 188
Shakespeare, William 161
Shamsie, Kamila 41
Shields, David 175
Shteyngart, Gary 56
Skarbakka, Kerry 45
Smith, Rachel Greenwald 23, 37
Snyder, Sharon 24
Sodom and Gomorrah 12
Sorenson, Lief 46
Speer, Albert 48–9
Spiegelman, Art 15–16, 61–79, 84, 95, 100
Stendhal, 14
Stern, Jessica 115–16
The Submission 18, 185–98
The Sun Also Rises 37
Survivors Fund 6

Tancke, Ulrike 126–7
Tennyson, Alfred Lord 17, 147, 161, 162–3
Terrorist 16–17, 105–21
"There were tears in her eyes" 13, 16, 72–4
"The Three Soldiers" 189
Tolstoy, Leo 8
Torres, Alissa 63, 78–9
Tower of Babel 11–12
transnational 22–3, 28, 36, 188
trauma 3, 14, 15, 16, 17, 21–37, 42, 44–5, 66, 68–9, 57, 74–6, 78–9, 84–101, 126, 128, 130, 131, 134, 135, 136, 138–43, 187, 188, 196
Tribeca Sunset: A Story of 9/11 61, 71, 78–9

Tribute in Light 94
Twin Towers Fund 6
Twitter 174

Unclaimed Experience 86
Underworld 15, 43, 47–8, 50
United 93 42, 62
Updike, John 4, 16–17, 105–21

"Varieties of Religious Experience" 107–8
Versluys, Kristiaan 31
Vietnam Veterans Memorial 188
Vietnam War 150–1, 157, 160
Vizenor, Gerald 41

Waiting for Godot 96
Waldman, Amy 18, 185–98
The Walking Dead 5–8, 11
Walkowitz, Rebecca 197
Wallace, David Foster 173
Walter, Jess 42
Walzer, Michael 114–15
The War of the Worlds 8–9, 11
War on Terror 56, 139
The Waste Land 92–4
The Waste Makers 48
Watergate 158
Watt, James G. 189
Wegner, Philip 50
Weilenberg, Erik 12
Weiner, Matthew 45
Wells, H. G. 8
Whitehead, Colson 41, 56
White Noise 48–9, 64
Wills, David 24
Winfrey, Oprah 2
Witt, Emily 190
Wood, James 13–14
Woolf, Virginia 37

World Trade Center 2, 13, 37, 42, 47, 48, 50–1, 55, 57, 61, 65, 66, 67, 74–5, 76, 94, 148–9, 153, 157, 159, 160, 185
The Writing on the Wall 12–13, 17, 125–43
WTC Memorial 56
WTC Relief Fund 6
Wyatt, David 52–3

Wyndham, John 7–8

Yeats, William Butler 13, 16, 88
Young, James E. 186, 196–7
YouTube 174

Zephaniah 11
The Zero 42
Žižek, Slavoj 64
Zola, Emile 14

www.ingramcontent.com/pod-product-compliance
Lightning Source LLC
Chambersburg PA
CBHW050138240426
43673CB00043B/1722